P. $2.98

We, the American Women

We, the American Women

A Documentary History

Beth Millstein

and

Jeanne Bodin

SCIENCE RESEARCH ASSOCIATES, INC.
Chicago, Palo Alto, Toronto, Henley-on-Thames, Sydney, Paris

A Subsidiary of IBM

The authors gratefully acknowledge the cooperation of the following in providing many of the illustrations used in this book: American Telephone and Telegraph Company; Associated Press; Brown Brothers; Library of Congress; M.I.T. Historical Collections; Minnesota Historical Society; National Archives; Nebraska Historical Society; Newark Public Library; New York Public Library Picture Collection; Schomburg Collection of the New York Public Library; Sophia Smith Collection, Smith College; United Press International; Vassar College Library.

Library of Congress Cataloging in Publication Data
Millstein, Beth.   We, the American women
Bibliography: p.
Includes index.
1. Women — History.   2. Women's rights.   3. Feminism.
I. Bodin, Jeanne, joint author. II. Title.
HQ 1426.W385   301.41′2′0973   75-28344
ISBN 0-574-42000-2 pbk.
ISBN 0-574-42003-7

Designed by Richard C. Lewis
Manufactured in the United States of America

Contents

4   AN ERA OF REFORM

5   ABOLITION AND WOMAN'S RIGHTS

6   THE CIVIL WAR AND RECONSTRUCTION

7 REFORM AND THE PROGRESSIVE ERA

8 SUFFRAGE AT LAST

Introduction

Can you name five prominent American women who lived before 1950? Without including Presidents' wives, many of us would not be able to recall more than one or two. If you had trouble how did you feel—angry, embarrassed, ashamed, surprised? You probably wondered why you could think of so few names.

In this book we have attempted to bring to life some of the "lost women" of our past. A look at your history books will quickly reveal that virtually all the authors are male. They choose their subjects, analyze their data, and draw conclusions based upon attitudes and values they have learned, for historians reflect the social values of their society. Since most Americans have believed that women "belonged in the home," historians have believed this also. As a result they have neglected or have been unable to see clearly the actual accomplishments of American women.

Historians have also assumed that certain activities were more important and more valuable to our developing civilization than others. War and politics have been the main themes of historical writing. Since women have been excluded from these pursuits they have generally not appeared in the history books. The average student, therefore, has learned almost nothing about the American woman's role in building our nation.

How does this affect us? Both females and males have a false picture of our past—an America shaped almost exclusively by white Protestant males, if one is to believe the history books. Both females and males tend to believe that women are less capable and of less value than men in our society. And young American women have few female models upon whom to pattern themselves.

From personal experience we know how crippling this lack of a past can be. Often, during our years of schooling, we found it difficult to perceive ourselves as serious and scholarly. These feelings can in part be attributed to the lack of such women in our own past. They existed, but until we became teachers and feminists we were never aware of them. We missed the experience of learning about the heroines and ordinary women of our past, and we wrote this book so students today will not miss them also.

We have attempted to do three things in each chapter. First, we have explained the general legal and social status of women in that period. Second, we have described the contributions of various outstanding women to the shaping of the nation at that time. Finally, we have analyzed the roles played by the "average woman" as a force in maintaining society and pressuring for change.

Each chapter contains two types of historical information. We begin with a narrative in which we analyze women's roles at a particular time in American life. Then we present excerpts from the writings of and about women of the period. In order to preserve their original character, we edited the documents as lightly as possible. However, spelling and punctuation have been modernized for clarity.

We appreciate the encouragement our editor and publisher, Jerome S. Ozer, has given us throughout the writing of this book. We are grateful to Bertram Linder, chairman of the social studies department at Adlai Stevenson High School in the Bronx, New York, for his confidence in our ability to write this book. We thank also the many librarians around the country who have been most helpful in difficult stages of our research. Our students at Stevenson High School and Harrison High School have provided us with insight into the need for a book like this as well as positive responses to our uses of parts of this material. As they have learned from us, we have learned even more from them. Finally, it is customary for authors to thank their wives for typing their manuscripts. We thank Jeff and Murray for their support, even though they can't type.

BETH MILLSTEIN

JEANNE BODIN

We, the American Women

1

Those Who Came First

When the women, men, and children of the *Mayflower* landed in America, they hoped they would be able to practice their religion freely, make a good living, and determine their own laws. Many of the settlers brought a favorite treasure from the Old World. But they also brought with them ideas and ways of acting they had learned in Europe, and many of their ideas dealt with the proper roles of women and men. These familiar roles shaped the way women were to act in building the colonies.

European Traditional Ideas Affect Colonial Thinking

All colonists brought the teachings of the Bible with them. When Margaret Winthrop, wife of the governor of Massachusetts went to church, she listened to the minister preach from *The Bible* and learned that as a wife she was to "submit [herself] unto [her] husband as unto the Lord for the husband is the head of the wife, even as Christ is the head of the Church." Women were also taught that they should "learn in silence with all subjection." Because Mrs. Winthrop lived where religious rules dictated people's dress, play, work, and family relationships, she tried to follow the teachings of *The Bible*.

1

In England, upper-class women often led lives of leisure amid elegant surroundings. However, English law gave their husbands complete control over their persons. Conditions in colonial America changed the status of women.

In Europe and England at the end of the seventeenth century, almost every writer accepted the idea that husbands should rule their wives. Education for women was believed to be unnecessary and even dangerous. With education women would begin to question the power of their husbands over them. These ideas were brought to the American colonies. Jean Jacques Rousseau, one of the most important European writers of the eighteenth century, described the beliefs held by Europeans and American colonists when he wrote in *Emile*, his famous book on education:

> To please, to be useful to us, to make us love and [value] them, to educate us when young, and take care of us when grown up, to advise, console us, to render our lives easy and agreeable; these are the duties of women.

Education for women was therefore designed to make them useful to men. Even Benjamin Franklin of Pennsylvania, who was forward-thinking, believed in the traditional European education for women. His daughter was taught to be a "notable woman"—that is, an able housewife with enough business sense to make her helpful to her husband.

Girls often resented the limited education they were given. The following letter, written by 11-year old Betty Pratt of Virginia to her brother in England in 1732, tells us a great deal about her feelings regarding what she was learning:

I find you have got the start of me in learning very much, for you write better already than I can expect to do as long as I live; and you are got as far as the rule of three in Arithmetic, but I can't cast up a sum in addition cleverly, but I am striving to do better every day. I can perform a great many dances and am now learning the Sibell [a dance], but I cannot speak a word of French.

Betty's grandmother inserted a note in the letter. She said that Betty had made a handkerchief and was hemming a neckerchief. The general attitude of the colonists was that although women could learn the basic skills of reading and writing, more important were their skills in running a household with graciousness and ability, and raising children properly.

Along with religious teachings and European social theory, American settlers brought with them English common law, which shaped lawmaking in both the Northern and Southern colonies. Under common law, the husband controlled his wife's property and earnings. A wife could not enter into a contract without the signature of her husband. He shared responsibility, or was held completely responsible, for his wife's crimes.

Sybilla Masters of Philadelphia might have been envious of a male inventor like Benjamin Franklin. In 1715 she invented a new way of cleaning and curing Indian corn, but the patent was granted to her husband. The following year Thomas Masters secured a patent for a new way of preparing straw for covering and decorating hats and bonnets. Sybilla had also invented this method.

Generally, too, a woman had no claim in law for the possession of her children because their father had the legal right to choose their guardian in his will. In addition, the husband was held responsible for supporting his wife and paying any of her debts. The English idea that husband and wife were legally one person was influential in America. This severely limited the rights of wives.

Common Law Treatment of Single Women and Widows

In common law single women and widows were treated much differently than married women. They were considered "feme soles", or women alone, and had much greater freedom and more legal rights than did married women. Although married women could not vote, there are records of widows with property voting in New York and New Jersey in colonial times. As a woman alone, Lady Deborah Moody headed the first English settlement in the area today called Brooklyn, New York.

Some single women succeeded brilliantly in colonial life. Margaret Brent arrived in Maryland in 1638. She received 1,000 acres from her brother Giles as repayment for money he owed her. Through her considerable business ability, Brent became wealthy and influential. She was unusual because as a woman she lived alone and managed her own affairs, and even appeared in court on business matters. In 1647 she demanded to be allowed to vote in the Maryland Assembly, but her request was denied. She protested that, if she had been a man, she would have been entitled to that vote because she owned land.

Another unmarried woman, Eliza Lucas, became a successful planter. She went to South Carolina in 1737 with her family, and by the time she was 16 this industrious young woman had taken charge of all of her father's business affairs. She began to experiment to find crops that would do well on her land, and by the late 1700's her work had made indigo, a new crop, the chief export of South Carolina.

In 1744 Eliza Lucas married Charles Pinckney, a widower 20 years older than herself. As a result she lost many of the rights she had held as a single woman under English common law. Why did she choose to marry when marriage meant the loss of many of her personal rights? Part of the answer lay in European religious and social beliefs that marriage was the natural state and that women could find meaning in life only as wives and mothers. As a result unmarried persons, especially women, were considered pitiable. Because of the limited opportunity for most women to support themselves, single women often became financial burdens on male relatives. Therefore, women were encouraged to marry, not only for religious and social reasons, but for economic ones as well.

Women dreaded becoming "old maids." The attitude toward old maids was described in the following excerpt from the *State Gazette* of North Carolina, March 22, 1764:

> An old maid is one of the most cranky, ill-natured, maggotty, peevish, conceited, disagreeable, hypocritical, fretful, noisy, gibing, canting, ... never to be pleased, good for nothing creatures .... She pretends to be very religious and visits the churches, in order to watch the signs—what tokens of love may be going on.

So most women married. The laws of marriage, which placed the man in charge of the woman, showed that the Old World attitude toward the woman's position in society continued to be powerful in the New World.

Women Participate in Colonial Life

If we were to describe woman's role in America solely on the basis of what the colonists brought with them, we would be most inaccurate. The environment of America was so different from that of England and other European countries that the role of women changed greatly in the colonies.

America was a frontier land. The main concern of settlers during much of the seventeenth century was survival: collecting food, building shelter, providing protection. Rugged conditions made the participation of every settler essential, for the colonists could not afford the wastefulness of a person doing less than she or he could do. In spite of theory, women worked as hard as and with as much responsibility as men. This helped to change religious and social thought as well as the legal system the colonists brought to America.

In some places in the colonies women were scarce. Many men had come to America for adventure and profit and had come without women. Since women were considered to be a stabilizing force, colonial leaders encouraged them to travel to America. Between 1619 and 1622, 140 young girls were brought by the London Company

The young women who were brought to Jamestown as prospective wives were described as "agreeable persons, young and incorrupt." They were "sold with their own consent to settlers as wives." The London Company hoped the migration of these young women would make the Virginia settlement more permanent.

from England to Jamestown, Virginia. They lived with married couples until chosen by one of the settlers, who paid the London Company 120 pounds of the best leaf tobacco for his bride. As more women arrived they helped to make the primitive homes more livable.

In numerous and varied ways, women became active in colonial life. Women appeared in newspapers and court records in such occupations as shopkeepers, teachers, blacksmiths, shipwrights, tanners, gunsmiths, butchers, publishers and printers, and barbers.

Ann Smith Franklin of Newport, Rhode Island, was probably the first woman printer in New England and one of 11 women known to have supported themselves as printers before the American Revolution. Enterprising Mary Spratt Provoost managed her dead husband's business affairs. Hardly a ship docked in New York without goods for her store.

The extent to which women participated in work "outside" the home is impressive when their household tasks are considered. In the home women were responsible for a wide variety of tasks. The poet Jane Colman Turell sometimes described scenes from her own life as a homemaker:

> My good fat Bacon, and our homely Bread,
> With which my healthful family is fed,
> Milk from the Cow, and Butter newly Churn'd,
> And new fresh Cheese, with Curds and Cream just turned.

Animals were generally raised and slaughtered, and the meat cured at home. Wheat, corn, and oats were grown and threshed, and

In colonial America, candles were the only source of artificial light. In addition to her other tasks, the colonial woman had to dip candles—a complex and painstaking process.

then frequently made into flour and meal at home. Fruit was dried and preserved. Colonial women also made the clothing: they did the spinning, weaving, and dyeing, and made the thread. They made candles and soap. Women, such as the hard-working Mrs. Turell, spent part of their time gathering herbs for ointments and salves, for women served as the earliest colonial doctors. Many women were midwives. A Mrs. Whitmore of Marlboro, Vermont, "possessed a vigorous constitution and frequently traveled through the woods on snowshoes . . . to relieve the distressed." Mrs. Whitmore delivered more than 2,000 babies in her 87 years.

Mrs. Cornelius Harnett, a Southern woman, was described as a "pattern of industry." She kept a garden and supplied much of her town with vegetables, pies, eggs, poultry, and butter.

Although mistresses of large plantations had domestic duties different from those of poorer women, both derived their value as human beings from the home. Society required that a woman keep a clean home, provide food for her family, tend to its clothing needs, and be a source of solace and understanding for her husband. It was in this way that a woman was free to show her intelligence and initiative.

Because large families were necessary in a frontier society in order to get the work done, women were expected to bear as many children as possible. The average family often included at least seven children, and families of 15 children were not uncommon. But frequent childbearing was dangerous to women's health, and as a result women often died young. The following tombstone inscription gives witness to the difficulties of childbirth:

> Underneath [lies] what was mortal of Mrs. Margaret Edwards, Wife of Mr. John Edwards, Merchant of this place. She died in Travail with her 10th child. Aged 34 years and about 4 months, a sincere modest and humble Christian . . . . She committed her soul to him whom she ardently loved and dies without fear or a groan. August 27, 1774.

Thomas Clap was the President of Yale University. At 24 he married a 15-year-old girl who bore six children. She died when she was 23. The description he wrote of her portrays an admired, hard-working colonial wife:

> She was a woman of Such great Prudence and Discretion in the conduct of Her Self and Affairs, that She Was Scarce ever taxed with taking a [wrong] Step. She was Diligent, neat and Saving, and always [tried] to make the best of What She had . . . .

The burden of bearing numerous children, and the enormous workload of maintaining a household made the additional responsibilities of running a business very difficult. Yet many women commonly did all of these things.

As a result of frontier conditions, the common law system changed. Americans began to see marriage more as a relationship of equals, and agreements made between husbands and wives about property and other matters gave wives greater rights. When men were frequently absent, as the seafaring men of Nantucket were, women often represented their husbands and were given some degree of contractual freedom. Divorces, though uncommon—there were 40 in Massachusetts between 1639 and 1692—were more easily secured than in Europe. But, in spite of their considerable participation in colonial life in the seventeenth and eighteenth centuries, women had extremely limited legal rights.

Witchcraft and Religious Intolerance

Two incidents in the history of the Massachusetts Bay colony show further the variety of roles women held and the conflicts they often faced. As a result of Puritan religious beliefs, life in Massachusetts was highly regulated and restrictive, especially for women. They

Rebecca Nurse was a victim of the witchcraft epidemic in Salem, Massachusetts. She was accused of being a witch by several teen-age girls. Found guilty by the Salem magistrates, Rebecca Nurse was hanged.

could not speak or hold office in the church and generally sat separately from the men.

Most Americans know that Roger Williams was expelled from Massachusetts because of his radical religious beliefs, but fewer have heard of Anne Hutchinson. She came from a large family and had 15 children of her own. She was well educated and, before she was expelled from the Puritan community, Hutchinson had many male followers who accepted her as an equal. When she began to challenge the accepted ideas of the Puritan leaders, she was accused of teaching untruths and of dividing the community. At her trial the leaders told her she had erred in stepping out of her place as a woman. For her crimes she was excommunicated and expelled from the colony. Anne Hutchinson is remembered as part of the struggle for freedom of thought in America and as a forerunner of the fight for women's rights.

The restrictive nature of Puritan society tended to limit free expression. This repressiveness often resulted in bizarre behavior. One example of this was the witchcraft hysteria that began in 1692. Tituba, a slave woman from Barbados, told stories of witchcraft to a group of children who started barking and mewing and accused others of bewitching them. The girls were taken seriously and many women were accused and executed for being witches, as were a few men. The majority of witnesses in the cases were women as well. Although in 1710 the convictions were reversed, it was too late for such women as the unfortunate Martha Corey and Rebecca Nurse, who had been hanged. Many explanations have been given for this hysterical outburst, ranging from the political problems of the Puritans to problems caused by the enormous restrictions on daily life. It is clear, however, that in Massachusetts and in other colonies where witches were hunted, women played a controversial and often unfortunate role.

Slaves and Indentured Servants

Not all colonial women were able to participate freely in the building of American society. Many women lived as slaves; others as indentured servants, people who were bound to serve a master for a specific period of time before receiving their freedom.

In 1619, 20 Africans were brought to Jamestown as laborers. Two generations later laws were passed by the Virginia House of Burgesses making newly-arrived Africans and their children slaves forever. Slavery expanded throughout the South and North.

Ironically, many of the black women who became slaves in colonial

Slavery was a brutal and dehumanizing institution. The slave owner, who considered his slaves as property, sometimes branded them like cattle to prove his ownership.

America had enjoyed greater freedom in West Africa than the women who became their mistresses. The African women had had the right to own property and conduct their own affairs. They had been bookkeepers, merchants, dyers, and spinners of wool. Upon arriving in America, however, these slave women became the most brutally treated of all American women.

Slave women suffered unspeakable treatment by both whites and African chieftains. Surviving the trip from Africa was an ordeal many slaves could not endure. Once in America the slave woman was expected to work from sunrise to sunset in the fields, given little if any time to recover from childbirth, separated from her children at will, and often sexually exploited by white men. Since slaves were considered property, not human beings, they had no personal or civil rights. In the eyes of the law, slaves were not considered married; therefore, husband and wife could be sold separately. As a result, traditional American patterns of family life could develop only with difficulty. The following excerpt was written by a slave, Jenny Proctor:

> When he go to sell a slave, he feed that one good for a few days, then when he goes to put 'em up on the auction block he takes a meat skin and greases all around that nigger's mouth and makes 'em look like they been eating plenty meat and such like and was good and strong and able to work. Sometimes he sell the babes from the breast, and

then again he sell the mothers from the babes and husbands and wives, and so on. He wouldn't let 'em holler much when the folks be sold away. He say, "I have you whupped . . ." The slave trader and his wife sure loved their six children, though. They wouldn't want nobody buying them.

To a great extent slavery shaped the role of the Southern white woman. As a result of the plantation system, Southern women often did little manual work and were generally not responsible for the care of their children. The Southern woman was considered to be a "lady"—fragile, delicate, and in need of continuous protection. In reality she was the manager of a household that often included more than 100 persons. However, she was seen as a decorative object, rather than a capable human being.

In the North slaves were generally not excluded from the lives of their masters, as in the South. Northern slave women had greater opportunity to secure education, for example, and slaves were often treated the same as white indentured servants. Black women served as cooks and nurses and were often assisted by the white women of the household. Phillis Wheatley, bought as a child by a Boston woman and educated by her owner, became a well-known poet. George Washington once invited her to visit because of a poem she had written about him. Many slave women rebelled and showed great independence, and there are records of slave women who successfully sued for their freedom. But the overwhelming experi-

This portrait of the poet Phillis Wheatley appeared in the front of a book of her poetry that was published in 1773.

ence of black women, in the North and South, was total dehumanization.

Women were also indentured servants. An indentured servant came to the American colonies under a contract binding her or him to labor. Some had volunteered to work for passage, others were kidnapped persons or criminals who had been deported. They generally served from four to seven years and were then given their freedom. Girls often learned useful skills during their indenture. Sarah Davis, who was bound out as a servant in Albany in 1684, was taught to read and knit stockings, had silk hoods and a silk scarf for church wear, and a variety of other clothes in return for her work. Servant girls often received good pay that helped them to become independent after they were freed.

Summary

Women thus had many roles in early American life: as free women serving in a variety of roles, but restricted in their legal rights; as indentured servants bound to a master for a specific period of time; as slaves with no freedom. American women were a vital part of society, although they suffered severe economic, political, and social hardships. The frontier conditions of colonial life broke down many traditional European attitudes and values that saw women as wives rather than capable human beings. Unfortunately, although the American Revolution was fought in part to establish the principle of equality, traditional attitudes worked to exclude women from that principle.

A PURITAN VIEW OF WOMAN'S ROLE

John Winthrop, the first governor of the Massachusetts Bay Colony, was a strict follower of Puritan teachings. In this excerpt from his writings, he describes a woman who did not conform to the ideal of a Puritan wife.

Mr. Hopkins, the governor of Hartford upon Connecticut, came to Boston, and brought his wife with him, (a godly young woman, and of special [talents],) who was fallen into a sad [sickness], the loss of her understanding and reason, which had been growing upon her [for] years, [because] of her giving herself wholly to reading and writing, and had written many books. Her husband, being very loving and tender of her, [didn't want to make her unhappy]; but he saw his error, when it was too late. For if she had attended [to] her household affairs, and such things as belong to women, and not gone out of her way and calling to meddle in such things as are proper for men, whose minds are stronger, etc., she [would have] kept her wits, and might have improved them usefully and honorably in the place God had set her. He brought her to Boston, and left her with her brother, one Mr. Yale, a merchant, to try what means might be had here for her. But no help could be had.

John Winthrop, *The History of New England from 1630 to 1649*, edited by James Savage (Boston: Little, Brown and Co., 1853), Vol. II, pp. 265-266.

ANNE BRADSTREET WRITES ABOUT BEING A NEW ENGLAND WOMAN

Anne Bradstreet achieved fame as a poet of colonial days. Although she had eight children and was frequently ill, she saw her poetry published in book form in 1678. Because there was little encouragement for a female poet in Puritan New England, her accomplishment was especially unusual.

From *The Prologue*

5

I am obnoxious to each carping [faultfinding] tongue,
Who says, my hand a needle better fits,
A Poets pen, all scorn, I should thus wrong;
For such despite [scorn] they cast on female wits:
If what I do prove well, it won't advance,
They'll say it's stolen, or else, it was by chance.

7

Let Greeks be Greeks, and Women what they are,

Men have precedency, and still excel,
It is but vain, unjustly to wage war,
Men can do best, and Women know it well;
Pre-eminence in each and all is yours,
Yet grant some small acknowledgement of ours.

Anne Bradstreet, *The Tenth Muse Lately Sprung up in America* . . . (London, 1650), pp. 3-4.

A MARRIAGE AGREEMENT

Married women were allowed almost no rights under English common law. However, colonial American conditions encouraged some changes in these laws. Sometimes husbands and wives made marriage agreements which gave the wives more power than they had possessed before. This is such an agreement, made in 1714, between John and Frances Custis of Virginia.

Articles of Agreement between Mr. John Custis and his Wife

There have been some differences and quarrels between Mr. John Custis of York County and Frances his wife concerning some money, plate and other things taken from him by Frances; and concerning a more plentiful maintenance of living for her . . . In order to stop all of this anger and unkindness and to renew a perfect love and friendship between them, they have together agreed upon the following articles in June of 1714.

1st. First it is agreed that Frances shall return to John all the money and other things that she has taken from him or removed out of the house. She will then be obliged never to take away by herself or by any other, anything of value from him again. She shall not put him in debt without his consent, nor sell, give away nor dispose of anything of value out of the family without his consent. However, John shall not dispose nor give away the plate or damask linen during Frances' life . . .

2nd. Frances shall from now on, cease calling John any vile names or giving him any ill language. He shall do the same for her and they will live lovingly together as a good husband and good wife ought to do. She shall not meddle with his affairs but shall allow all business which belongs to his management to be transacted by him. In turn, he shall not meddle in her domestic affairs but all business properly belonging to the management of the wife shall be transacted by her.

3rd. John shall pay all the debts he has contracted. And after all debts he must make for buying clothes, tools and all the necessary things for the servants and plantations and the making of repairs are deducted and paid, he shall freely and without resenting it allow one half of all the production of the estate annually to Frances for clothing herself and the children. This shall also be for education of the children and for furnishing and providing all things that are necessary for housekeeping (that are to be brought from England) so long as Frances shall live peacefully and quietly with him. He shall also provide for the servants and family one bushel of wheat a week, sufficient Indian corn and meat and cider and brandy.

Nothing in this agreement shall be understood to stop John from the free command and use of anything that shall be provided for housekeeping so long as he does not sell any of it without Frances' consent. Also, if Frances exceeds her allowance, or runs John into debt her allowance will be stopped.

4th. John shall allow Frances to keep in the house to do the necessary work in and about, the same servants she has now . . .

5th. John shall allow Frances fifteen pounds of wool and fifteen pounds of finest dress material . . . to spin for any use in the family she shall think necessary.

6th. Frances shall be free to give away twenty yard of Virginia cloth every year to charitable uses . . .

7th. That Frances shall be free to keep a white servant if she shall think it possible out of the above allowance so long as that servant is also subject to John.

8th. In order to supply the present wants of Frances, the children and the house, John shall allow Frances fifty pounds in money if there is that much left after the debts now due are paid.

9th. Frances shall give a true account under oath to John, if he wants it, of how that fifty pounds and other profits are spent . . .

"A Marriage Agreement", *The Virginia Magazine of History and Biography,* Vol. IV (1896-1897), pp. 64-66, adapted.

EDUCATING THE SOUTHERN LADY

The large majority of Southern women were not educated to be literate citizens but rather were taught the skills necessary to manage a home gracefully. In the following letter, Thomas Jefferson proposed an unusual education for his daughter. He recommended she learn a wide variety of things, including reading.

Annapolis Nov. 28, 1783

Dear Patsy,
    After four days' journey, I arrived here without any accident, and

in as good health as when I left Philadelphia . . . The conviction that you would be [better off] in the situation I have placed you than if still with me, has [comforted] me on my parting with you . . .

With respect to the distribution of your time, the following is what I should approve:

from 8 to 10, practice music.

from 10 to 1, dance one day and draw another.

from 1 to 2, draw on the day you dance, and write a letter next day.

from 3 to 4, read French.

from 4 to 5, exercise yourself in music.

from 5 till bedtime, read English, write, etc.

Communicate this plan to Mrs. Hopkinson [her guardian], and if she approves of it, pursue it . . . I expect you will write me by every post. Inform me what books you read, what tunes you learn, and enclose me your best copy of every lesson in drawing . . . Take care that you never spell a word wrong. Always before you write a word, consider how it is spelt, and, if you do not remember it, turn to a dictionary. It produces great praise to a lady to spell well. I have placed my happiness on seeing you good and accomplished; and no distress this world can now bring on me would equal that of your disappointing my hopes . . .

TH: [OMAS] JEFFERSON

Paul Leicester Ford, editor, *The Writings of Thomas Jefferson* (New York: G.P. Putnam's Sons, 1894), Vol. 3, pp. 344-346.

MARTHA COREY IS CONVICTED OF WITCHCRAFT

Martha Corey was accused of witchcraft in 1692 by several young girls and older women who claimed to have been bewitched by her. She refused to confess and was convicted and then hanged on September 22. In 1710, the Massachusetts General Court reversed this decision as well as other witchcraft convictions. This is an account of her trial.

At the sermon time, when Goodwife Corey was present in the meeting-house, Abigail Williams called out, "Look where Goodwife Corey sits on the Beam suckling her Yellow Bird betwixt her fingers!" Anne Putnam, another girl who showed signs of being bewitched, said there was a Yellow-bird "sitting on my hat as it hung on the pin in the pulpit", but those that were around her stopped her from speaking out about it.

On Monday, the 21st of March, the Magistrates of Salem came to examine Goodwife Corey. At about twelve o'clock, they went into the meeting-house, which was crowded with spectators. The minister began with a very pertinent and pathetic prayer. Goodwife Corey, being called to reply to the charges that had been made against her, wanted to pray, which was much wondered at in the presence of so many people. The Magistrates told her they would not allow it; they did not come to hear her pray but to examine her about the charges against her. The worshipful Mr. Hathorne, a magistrate, asked her, "Why do you afflict those children?" She said, "I do not afflict them." He asked her who had made them act as they did and she said, " I do not know; how should I know?" The number of afflicted persons was about ten—four married women, three young women, and three girls, from nine to twelve years of age. They were Elizabeth Parris, Abigail Williams and Anne Putnam. Most of these people were at the trial of Goodwife Corey and strongly accused her in the Assembly of afflicting them by biting, pinching, strangling, etc. And when they were afflicted they saw her likeness coming to them and bringing a Book to them. She said she had no Book. They said she had a Yellow-Bird that used to suck betwixt her fingers, and being asked about it, she said she had no familiarity with spirits or any such thing. She was a good woman which she called herself. The afflicted persons told her, "Ah! You are a good witch." Anne Putnam said that one day when Lieutenant Fuller was at prayer at her father's house, she saw the shape of Goodwife Corey praying to the Devil. Goodwife Corey answered that they were poor, distracted children and should not be listened to. Mr. Hathorne and Mr. Noyes replied that it was the judgement of all that were present that the girls were bewitched and that only she, the accused person, said that they were distracted.

It was observed several times that if Goodwife Corey bit her lip while she was being examined, the afflicted persons were bitten on their arms and wrists and produced the marks before the magistrates and others. And while she was being watched for that, if she pinched her fingers, or grasped one hand in another, they were pinched and produced their marks before the magistrates and spectators. After that it was observed that if she but leaned her breast against the seat in the meeting-house, they were afflicted. Especially Mrs. Pope complained of great torment. She strongly accused Goodwife Corey as the cause and first threw her muff at Corey, but when that did not hit her, she took off her shoe and hit Goodwife Corey on the head with it. After the movements were watched, the afflicted stamped their feet fearfully if Goodwife Corey only slightly moved her feet.

The afflicted persons asked why she did not go to the company of witches. Did she not hear the drum beat? They accused her of having familiarity with the Devil, in the time of the questioning. He was in the shape of a Black man whispering in her ear.

They told her that she had made an agreement with the Devil for ten years; six of them were gone and four more to come. She was then required by the magistrates to answer a religious question and she answered it, but oddly. She denied all that was charged against her and said, "They could not prove a witch." That afternoon Goodwife Corey was committed to Salem prison, and after she was in custody she did not appear to the young girls and women and afflict them as before.

Deodat Lawson, *A Brief and True Narrative of Some Remarkable Passages Relating to Sundry Persons Afflicted by Witchcraft* (Boston, 1692) Facsimile: Photostat Americana, second series, (Boston, 1936), adapted.

THE TRIAL OF ANNE HUTCHINSON

In 1638 Anne Hutchinson was excommunicated by the Puritans of Massachusetts Bay and forced to leave the colony. The record of her trial shows the divisions among the Puritans and the threat they saw in Mrs. Hutchinson's ideas.

March 15, 1638

Mr. Leverit [A Puritan Elder of the Church of Boston]. Sister Hutchinson: Here are the opinions you are accused of having and I must request you in the name of the Church to declare whether you hold them or renounce them, as they are read to you. [He reads the charges.] It is desired by the Church, Sister Hutchinson, that you express whether this is your opinion or not.

Mrs. Hutchinson. If this is Error, then it is mine and I ought to stop believing it; if it is the truth it is not mine but Jesus Christ's and then I must continue to believe it. [There follows a long argument between the Elders and Mrs. Hutchinson over her religious beliefs which are different from theirs.]

Mr. Cotton [A leader of the Boston Church]. I do in the first place bless the Lord and thank, in my own name and in the name of our Church, these our friends for their care in watching over our Church and for bringing to light what ourselves have not been so ready to see in any of our own members . . . I confess I have not been ready to believe reports and have been slow in proceeding. [The charges against Hutchinson are judged true.] And therefore in the first place I shall direct my speech to those who are Mrs.

Hutchinson's sons and sons-in-law. Let me tell you from the Lord though natural affection may lead you to speak in defense of your mother, and to take her part, which may be lawful and praiseworthy in some cases and at some times, yet in the cause of God you are neither to know father nor mother, sister nor brother. You have not helped your mother by pleading for her but you have hardened her heart and encouraged her wrong opinion.

Now let me speak to the sisters of our Congregation, many of whom I feel have been led astray by Mrs. Hutchinson. I warn you in the name of the Lord to look to yourselves and to take care that you accept nothing as Truth which has not the stamp of the word of God on it. Let me say this to you all, let not the good you have received from Mrs. Hutchinson make you believe all she says, for you see she is only a woman and many unsound and dangerous principles are held by her . . .

March 22, 1638

[Her errors of belief are read to the Elders again.]
Mrs. Hutchinson. As my sin has been open, so I think it necessary to acknowledge how I first came to fall into these errors. Instead of looking upon myself I looked at men. I know my concealing will do no good. I spoke hastily and unwisely. I do not allow the slighting of ministers or of the Scriptures, nor anything that is set up by God: if my accusers believe that I had any of these things in mind then they have been tricked. It was never in my heart to slight any man, but only that man should be kept in his own place and not set in the room of God.

[They continue to discuss her errors.]
Mr. Peters. I would desire Mrs. Hutchinson in the name of the Lord that she would search into her heart farther to help on her repentance, for though she has confessed some things yet it is far short of what it should be and therefore:

1. I fear you are not well principled and grounded in your religious beliefs.

2. I would commend this to your consideration; that you have stepped out of your place, you have rather been a husband than a wife and a preacher rather than a hearer; and a magistrate rather than a subject. So you have thought to do all things in Church and commonwealth in your own way and you have not been humbled for this. [She is excommunicated.]

Ezra Stiles, "Report of the Trial of Mrs. Anne Hutchinson," *Proceedings of the Massachusetts Historical Society,* Vol. IV, Series II (Boston, 1889), pp. 161-191, adapted.

SELF-RELIANT WOMEN OF THE NORTHERN COLONIES

The newspapers of the period are a good source of information about the activity of colonial women. The following advertisements, taken from several 18th century newspapers in northern colonies, show the business ability of early American women.

From the *Pennsylvania Gazette:*

October 25, 1739   Choice RICE to be SOLD, either by the Barrel, or smaller Quantity, by Mrs. Margaret Magee next door but one to the Adam and Eve, in Arch-Street.

May 30, 1771   PICKLED STURGEON, of this Season's putting up, by ELIZABETH PHILLIPS ... Where the Public may be supplied with Kegs of different Prices, done in the Baltick Manner, different from any cured in this Province, she having served a regular Time to that Branch of Business ...

May 30, 1771   The subscriber takes this method of informing the public, that she carries on the business of Tavern-Keeping, in the house where her late husband (Joseph Yeates) formerly lived, at the Sign of the Fountain and Three Tons ... where she hopes to give satisfaction ...
   MARY YEATES
   All persons indebted to the estate of JOSEPH YEATES, late of the said city of Philadelphia, deceased, are desired to make speedy payment ...
   MARY YEATES
   administratrix

From the *Boston Evening-Post:*

August 30, 1762   A WET NURSE with a young Breast of Milk, would either go into a Family, or take a Child Home to nurse.

February 1, 1748   This may inform young Gentlewomen in Town and Country, That early in the Spring, Mrs. Hiller designs to open a Boarding-School at the House where she lives, in Fish-Street ... where they may be taught Wax-works, Transparent and Filligree, Painting upon Glass, Japanning, Quilt-Work, Feather-Work and embroidery with Gold and Silver, and several other sorts of Work not here enumerated, and may be supplied with Patterns and all sorts of Drawing, and Materials for their Work.

February 1, 1748   To be sold by Elizabeth Decoster in Milk-Street, in Boston, at the Sign of the Walnut Tree . . . pickled Pepper and fine Celery, Endive, Windsor Beans, early Peas, and Garden seeds of several sorts, Flower seeds and fine English Walnut Trees, and grafted Pear Trees, all at Reasonable Rates.

From the *New York Gazette or The Weekly Post-Boy:*
May 21, 1753   Notice is hereby given, that the Widow of Balthaser Sommer . . . Grinds all sorts of Optic Glasses to the greatest Perfection, such as Microscope Glasses, Spying Glasses of all Lengths, Spectacles, Reading-Glasses, . . . all at the most reasonable Rates.

June 13, 1765   Mrs. RIDGELY, MIDWIFE FROM LONDON: she intends during her Stay [in New York] to resume that Practice . . . and will most carefully, tenderly and punctually attend those Ladies who may please to favor her with their Commands . . .

From the *New York Gazette and the Weekly Mercury:*
May 7, 1770   Mary Morcomb, Mantua-Maker [loose gown] . . . Makes all sorts of negligees, Brunswick dresses, gowns, and every other sort of lady's apparel: And also covers Umbrellas in the neatest and most fashionable manner, at the lowest prices . . .

(Some advertisements involved women in other ways, as shown in these notices from the *Pennsylvania Gazette*)
August 23, 1739   TO BE SOLD. A Likely Servant Girl, who can do any sort of Household Work, either in Town or Country.
TO BE SOLD. A Likely Welch Servant Maid, who has four Years to serve, and can do any Household Work, either in Town or Country.

September 29, 1748   TO BE SOLD. A Likely Negro Woman, about 27 years of age, very fit for town or country business.

MARY PROVOOST ALEXANDER–COLONIAL BUSINESSWOMAN

Mary Provoost was born in New York City in 1693. She inherited money from her father and invested it in her husband's business ventures. After her husband died she continued to manage his business affairs as was usual with the Dutch of the colony. The following letter was written by her second husband on October 21, 1721.

Two nights ago at eleven o'clock, my wife [gave birth to] a daughter and is in as good health as can be expected, and does more than can be expected of any women, for till within a few hours of her being brought to bed she was in her shop, and ever since has given the price of goods to her apprentice, who comes to her and asks it when customers come in. The very next day after she was brought to bed she sold goods to above thirty pounds value. And here the business matters of her shop, which is generally esteemed the best in New York, she with an apprentice of about 16 years of age perfectly well manages without the least help from me, you may guess a little of her success . . . The greatest of my good fortune is in getting so good a wife as I have, who alone would make a man easy and happy had he nothing else to depend on.

Alice Morse Earle, *Colonial Days in Old New York* (New York: Charles Scribner's Sons, 1896), p. 163.

NEW YORK WOMEN PROTEST THEIR LACK OF RIGHTS

Although many colonial women were active in business throughout the northern settlements, in other areas of daily life their participation was not permitted. This letter, which appeared in 1733 in John Peter Zenger's New York Weekly Journal, was written by a group of women who were concerned about this problem.

Mr. Zenger,
    We the widows of this city, have had a meeting and as our case is something deplorable we beg you will give it [a] place in your Weekly Journal, that we may be relieved. [Our case] is as follows.
    We are housekeepers, pay our taxes, carry on trade, and most of us are she merchants, and as we in some measure contribute to the

support of the government, we ought to be entitled to some of the sweets of it; but we find ourselves entirely neglected, while the husbands that live in our neighborhood are daily invited to dine at Court: we have the vanity to think we can be [just] as entertaining, and make as brave a defense in case of an invasion, and perhaps not turn tail so soon as some of them . . .

New York Weekly Journal, January 21, 1733/4, pp. 3-4.

ELIZA LUCAS PINCKNEY–COLONIAL FARMER

One of the outstanding Southern women of colonial times was Eliza Lucas Pinckney. The two letters which follow describe her lifestyle and expectations for herself and give a picture of a spirited and talented woman.

I. Here she describes to a friend what keeps her busy.

In general then, I rise at five o'clock in the morning, read till seven—then take a walk in the garden or fields, see that the servants are at their respective business, then to breakfast. The first hour after breakfast is spent in music, the next is constantly employed in recollecting something I have learned, lest for [lack] of practice it should be quite lost, such as French and shorthand. After that, I devote the rest of the time till I dress for dinner, to our little Polly and two black girls who I teach to read, and if I have my papa's [approval] (my mama's I have got) I intend [to get] school mistresses for the rest of the Negro children. Another scheme you see, but to proceed, the first hour after dinner, as the first after breakfast, at music, the rest of the afternoon in needle work till candle light, and from that time to bed time read or write . . . Monday's my music Master is here. Tuesday my friend Mrs. Chardon . . . and this is one of the happiest days I spend . . . Thursday the whole day except what the necessary affairs of the family take up, is spent in writing, either on the business of the plantations or on letters to my friends. Every other Friday, if no company, we go avisiting, so that I go [out] once a week and no oftener . . .

O! I had [forgotten] the last thing I have done in a great while. I have planted a large fig orchard, [with the plan] to dry them out and export them . . . I love the vegetable world extremely. I think it an innocent and useful amusement . . .

II. Her father has suggested two men for Eliza to consider marrying and here she answers his request.

Honoured Sir,—. . . As you propose Mr. L. to me I am sorry I can't have sentiments favorable enough to him to take time to think on the subject . . . But as I know 'tis my happiness you consult, I must beg the favor of you to pay my compliments to the old gentleman for his generosity and favorable sentiments of me, and let him know my thoughts on the affair in such civil terms as you know much better than any I can dictate; and beg leave to say to you that the riches of Chile and Peru put together if he had them, could not purchase a sufficient esteem for him to make him my husband.

As to the other gentleman you mention, Mr. W., you know Sir I have so slight a knowledge of him I can form no judgement . . .

But give me leave to assure you my dear Sir that a single life is my only choice;—and if it were not as I am yet but eighteen hope you will put aside the thoughts of my marrying yet these two or three years at least . . .

> Your most dutiful and affect. Daughter
> E. Lucas

Harriott Ravenal, *Eliza Pinckney* (New York: Charles Scribner's Sons, 1896), pp. 30-32, 55-57.

THE LIFE OF THE PRIVILEGED SOUTHERN WOMAN

As a young man Philip Vickers Fithian was a tutor at Nomini Hall, one of the large Virginia plantations. He kept a journal of his experiences there from 1773 to 1774. In the following excerpt Fithian describes the women of Nomini Hall.

Thursday 16 [Dec] . . . I had the pleasure of walking today at twelve o'clock with Mrs. Carter [the plantation mistress]; she showed me her stock of fowls and muttons for the winter; she observed, with great truth, that to live in the country, and take no pleasure at all in groves, fields, or meadows; nor in cattle, horses, and domestic poultry, would be a manner of life too tedious to endure . . .

Tuesday 4 [Jan] . . . Mrs. Carter is prudent, always cheerful, never without something pleasant, a remarkable economist, perfectly acquainted (in my opinion) with the good management of children, entirely free from all foolish and unnecessary fondness, and is also well acquainted . . . with the formality and ceremony which we find commonly in high life . . .

. . . Miss Priscilla, the eldest daughter about 16, is steady, studious, docile, quick [of understanding], and makes good progress in what she undertakes; if I could with propriety continue in the family, I should require no stronger inducement than the satisfaction I should receive by seeing this young lady become perfectly acquainted with anything I propose so soon as I communicated it to her . . . She is small of her age, has a mild, winning presence, a sweet obliging temper, never swears, which is here a distinguished virtue, dances finely, plays well on keyed instruments, and is upon the whole in the first class of the female sex.

Philip Vickers Fithian, *Journal and Letters 1773-4: A Plantation Tutor of the Old Dominion* (Williamsburg: Colonial Williamsburg Inc., 1943), pp. 42, 64-65.

A SOUTHERN BACKCOUNTRY WOMAN

The traditional picture of the "Southern lady" did not generally apply to those women who lived in frontier societies in the Southern colonies. Mrs. Jones, one of these women, led a very different life from the "Southern lady."

It is said of this Mrs. Jones from whose house we came that she is a very civil woman and shows nothing of ruggedness or immodesty in her [appearance], yet she will carry a gun in the woods and kill deer, turkeys, etc., shoot down wild cattle, catch and tie hogs, knock down beeves [beef] with an ax, and perform the most manful exercises as well as most men in these parts.

Philip Ludwell and Nathaniell Harrison, "Boundary Line Proceeding, 1710," *The Virginia Magazine of History and Biography,* Vol. V (1897-1898), p. 10.

A SOUTHERN WOMAN COMPLAINS ABOUT HER ROLE

The poem below was printed anonymously in the *Virginia Gazette* in 1736. Its author, who was quite dissatisfied with the role woman were expected to play, made one of the earliest pleas for legal equality for women.

Mr. Parks [Publisher], The following Lines were some Years ago, presented to me by a Lady; and as I don't remember I ever saw them in Print, you inserting them in your Paper will, I dare say, oblige many of your Readers, as well as your humble Servant.

The Lady's COMPLAINT

CUSTOM, alas! doth partial prove,
    Nor gives us equal Measure;
A Pain for us it is to love,
    But is to Men a Pleasure.

They plainly can their Thoughts disclose,
    Whilst ours must burn within:
We have got Tongues, and Eyes, in Vain,
    And Truth from us is Sin.

Men to new Joys and Conquests fly,
 And yet no Hazard run:
Poor we are left, if we deny,
 And if we yield, undone,

Then Equal Laws let Custom find,
 And neither Sex oppress;
More Freedom give to Womankind,
 Or give to Mankind less.

Virginia Gazette, October 15-October 22, 1736, p. 3, column 2.

PHILLIS WHEATLEY–BLACK POET

In 1761 Phillis Wheatley was bought from a slave ship in Boston by John Wheatley, a wealthy merchant whose wife wanted a personal servant. Although a slave, Wheatley was treated like a daughter of the family and given an excellent education. Her poetry drew much attention and her first book of poems was most likely the first book by a black American.

Copy of a letter sent by Author's Master to Publisher in 1772.

Phillis was brought from Africa to America, in the year 1761, between seven and eight years of age. Without any assistance from school education, and by only what she was taught in the family, she, in sixteen months time from her arrival, attained [learned] the English language, to which she was an utter stranger before, to such a degree, as to read any, the most difficult parts of the sacred writings, to the great astonishment of all who heard her.

As to her writing, her own curiosity led her to it; and this she learnt in so short a time, that in the year 1765, she wrote a letter to the Reverend Mr. Occum, the Indian minister, while in England.

She has a great inclination to learn the Latin tongue, and has made some progress in it. This relation [account] is given by her master who bought her, and with whom she now lives.

                                    John Wheatley
Boston, November 14, 1772

(The following is probably Phillis Wheatley's first poem.)

On being brought from AFRICA to AMERICA

'Twas mercy brought me from my *pagan* land,
Taught my benighted [ignorant] soul to understand
That there's a God, that there's a *Savior* too:

Once I redemption neither sought nor knew.
Some view our sable race with scornful eye,
"Their color is a diabolic [devilish] die."
Remember, *Christians*, *Negroes*, black as *Cain*,
Many be refin'd, and join th' angelic train.

(This poem shows a different attitude about being a slave.)

No more, *America*, in mournful strain
Of wrongs, and grievance unredress'd complain,
No longer shall thou dread the iron chain,
Which wanton *Tyranny* with lawless hand
Has made, and which it meant t' enslave the land.
Should you, my lord, while you puruse my song,
Wonder from whence my love of Freedom sprung,
Whence flow these wishes for the common good,
By feeling hearts alone best understood,
I, young in life, by seeming cruel fate
Was snatched from *Afric's* fancy'd happy seat:
What pangs excruciating must molest,
What sorrows labour in my parent's breast?
Steel'd was that soul and by no misery mov'd
That from a father seiz'd his babe belov'd:
Such, such is my case. And can I then but pray
Others may never feel tyrannic sway?

Phillis Wheatley, *Poems on Various Subjects* (London, 1773), pp. vi, 18, 74.

A YOUNG GIRL BECOMES AN INDENTURED SERVANT

During colonial times, white women and men, and, very rarely, blacks, became indentured servants. Often young children were bound out. This agreement binds out young Aulkey Hubertse as a house servant in Albany, New York, in 1710.

   This Indenture witnesses that Aulkey Hubertse, daughter of the deceased John Hubertse, of the Colony of Rensselaerwyck, has bound herself as a menial servant. She has voluntarily and of her own free will and accord bound herself as a menial servant to John Delemont, a weaver of the City of Albany, with the consent of the Deacons of the Reformed Dutch Church. She will serve from the date of these present Indentures [1710] to the time that the said Aulkey Hubertse shall come to Age. During this term the said servant shall serve her Master faithfully, keep his secrets, gladly obey his lawful commands. She shall do not damage to her said Master nor see it to be done by others without telling her Master; she shall not waste her Master's goods, nor lend them unlawfully to anyone. At cards, dice or any other game she shall not play. She shall not buy or sell with her own goods or the goods of others during the said term; she shall not absent herself day or night from her Master's service without his permission. She shall not go to ale-houses, taverns or playhouses, but in all things she shall behave as a faithful servant. And the said Master, during the said term, shall find and provide sufficient and complete meat and drink, washing, lodging and apparel, and all other necessities fit for such a servant. It is further agreed between the Master and Servant that in case the said Aulkey Hubertse should [get married] before she shall come to Age, then the servant is free from her service. At the end of her servitude, John Delemont shall find, provide for and deliver to the servant double apparel, that is to say, apparel fit for wearing on the Lord's Day as well as on working days, both linen and woolen stockings and shoes and other necessities. For the true performance of all and every part of this agreement, the said parties bind themselves to each other.

Alice Morse Earle, *Colonial Days in Old New York* (New York: Charles Scribner's Son, 1896), pp. 84-86, adapted.

DISSATISFACTIONS OF INDENTURED SERVANTS

Because of the harsh conditions under which they worked, many indentured servants tried to escape. The following advertisements are typical of the many notices that appeared in colonial newspapers as masters searched out their servants.

Run away from the Subscriber, of Essex County, on Wednesday the 9th of this . . . November, a Convict Servant Woman, nam'd Ann Wheatley; she is a lusty, well-set Woman, with very dark Hair black Eyes, and a fresh Complexion . . .

The Virginia Gazette, Friday November 11-Friday November 18, 1737.

Ran away from the Subscriber, living in *Fairfax* County, on the 30th Day of March last, an English, Convict Servant Woman, named *Isabella Pierce;* of a middle Stature, thin Visage, limps with her right leg, which, if examin'd, will appear to be a large Scar on each Side of the Ankle of her said leg . . .

The Virginia Gazette, Friday May 2-Friday May 9, 1745.

Run away from the subscriber, in *Northumberland* county, two Irish convict servants named WILLIAM and HANNAH DAYLIES, tinkers by trade, of which the woman is extremely good; they had a note of leave to go out and work in *Richmond* county and *Hobb's Hole*, the money to be paid to *Job Thomas,* in said county; soon after I heard they were run away . . .

The Virginia Gazette, March 26, 1767.

2
Formation of a New Nation

On March 31, 1776, Abigail Adams wrote to her husband, John, who was in Philadelphia with the Continental Congress. She wrote that she hoped he would "remember the ladies" in the new code of laws that she thought it would be necessary to write and "be more generous and favorable to them" than his ancestors had been. "Remember," she reminded him, "all men would be tyrants if they could." Perhaps he was amazed when she threatened to "foment a rebellion" if women had no voice in the new government. Perhaps he was amused. On July 4, 1776, Abigail Adams and the other American women and men were able to read the finished Declaration of Independence, which contained the words, "We hold these truths to be self-evident, that all *men* are created equal . . ." Apparently traditional ideas about the proper role of women had influenced the fathers of the new nation much more than Abigail Adams' radical and unusual beliefs.

Women Participate in the War Effort

The Declaration of Independence was the response of the American colonists to British restrictions in the decades before 1776. The col-

30

Abigail Adams.

onists objected to unfair taxes, trade limitations, and lack of representation in the British Parliament. As the relationship between England and the colonies worsened, writers began to encourage women to participate in patriotic activities.

While men formed the Sons of Liberty and boycotted British goods, groups of women organized Daughters of Liberty societies. A woman who joined this group would have spun thread and made clothes to replace goods that were no longer imported from England. She would also have urged people to stop drinking tea, because tea was supplied by the English. The Daughters of Liberty publicized substitutes for tea such as sage, birch brew, rosemary, and a difficult to prepare mixture called "liberty tea."

Abigail Adams wrote in 1773, "The tea that bainfull weed is arrived. Great and I hope effectual opposition has been made to the landing of it." Her words reflected women's growing political awareness and economic power in the years before the Revolution.

Mercy Otis Warren, a patriot and an outstanding writer of the period, was even more politically aware than her friend Abigail. She corresponded with and was listened to by some of the foremost male leaders of the day. In 1775 she wrote to John Adams:

Throughout the colonies, many women voted to boycott English tea. This cartoon of a group of North Carolina women shows that often their efforts were not taken seriously.

> How much longer, sir, do you think the political scale can hang [in the balance]? Will not justice and freedom soon dominate? . . . If you attempt to repair the shattered Constitution or to erect a new one may it be constructed . . .[so] that it may never be in the power of ambition or tyranny to shake the durable fabric . . .

Her strong beliefs in freedom expressed the ideas of a number of colonial women who could not write as well.

The Battles of Lexington and Concord in 1775 started the Revolutionary War. As men left home for the battlefields many women became involved with business affairs that supported the war effort.

Mrs. Peter Coffin, the wife of a New Hampshire farmer, took over his responsibilities when he went to war. She harvested the farm's wheat crop with the help of a 14-year-old youth. Resourceful Mary Sescumb, an 18-year-old bride, took charge of an entire North Carolina plantation, and split rails and managed all the other affairs of her home. Even wealthy women assumed economic responsibilities. While John Adams was away from home, Abigail Adams ran the household, caring for the education of her children, the farming, and all business affairs.

Clever management of these business affairs enabled some women to contribute money to the war effort. Elizabeth Peck Perkins was widowed in 1773 with eight children to support. She established her own business, a shop where she sold chinaware, glass, wine, and other imported goods. Doing this, she was able to provide for her family throughout the war and in 1780 to give $1,000 to the Continental Army. Active in many other business and domestic areas, women kept colonial life stable throughout the Revolutionary period.

Military Activities

Today weapons are produced in factories by machines. During the Revolutionary War period, many citizens helped to supply the army by using materials from their homes. Women's military activities grew. They helped to make munitions, sometimes even giving up a cherished pewter dish so that musket balls could be made. Statues of the British King George III were melted down for ammunition— one statue in Bowling Green, New York City, produced 42,000 musket balls. Women also were largely responsible for supplying the hard-pressed Continental Army with food and clothing. Even

During the American Revolution women participated on the home front in many ways. Here a patriot sets fire to her fields to prevent the crop from falling into English hands.

Molly Pitcher.

Martha Washington became an army wife during the struggle and brought food to soldiers from her home at Mount Vernon. In 1780 Esther De Berdt Reed and Sarah Bache organized a campaign of Philadelphia women to raise money and were able to turn over more than $300,000 to the Revolutionary government. Part of the money was used to buy material to make shirts, and by December 26, 1780, just over 2,000 shirts were delivered to the soldiers by hardworking, competent seamstresses.

Not all women remained at home during the 1770's. Many went along with the army. Families were permitted to travel with the troops when the British advanced toward their home towns. Army pay was irregular, and poor women were often better able to survive when traveling with their men. Army women performed essential services such as washing, mending, and cooking, as well as nursing the sick and wounded.

Sometimes courageous women participated actively in the fighting. Mary Ludwig married John Hays and followed him to his army camp where she worked as a cook and nurse. Ludwig became famous at the Battle of Monmouth on June 28, 1778, when she spent hours carrying water back and forth to the men, who were fainting from the heat. The men gave her the name Molly Pitcher (Molly with her pitcher). On one of her trips she saw her husband wounded by gunfire and immediately took over his position in the battle. General Washington made her a sergeant and placed her on officer's half-pay as a reward for her heroic actions. Two years earlier, in a battle at Fort Washington in New York, Molly Corbin replaced a gunner who had been shot. She was seriously wounded herself in the fighting. Corbin appears to have been the first woman to fight for the United States.

Most exciting of all the army women was Deborah Sampson, who enlisted as a Continental soldier disguised as a man named "Robert Shurtleff." She fought in several battles and remained undiscovered for over a year. When she was wounded the shocked doctor discovered that she was a woman. She was honorably discharged, though in secret, and eventually Sampson received a pension of $8 a month. Her husband asked for and got ten times that amount for taking care of her wounds. Apparently the government valued her husband's nursing care more than her participation in the war.

Lydia Darragh also helped the colonies achieve independence. Her home in Philadelphia was often chosen for conferences by British officers because she was a Quaker, and the officers believed she would not become involved in the war because of her religion. On December 2, 1777, a meeting took place and although Darragh pretended to be asleep, she actually listened at the door, where she heard the order for a surprise attack on American troops outside Philadelphia. The following day she told her husband she was going for flour, but actually walked until she found an American officer to whom she told her story. She thus prevented an American defeat. Perhaps her walk was important as Paul Revere's ride.

Hardy Jane Thomas rode 66 miles to warn of a coming attack by the British, and Sybil Ludington, who lived in Putnam County, New York, rode 25 to 40 miles over difficult terrain to warn scattered troops about supplies that the British had taken. The roused soldiers then defeated the British and recaptured the supplies.

Stories like those of Sampson and Darragh are many and show the vital but neglected role women played in the military actions of the Revolution. The one woman of this time with whom most Americans are familiar is Betsy Ross, the legendary creator of the first American flag. There appear to be no records that confirm this story, and George Washington was not even in Philadelphia, Ross' home, at the time. It is interesting to speculate why Americans know of Ross but not of Sampson or Corbin. Perhaps this is because Ross was engaged in an acceptable feminine activity.

Political Life

Although in wartime it was acceptable for women to raise money, provide food for the troops, act as messengers, and perform other patriotic tasks, tradition and legal restrictions kept these same

All the signers of the Declaration of Independence were men. This picture accurately illustrates the situation after the Revolution as well as before it. Abigail Adams' plea to the politicians to "remember the ladies" went unheeded.

women out of politics. Abigail Adams and Mercy Warren understood what was occurring politically in the nation, but they could not serve as political leaders. When Mary Goddard was appointed postmaster of Baltimore in 1775, she served in one of the few political jobs in which women could be found at this time.

Some American women stood outside this tradition, however. American Indian women were frequently leaders in their societies. During the Revolution Nancy Ward, a Cherokee leader, was the head of the influential women's council of that tribe and a member of the council of chiefs. In 1776 she secretly warned a leader of the Tennessee settlers of a planned pro-British Cherokee attack against American whites. As a result she was not killed when colonial troops retaliated against the Loyalist Cherokees. In another instance of female Indian leadership, Molly Brant, a spirited Mohawk, aided the British during the war. She sent ammunition to them and helped their soldiers who were in hiding. Her influence in her tribe enabled her to keep the New York tribes on the side of the British throughout much of the war.

Women played important roles in the economic, social, and political activities of the Revolutionary years. Yet at the end of the struggle they found that their legal and social roles had not changed very much. In fact, as laws were written for the new nation, women's rights often became more limited than before. For example, women, who had occasionally voted in colonial New Jersey, could not vote there after the Revolution because the new laws restricted voting to free white males. Women's activities had helped to free the colonists from British rule but did little to change discriminatory practices against their sex.

Summary

The traditional idea of Revolutionary women held by most historians was shown by a plaque unveiled in Continental Village, New York, in 1921. It was dedicated to the "Mothers of the American Revolution" and read as follows:

1776–1783
A MILITARY POST AND DEPOT OF SUPPLIES
BURNED BY THE BRITISH OCTOBER 9, 1777

———

IN MEMORY OF
MOTHERS OF THE REVOLUTION
WHO WATCHED AND PRAYED WHILE OUR
FATHERS FOUGHT THAT WE MIGHT BE FREE

———

THEY ALSO SERVE WHO ONLY STAND AND WAIT

Perhaps this conception of Revolutionary women became popular when the history of the period was originally written, but it does not accurately describe the role of American women during the Revolution. Although their participation in the war resulted in little progress for women, there were signs in the late 1700's that change was coming. Judith Sargent Murray, author and feminist, wrote an essay in 1779 in which she made a radical statement for the time—that women and men had equal minds and thus better education for women was a necessity. More than a decade later, an Englishwoman, Mary Wollstonecraft, was to write *A Vindication of the Rights of Women* which spread throughout America the idea that no society could be healthy unless all groups, including women, were equal.

ABIGAIL ADAMS URGES HER HUSBAND TO "REMEMBER THE LADIES."

Abigail Adams and her husband John were separated for long periods during the years of the Revolution and the formation of the new nation. This separation led to an extensive series of letters in which she recorded her ideas and concerns about the events she observed. She was especially concerned about the role women would play in the new nation.

Saturday Evening, 2 March, 1776

I was greatly rejoiced at the return of your servant, to find you had safely arrived, and that you were well. I had never heard a word from you after you had left New York, and a most ridiculous story had been [spread] in this and the neighboring towns to injure the cause and blast your reputation; namely, that you and your President [Hancock] had gone on board of a man-of-war from New York, and sailed for England. I should not mention so idle a report, but that it had given uneasiness to some of your friends; . . .

I am charmed with the sentiments of "Common Sense," and wonder how an honest heart, one who wishes the welfare of his country and the happiness of [the future], can hesitate one moment at adopting them. I want to know how these sentiments are received in Congress . . .

I have been kept in a continual state of anxiety and expectation ever since you left me. It has been said "tomorrow" and "tomorrow," for this month, but when the dreadful tomorrow will be, I know not. But hark! The house this instant shakes with the roar of cannon . . . No sleep for me tonight . . .

Braintree, 31 March, 1776

. . . I feel very differently at the approach of spring from what I did a month ago. We knew not then whether we could plant or sow with safety, whether where we had tilled we could reap the fruits of our own industry, whether we could rest in our own cottages or whether we should be driven from the seacoast to seek shelter in the wilderness; but now we feel a temporary peace, and the poor fugitives are returning to their deserted [homes] . . .

I long to hear that you have declared an independency. And, by the way, in the new code of laws which I suppose it will be necessary for you to make, I desire you would remember the ladies and be more generous and favorable to them than your ancestors. Do not put such unlimited power into the hands of the husbands. Remember, all men would be tyrants if they could. If particular care and attention is not paid to the ladies, we are determined to foment a rebellion, and will not hold ourselves bound by any laws in which we have no voice or representation.

That your sex are naturally tyrannical is a truth so thoroughly established as to admit of no dispute; but such of you as wish to be happy willingly give up the harsh title of master for the more tender and endearing one of friend. Why, then, not put it out of the power of the vicious and the lawless to use us with cruelty and indignity with impunity? Men of sense in all ages abhor those customs which treat us only as the [servants] of your sex; regard us then as being placed by Providence under your protection, and in imitation of the Supreme Being make use of that power only for our happiness.

From John Adams to Abigail Adams, April 14, 1776

. . . As to your extraordinary code of laws, I cannot but laugh. We have been told that our struggle has loosened the bonds of government everywhere; that children and apprentices were disobedient; that schools and colleges were grown turbulent; that Indians slighted their guardians, and negroes grew insolent to their masters. But your letter was the first [hint] that another tribe, more numerous and powerful than all the rest, were grown discontented. This is rather too coarse a compliment, but you are so saucy, I won't blot it out. Depend upon it, we know better than to repeal our masculine systems. Although they are in full force, you know they are little more than theory. We dare not exert our power [to the fullest]. We are obliged to go fair and softly, and, in practice, you know we are the subjects. We have only the name of masters, and rather than give up this, which would completely subject us to the despotism of the petticoat, I hope General Washington and all our brave heroes would fight . . .

From Abigail Adams to John Adams, Braintree, 7 May, 1776

How many are the solitary hours I spend [thinking] upon the past and anticipating the future . . .

I cannot say that I think you are very generous to the ladies; for, whilst you are proclaiming peace and good-will to men, emancipating all nations, you insist upon retaining an absolute power over wives. But you must remember that arbitrary power is like most other things which are very hard, very liable to be broken; and, notwithstanding all your wise laws and maxims, we have it in our power, not only to free ourselves, but to subdue our masters, and without violence, throw both your natural and legal authority at our feet . . .

Our little ones, whom you so often recommend to my care and instruction, shall not be deficient in virtue or [honesty], if the [teachings] of a mother have their desired effect; but they would be doubly enforced, could they be indulged with the example of a father alternately before them . . .

Charles F. Adams, editor, *Familiar Letters of John Adams and His Wife Abigail Adams During the Revolution* (New York, 1875), pp. 136-137, 149-150, 155, 168-170.

LETTER FROM AN ANONYMOUS WOMAN TO A BRITISH OFFICER

During the Revolution, many women were outspoken in their loyalty to the colonial cause. They showed this concern and commitment in the letters and the diaries that they wrote.

[Dear Sir]:

I will tell you what I have done. My only brother I have sent to the camp with my prayers and blessings. I hope he will not disgrace me; I am confident he will behave with honor, and [follow] the great examples he has before him; and had I twenty sons and brothers they should go. I have [stopped every extra] expense in my table and family; tea I have not drunk since last Christmas, nor bought a new cap or gown since your defeat at Lexington; and what I never did before, have learned to knit, and am now making stockings of American wool for my servants; and this way do I throw in my [little bit] to the public good. I know this—that as free I can die but once; but as a slave [to the British] I shall not be worthy of life. I have the pleasure to assure you that these are the sentiments of all my sister Americans. They have sacrificed assemblies, parties of pleasure, tea drinking and finery, to that great spirit of patriotism . . . If these are the sentiments of females, what must glow in the breasts of our husbands, brothers, and sons! They are as with one heart determined to die or be free . . . Heaven seems to smile on us . . . We are making powder fast, and do not want for ammunition.

Elizabeth Ellet, *The Women of the American Revolution* (New York: Baker and Scribner, 1849), Vol. 1, pp. 19-21.

AMERICAN WOMEN ORGANIZE ECONOMIC BOYCOTTS

In the period of the American Revolution, colonists were urged to boycott British-made goods in an "economic war" on the mother country.

The following Agreement has lately been come into by upwards of 300 Mistresses of Families in this Town; in which Number the Ladies of the highest Rank and Influence, that could be waited upon in so short a Time are included.

Boston, January 31, 1770

At a Time when our invaluable Rights and Privileges are attacked in an unconstitutional and most alarming Manner, and as we find we are reproached for not being so ready as could be desired, to lend our Assistance, we think it our Duty perfectly to concur with the true Friends of Liberty, in all the Measures they have taken to save this abused Country from Ruin and Slavery: And particularly we join with the very respectable Body of Merchants and other Inhabitants of this Town . . . in their Resolutions, *totally* to abstain from the Use of TEA: And as the greatest Part of the Revenue arising [from the latest acts from England] is produced from the duty paid on Tea . . . We the Subscribers do strictly [agree] that we will *totally* abstain from the Use of [Tea] (Sickness excepted) not only in our respective Families; but that we will absolutely refuse it, if it should be offered to us upon any occasion whatsoever . . .

Boston Evening Post, February 12, 1770.

The patriotic ladies of Halifax-town, in North Carolina, have entered into an association to refrain, as far as possible, from all unnecessary expenses and superfluous decorations; and are determined, in future, until their country shall be extricated from its present difficulties and distress, to pay strict attention to economy and frugality, and to give all due preference to the manufactures of their country.

American Museum, August, 1787, p.165.

To The Ladies of South Carolina

My Sisters and Countrywomen,

At a time when . . . one of our sister colonies [is] . . . suffering under the iron hand of power.[Massachusetts under British control], in the general cause of American liberty . . . surely, my sisters, we cannot be tame spectators, when so much remains to us to do, and may be reasonably expected of us. By our persisting hitherto in the use of East India Tea, we have opposed our friends, and assisted the enemies of America to enslave ourselves and posterity. Let us now make it evident to the world that we have some regard for our country, and our offspring, by joining cheerfully, under the faith of a promise to each other, to forego the use of all foreign tea, as also every kind of East India goods ... On Heaven alone, and our general unanimity, the salvation of America depends ...

A Planter's Wife

The Virginia Gazette, September 15, 1774.

WOMEN ARE ADVISED TO CHOOSE THEIR MEN CAREFULLY

Women had many ways of persuading men to join the patriot's cause. The author of this poem suggests one way of dealing with men who did not support the Revolution.

To the Printer
Poet's Corner

Permit a giddy, trifling Girl,
    For Once to fill your Poet's Corner,
She cares not though the Critics snarl,
    Or Beaus and Macaronies [vain men] scorn her.
She longs, in Print, her Lines to see;
    Oblige her (sure you can't refuse it)
And if you find her out, your Fee
    Shall be—to *kiss her*—if you choose it . . .

The Favor that to you she proffers [offers]
    Has been solicited in vain,
And many flattering, splendid Offers,
    Rejected with a cold Disdain.
She scorns the Man, however pretty,
    However Riches round him flow,
However wise, or great, or witty,
    That's to his Country's Rights a Foe.
He that, to flatter Folks in Power,
    His Country's Freedom would betray,
Deserves the Gallows every Hour,
    Or worse—to feel a Tyrant's Sway.
May such, alone, be unprotected

By justice and by Nature's Laws;
And, to despotic Power subjected,
    Suffer the miseries they cause.
To scorn them is each Female's Duty,
    Let them no Children have, or Wife;
May they ne'er meet the Smiles of Beauty,
    Nor any social Joys of Life.

The Virginia Gazette, June 2, 1774.

HARDSHIP DURING THE REVOLUTION

Women had great difficulties running their homes because of shortages of ordinary products during the years of the Revolution. In the following poem, Molly Gutridge describes the hardships she faced during "hard and cruel times."

It's hard and cruel times to live,
Takes thirty dollars to buy a sieve
To buy sieves and other things too,
To go thro' the world how can we do?

For salt is all the Farmer's cry,
If we've no salt we sure must die.
We can't get fire nor yet food,
Takes 20 weight of sugar for two feet of wood,
We cannot get bread nor yet meat,
We see the world is nought but cheat.

All we can get it is but rice
And that is of a wretched price.

These times will learn us to be wise,
We now do eat what we despis'd,
I now have something more to say,
We must go up and down the Bay,
To get a fish-a-days to fry,
We can't get fat were we to die.

New England Quarterly, Vol. 20 (September, 1947), p. 335.

DEBORAH SAMPSON FIGHTS IN THE REVOLUTION

Deborah Sampson was an indentured servant whose early life was one of poverty and hardship. At the end of her indenture she worked to give herself the opportunity to go to school. She recounts her adventures as a woman who disguised herself as a man to fight in the Continental Army.

In March 1781 [this date has been questioned] the season being too rough to commence her excursion, she proposed to equip herself at her leisure: and then [decide on] the time for her departure. A handsome piece of cloth was to be put to a use, of which she little thought, during the time she was employed in manufacturing it . . . She made her[self] a genteel coat, waistcoat and breeches without any other assistance, than the uncouth patterns belonging to her former master's family. The other articles, hats, shoes, etc., were purchased under invented pretexts. [She seems to have had doubts about her plan and hesitated, then continued, traveling for several days.] She acted her part [in her travels]: and having a natural taste for refinement, she was every where received as a blithe, handsome and agreeable young gentleman . . .

In Bellingham, she met with a speculator; with whom . . . she engaged . . . as a Continental Soldier. Instead, then, of going to Boston, she went back and was immediately conducted to Worcester; where she was . . . enrolled by the name of ROBERT SHURTLEFF . . .

On May 13, she arrived at West-Point in company with about fifty other soldiers, who were conducted there by a sergeant sent for that purpose. West-Point was then an important post, where was stationed a large division of the American army . . .

The second day, she drew a French fusee, a knapsack, cartridge-box and thirty cartridges. Her next business was to clean her [weapon], and to exercise once every morning in the drill, and at four o'clock, P.M. on the grand parade. Her garb was exchanged for a uniform peculiar to the infantry . . .

Passing over many marches, forward and [back], and numberless incidental adventures and hardships peculiar to war, I come to other MEMOIRS . . .

Sometime in June of this year, she, with two sergeants, requested leave of their Captain to retaliate on the enemy . . . for their outrageous insults to the inhabitants beyond their lines . . . near the close of the day they [began] their expedition . . .

About four in the morning . . . a severe combat [started]. The Americans found horses without riders; they had then light-horse and foot. Our [heroine] having previously become a good horseman, immediately mounted an excellent horse. [They pursued the enemy and fought with them.] The dauntless [Sampson] at this instant, thought she felt something warmer than sweat run down her neck. Putting her hand to the place, she found the blood gushed from the left side of her head very freely. She said nothing; as she thought it no time to tell of wounds, unless mortal. Coming to a stand, she dismounted, but had not strength to walk, or stand alone. [She was also wounded in the thigh.]

She told one of the sergeants, she was so wounded, she chose rather to be left in that horrid place, than be carried any further. They all, as one, concluded to carry her, in case she could not ride. Here was her trial! A thousand thoughts and spectres at once darted before her. She had always thought she should rather die, than disclose her sex to the army! [She is hospitalized and in order to avoid discovery] she requested the favor of more medicine than she needed for her head; and taking an opportunity, with a penknife and needle, she extracted the [bullet] from her thigh . . . [She became a victim of an epidemic and is taken to a hospital again where she worries about discovery.] Doctor Bana . . . entered; and putting his hand in her bosom to feel her pulse, was surprised to find an inner waist-coat tightly compressing her breasts. Ripping it in haste, he was still more shocked, not only on finding [her alive] but the breasts and other tokens of a female. Immediately, she was removed into the Matron's own apartment . . . [She eventually is honorably discharged with no general awareness of her sex.]

The following document was used as proof of service when Deborah Sampson Gannett tried to get a pension awarded to her including back pay.

To all whom it may concern,

These may certify, that Robert Shurtleff was a Soldier in my Regiment, in the Continental Army, for the town of Uxbridge in the Commonwealth of Massachusetts, and was enlisted for the term of three years—that he had the confidence of his Officers, did his duty, as a faithful and good Soldier, and was honorably discharged from the army of the United States.

HENRY JACKSON late Colonel
in American army.

Herman Mann, *The Female Review: Life of Deborah Sampson* (Boston, 1797), pp. 113, 127-129, 131-132, 170-175, 194, 255.

DEBORAH CHAMPION ROUSES THE PATRIOTS

During the Revolution several women warned the colonial troops of approaching dangers from British ambush. Deborah Champion was the daughter of General Henry Champion of the Revolutionary Army. At the age of 22, she was asked by her father to take an important message to General Washington, who was in Boston at the time. She successfully delivered the message to Washington who complimented her on her courage and patriotism. She tells of her ride in a letter to a friend.

My Dear Patience:

I know that you will think it a weary long time since I have written to you, and indeed I would have answered your last sweet letter long before now, but I have been away from home. Think of it! I know that you will hardly believe that such a stay-at-home as I should go and all alone too, to where do you think? To Boston! Really and truly to Boston. Before you suffer too much with amazement and curiosity, I will hasten to tell you all about it. About a week after receiving your letter I had settled with myself to spend a long day with my spinning, being anxious to prepare for some cloth which my mother needed to make some small clothes for father. Just as I was busily engaged I noticed a horseman enter the yard, and, knocking on the door with the handle of his whip, he asked for General Champion, and after a brief [conversation] he entered the house with father . . . When I returned [from having done errands for her mother], the visitor was gone, but my father was walking up and down the long hall with hasty steps, and worried and perturbed aspect. You know father has always been kind and good to me, but none know better than you the stern self-repression our New England character engenders, and he would not have thought seemly that a child of his should question him, so I passed on to find mother and deliver my purchases. "My father is troubled, Mother, is aught [anything] amiss?" "I cannot say, Deborah; you know he has many cares, and the public business presses heavily at times; it may be he will tell us." Just then my father stood in the doorway. "Wife, I would speak with you." Mother hastily joined him in the keeping room, and they seemed to have long and anxious [conversation]. Finally, to my astonishment, I was called to attend them. Father laid his hand on my shoulder (a most unusual caress with him) and said solemnly: "Deborah, I have need of thee; hast thou the heart and the courage to go out in the dark and in the night and ride as fast as may be until thou comest to Boston town?" "Surely, my Father, if it is thy wish, and will please thee."

"I do not believe, Deborah, that there will be actual danger to threaten thee, else I would not ask it of thee, but the way is long and the business urgent. The horseman that was here awhile back brought dispatches which it is desperately necessary that General Washington should receive as soon as possible. I cannot go, the wants of the army call me at once to Hartford, and I have no one to send but my daughter. Dare you go?"

"Dare! father, and I your daughter—and the chance to do my country and General Washington a service. I am glad to go."

So, dear Patience, it was finally settled that I should start in the early morning and Aristarchus should go with me . . . . Early in the morning, before it was fairly light, mother called me, though I had seemed to have hardly slept at all. I found a nice hot breakfast ready, and a pair of saddle-bags packed with such things as mother thought might be needed. Father told me again of the haste with which I must ride and the care to use for the safety of the dispatches, and I set forth on my journey with a light heart and my father's blessing. The British were at Providence, in Rhode Island, so it was thought best I should ride due north to the Massachusetts line, and then east, as best I could to Boston. The weather was perfect, but the roads none too good as there had been recent rains, but we made fairly good time . . . All went as well as I could expect. We met few people on the road, almost all the men being with the army and only the very old men and the women at work in the villages and farms. Dear heart, but war is a cruel thing! but I was glad, so glad that I could do even so little to help! . . . I heard that it would be almost impossible to avoid the British unless by going so far out of the way that too much time would be lost, so I plucked up what courage I could and secreting my papers in a small pocket in the saddle-bags, under all the eatables mother had filled them with I rode on determined to ride all night. It was late at night, or rather very early in the morning, that I heard the call of the sentry and knew that now, if at all, the danger point was reached, but pulling my calash [bonnet] still farther over my face, I went on with what boldness I could muster. Suddenly, I was ordered to halt; as I couldn't help myself I did so . . . A soldier in a red coat proceeded to take me to headquarters, but I told him it was early to wake the captain, and to please to let me pass for I had been sent in urgent haste to see a friend in need, which was true if ambiguous. To my joy, he let me go on, saying; "Well, you are only an old woman anyway," evidently as glad to get rid of me as I of him. Will you believe me, that is the only bit of adventure that befell me in the whole long ride. When I arrived in Boston, I was so very fortunate as to find friends who took me at once to General Washington and I gave him the papers, which proved to be of utmost importance, and was pleased to compliment me most highly both as to what he was pleased to call the courage I had displayed and my patriotism. Oh, Patience, what a man he is, so grand, so kind, so noble, I am sure we will not look to him in vain to save our fair country to us.

Mary Beard, *America Through Women's Eyes* (New York: Macmillan Co., 1933), pp. 73-75.

THOMAS PAINE WRITES ABOUT THE OPPRESSION OF WOMEN

Thomas Paine was a well-known writer of the Revolutionary period. He worked and wrote for freedom from English rule in the years before and during the American Revolution. His concern for the rights of the oppressed led him to examine the position of women in this magazine article of 1775. His ideas about women were considered radical for his era.

An Occasional Letter on the Female Sex

If we take a survey of ages and of countries, we shall find the women, almost—without exception—at all times, and in all places, adored and oppressed. Man, who has never neglected an opportunity of exerting his power, in paying homage to their beauty, has always availed himself of their weakness. He has been at once their tyrant and their slave. [He describes the condition of women in various parts of the world.] Even in countries where they may be esteemed most happy, constrained in their desires in the disposal of their goods, robbed of freedom of will by the laws, the slaves of opinion, which rules them with absolute sway, . . . surrounded on all sides by judges, who are at once tyrants and their seducers, and who, after having prepared their faults, punish every lapse with dishonor . . . Who does not feel for the tender sex? Yet such, I am sorry to say, is the lot of women over the whole earth . . . Over three-quarters of the globe Nature has placed them between contempt and misery . . .

If a woman were to defend the cause of her sex, she might address [man] in the following manner:

'How great is your injustice? . . . Our duties are different from yours, but they are not therefore less difficult to fulfil, or of less consequence to society. They are the fountains of your felicity, and the sweeteners of life. We are wives and mothers. 'Tis we who form the union . . . of families . . . Permit our names to be some time pronounced, beyond the narrow circle in which we live . . .'

Pennsylvania Magazine, Vol. I (August 1775), pp. 362-364.

JUDITH SARGENT MURRAY ANTICIPATES FUTURE FEMINIST CONCERNS

As a child, Judith Sargent Murray received an unusual education. She was allowed to share her brother's lessons as he prepared for Harvard. In calling for better educational opportunities for women, Murray anticipated feminist developments of the nineteenth century.

Much, in this momentous department, [of educating the young] depends on *female administration;* and the mother, or the woman to whom she may delegate her office, will imprint on the opening mind [of the child], characters, ideas, and conclusions, which time . . . will never be able to erase.

Surely then, it is [wise] to bestow upon the education of girls the most exact attention: Let them be able to converse correctly and elegantly . . . with the children they may usher into being; and, since the pronunciation is best fixed in the early part of life, let them be qualified to give [the children] a pleasing impression of the French language; nor, it is conceived, ought it to be considered as *unsexual,* if they [were able] to familiarize the children with Latin. An acquaintance with history would enable mothers to select their nursery tales from those . . . which have actually taken place upon our globe, and thus useful knowledge would [replace] fairy legendary witches, and hob-goblins. Geography also might be introduced, . . . astronomy too may lend its aid . . .

. . . I take leave to congratulate my fair country-women, on the happy revolution which the past few years has made in their favor; that in these infant republics, where, within my remembrance, the use of the needle was the principal attainment which was thought *necessary* for a woman, [she] is now permitted to appropriate a [portion] of her time to studies of a more elevated and elevating nature. Female academies are everywhere establishing, and right pleasant is the [name] to my ear.

Yes, in this younger world, "The Rights of Women" begin to be understood; we seem, at length, determined to do justice to the SEX; and . . . we are ready to contend for the quantity, as well as the quality, of mind . . .

The idea of the incapability of women is, we conceive, in this *enlightened age,* totally *inadmissable;* Our evidence tend to prove them—

First, Alike capable of enduring hardships.

Secondly, Equally ingenious, and fruitful in resources.

Thirdly, Their fortitude and heroism cannot be surpassed.

Fourthly, They are equally brave.

Fifthly, They are as patriotic.

Sixthly, As influential.

Seventhly, As energetic, and as eloquent.

Eighthly, As faithful, and as perservering in their attachments.

Ninthly, As capable of supporting, with honor, the toils of government, And

Tenthly, and Lastly, They are equally susceptible of every literary acquirement.

Judith Sargent Murray, *The Gleaner* (Boston, 1798) Vol. II, pp. 6-7, Vol. III, pp. 188, 191, 198.

3
Westward the Nation

... early in the morning of May 15 [1855] we began yoking the oxen. There were twenty head and two cows and only one pair had ever been yoked before.

Lydia Milner Walters was on her way to California. Her statement shows that the men and women who traveled west had equal responsibilities and duties. Yet what do you think of when you hear or see the words "the West"? Most people probably imagine cowboys and buffalo, log cabins, and bucking broncos. Certainly they include American Indians in this picture. You may also think of women carrying heavy pots from fire to table, being captured by Indians, or being romanced by wild cowboys.

Much of our understanding of the history of our western settlement has been distorted by books, magazines, films, and television. These media have shown the West in a highly romantic way, with little concern for truth. Pioneer women are shown either meekly and quietly following their husbands or wearing sixguns and buckskin pants and shooting their way through history (inevitably missing the target). Yet thousands of women played important and varied roles in building the West under conditions of great hardship.

Reasons for Traveling West

To what did these women look forward as they started their journey across the plains to Oregon, Washington, Wyoming, or California? In the early 1800's people of the Eastern states knew very little about the country beyond the Mississippi River. Congressmen spoke of cannibalism, wild beasts, deserts, mountains, and uncrossable rivers. One said, "The whole country is the most irreclaimable barren waste known to mankind except the desert of Sahara." In spite of these difficult conditions, however, pioneer women went west in ever-increasing numbers throughout the nineteenth century.

Many women left the East to establish new homes in a land that provided great opportunity and permitted the individualism American women and men valued. These women had tremendous duties and responsibilities which often equaled or surpassed those of men.

Some women traveled west for economic opportunity, such as Florinda Washburn, who arrived in the California gold-mining territory in the 1850's. A milliner by trade, and unmarried, she financed her own wagon, with a "strapping youth" to drive it, arrived at the mines, and set up a millinery shop. Eventually, Washburn became a woman of great wealth.

Some women went west to serve as teachers and missionaries. Eliza Spalding left Holland Patent, New York, with her husband and another couple in 1836. She became one of the first white women to cross the Rockies. Mrs. Spalding, an invalid, left on the difficult journey to Oregon and became even sicker from the buffalo meat the group ate regularly. She finally reached the West where she taught religion, weaving, and knitting to the Nez Percés tribes for many years.

Mary Atkins, an educated Midwestern woman, reached California in 1855 and became the head of the Young Ladies' Seminary in Benicia. An educator, publicist, and financial coordinator, she was compared by an admirer to a "sculptor chiseling the character of California womanhood from the primitive marble . . . " In the mining world of the 1850's, Atkins provided much needed education for women.

Jane Barnes was one of a number of women who went west for adventure and excitement. She was a barmaid who left England to travel to Oregon by ship with the man who was to become governor of a trading post. There, in 1814, she became the first white woman to land on the northwest coast of North America. Barnes was the first of a group of "loose" women who went west. Although most women in the West were busy with their homes and families, much

Narcissa Whitman was one of the many missionary women who went west in the nineteenth century.

attention has been paid to frontier women like Barnes who were often very successful financially and benefactors of the communities in which they lived.

Also going west, most often as slaves, were many black women, some of whom were to become quite well known in frontier communities. Many slave women gained their freedom in the Western territories, established businesses, taught school, and farmed. Mrs. Joe Scott founded the first school for blacks in Alameda County, California. Mary Ann Israel Ash mortgaged her home in order to buy slaves and set them free. One of the best known of the black women of the West was Biddy Mason, who secured her freedom in Los Angeles, became a nurse, and did extensive charitable work in California. She died a wealthy, famous woman.

A variety of women went to the West for many reasons. The common stereotype of the pioneer woman, hiding from danger in the covered wagon, pale features protected by the ever-present sunbonnet, is one that is contradicted by the real experience of Western pioneers.

American Indian Women

Not all women of the West had to travel great distances to get there. The first women in the West were American Indian women. They were responsible, to a great extent, for the opening of the West to white settlers. Journals written by early pioneers tell how important Indian women were because of their knowledge and hardiness. They taught settlers to live off the land, helped them establish relationships with the western tribes, and often served as guides in unfamiliar territory.

The most famous of the early Western women was Sacajawea, who was a member of the 1804 to 1806 Lewis and Clark expedition to Oregon, Washington, Idaho, and Montana. She was given great credit by the men for the success of their explorations, which led to the acquisition of those territories by the United States. The contribution of American Indian women to the settlement of the West in the 1800's was of great importance and has generally been overlooked by historians.

Daily Life in the West

Once settled in frontier homes, women in the West were affected in many different ways by the pioneer life. All faced the common frontier conditions of dirt, disease, early death, fear of Indian attack, and great loneliness. It is hard for Americans today to imagine the isolation of a woman working alone in a small log cabin in the towering forests of the Pacific Northwest. Children of these women remember traveling through forests to school and never seeing the sky because of the thick tree cover. The early frontier experience was one of great hardship for the pioneer woman.

Many frontier women had similar daily routines. Mary Walker, a missionary's wife living near Spokane, Washington in the 1830's, described in her diary her role as shoemaker, carpenter, tailor, weaver, soapmaker, milkmaid, doctor, cook, candlemaker, and childbearer:

> Rose about five. Had early breakfast. Got my housework done about nine. Baked six loaves of bread. Made a kettle of mush and have now a suet pudding and beef boiling. My girl [American Indian] has ironed and I have managed to put my clothes away and set my house in order. May the merciful [Lord] be with me through the unexpected scene. Nine o'clock p.m. was delivered of another son.

In addition to their homemaking chores, pioneer women protected their homes from attack, taught school, and sometimes ran businesses. Survival on the frontier depended upon their strength and the variety of their skills. It is no wonder, then, that women were in great demand in pioneer communities. One man, Asa Mercer, even began a business of bringing women from the East to the West.

A family of Nebraska homesteaders. Their one-story sod house contained few comforts.

He advertised in Eastern newspapers for women who wanted positions as schoolteachers, nurses, and dressmakers. Soon after they arrived most of them became brides.

In the early years of its development, the West was "a man's world." For example, in the summer of 1851 at Fort Laramie, in the Wyoming territory, a count showed 37,171 men to 803 women. In the California gold-rush towns, women were often no more than 2 percent of the population. Because of this shortage, the rare woman who worked as a washer could make $100 a week—a considerable income at that time. Horace Greeley's famous advice, "Go West, young man," also reached women, many of whom followed it.

In addition to providing the valuable work that enabled frontier life to continue, women were vital to the establishment of community cooperation in the West. To overcome the isolation of the vast unsettled Western territories, women formed organizations and informal groups that unified the widely-scattered communities. One of the earliest was the Columbia Maternal Association, established in the 1840's by missionary women of the Pacific Northwest. This organization kept detailed records of births and deaths and provided communication among isolated settlements. By this and similar groups, women created permanence and stability in frontier life.

Involved with the day-to-day tasks of survival, pioneer women were very conscious of the passage of time and often kept detailed records and accounts of their daily existence. Today these diaries are invaluable to historians attempting to describe life in the West.

Women Demand Equality

The frontier environment and pioneer women interacted in many ways. But the most significant result of the presence of women in the West was the opportunity for both sexes to perform tasks of equal value and difficulty. The West created a society in which women had to pull their own weight. Not only were they responsible for cooking, baking, canning, sewing, and childrearing, but also for finding food and establishing community services. Women thus were in a strong position to demand legal equality. Since they had coped with the same hardships that men had and had often run even greater risks because of pregnancy and childbirth, women would not accept a secondary place in the legal and social structure of Western communities.

So, when Mary Walker was told by her husband that it was improper for her to pray in public, she questioned his judgment. A woman who worked long hours to make butter to sell so that she could have spending money was angered because that income belonged legally to her husband. Abigail Duniway, an active woman throughout her long life, struggled against ridicule to get the vote

A "quilting bee." Because isolation was a major problem on the frontier, any reason for getting together was welcome. A communal project, such as a "quilting bee," gave pioneer women a chance to talk about their common experiences.

Women voted for the first time in Wyoming on September 6, 1870. Some accused Wyoming of passing "freak" legislation, while others hailed it as the landmark decision of the century.

for women in the Far West. Thus, the social and cultural experience of the pioneers created a demand for equality between women and men.

Many of the women of the West added their voices to this growing insistence on changes in laws and attitudes. Since pioneer women could prove that they were as capable, as self-reliant, and as responsible as men, it became more and more difficult for lawmakers to argue otherwise. In 1869 Wyoming became the first state to grant female suffrage. The following year, in Laramie, Wyoming, women sat on a jury for the first time. The democratizing effect of the frontier experience had been proven.

Summary

When discussing the West, many books refer to the people who went west as "the pioneers and their wives." This assumes that the only pioneers were men. In reality, women as well as men were pioneers. The greater equality experienced by Western women encouraged other Americans to work for social reform.

NARCISSA WHITMAN, FIRST WHITE WOMAN TO CROSS THE ROCKY MOUNTAINS

Narcissa Prentiss grew up in the 1820's in Amity, New York. Her religious training developed her interest in Christianizing Western Indians, one of the few adventuresome careers open to women at the time. She married Marcus Whitman, a missionary-doctor, and left for Oregon in 1836. Eleven years later she was killed by Indians.

Platte River Just Above the Forks

[June 4, 1836] We have two wagons in our company. Mr. and Mrs. S. and Husband and myself ride on one, Mr. Gray and the baggage in the other. Our Indian boys drive the cows and Dulin the horses . . . I wish I could describe to you how we live so that you can realize it. Our manner of living is far preferable to any in the States. I never was so contented and happy before. Neither have I enjoyed such health for years. In the morn as soon as the day breaks the first that we hear is the word—arise, arise, then the mules set up such noise as you never heard which puts the whole camp in motion.

We encamp in a large ring, baggage and men, tents and wagons on the outside and all the animals except the cows are fastened to pickets within the circle. This arrangement is to accomodate the guard who stand regularly every night and day, also when we are not in motion, to protect our animals from the approach of Indians who would steal them . . .

. . . You must think it very hard to have to get up so early after sleeping on the soft ground . . . While the horses are feeding we get our breakfast in a hurry and eat it . . . we are ready to start, usually at six, travel till eleven, encamp, rest and feed, start again about two, travel until six . . .

Since we have been in the prairie we have done all our cooking. When we left Liberty we expected to take bread to last us part of the way but could not get enough to carry us any distance. We found it awkward work to bake at first out of doors but we have become so accustomed to [it]. Now we do it very easy. Tell Mother I am a very good housekeeper in the prairie . . . We have tea and plenty of milk which is a luxury in this country . . . I never saw anything like buffalo meat to satisfy hunger. We do not want anything else with it. I have eaten three meals of it and it [tastes] well. Supper and breakfast we eat in our tent. We do not pitch it at noon, have worship immediately after supper and breakfast.

T. C. Elliot, compiler, *The Coming of the White Women*, 1836, *as told in Letters and Journal of Narcissa Prentiss Whitman* (Portland, Oregon: Oregon Historical Society, 1937), pp. 4-6.

MARY ATKINS EDUCATES WESTERN WOMEN

In California's rough-and-tumble gold-mining days little thought was given to education and culture. The Young Ladies' Seminary at Benicia, California, was established to fill these needs. Mary Atkins, a prominent educator from Ohio who went west in 1855, was responsible for the school's fame in training girls from California's towns, farms, and mining camps. The school's catalog described the purposes of the Seminary.

The teachers deem it of the highest importance that all ladies should be able to spell correctly, to read naturally, to write legibly, and to converse intelligently; and therefore they give constant attention to [spelling], reading, writing, English grammar, geography, and the history of the United States . . . The English course of study occupies from three to five years, according to the health and capacity of the pupil . . . [music, drawing, crayoning, painting and ornamental needle work were also included.]

[The object of the school was to] train healthy, companionable, self-reliant women—those prepared to be useful and acceptable in the school, in the family, and in society . . .

. . . As the present and future health of the young ladies is of the first importance, great pains have been taken, not only to proportion their studies to their strength, but also to develop their physical powers by appropriate exercises, and to observe in every possible way the laws of health . . . There are regular daily exercises in gymnastics, ample facilities for bathing, large, well-furnished grounds . . . and, what is of the utmost importance, a table abundantly supplied with wholesome food.

Rosalind Keep, *Fourscore Years: A History of Mills College* (Mills College, 1931), pp. 17, 18.

SACAJAWEA GUIDES THE LEWIS AND CLARK EXPEDITION, 1804-1806

Sacajawea was a member of the Shoshone tribe. Charbonneau, the interpreter of the Lewis and Clark expedition, won her in a gambling game. Lewis and Clark thought Sacajawea would be an important addition to their explorations of the Pacific Northwest because they were traveling through Shoshone lands. This excerpt from the diaries of the expedition shows how she helped the venture.

April 9, 1805

When we halted for dinner the squaw [Sacajawea] busied herself in searching for the wild artichokes which the mice collect and deposit in large hordes. This operation she performed by penetrating the earth with a sharp stick about some small collections of drift wood. Her labor soon proved successful, and she procured a good quantity of these roots.

May 16, 1805

[Their boat has overturned] The loss we sustained was not so great as we had at first apprehended; our medicine sustained the greatest injury, several articles of which were entirely spoiled, and many others considerably injured. The balance of our losses consisted of some garden seeds, a small quantity of gunpowder, and a few culinary articles which fell overboard and sunk. The Indian woman to whom I ascribe equal fortitude and resolution with any person onboard at the time of the accident, caught and preserved most of the light articles which were washed overboard . . .

July 22, 1805

The Indian woman recognizes the country and assures us that this is the river on which her relations live, and that the three forks are at no great distance. This piece of information has cheered the spirits of the party who now begin to console themselves with the anticipation of shortly seeing the head of the Missouri yet unknown to the civilized world.

Reuben Gold Thwaites, editor, *Original Journals of the Lewis and Clark Expedition* (New York: Dodd, Mead & Co., 1904), Vol. I, p. 290; Vol. II, pp. 39, 260.

JANETTE RIKER SURVIVES ALONE, 1849

Janette Riker, her father, and two brothers were traveling through the Dakota country on their way to Oregon. One day the men went hunting and did not return. Riker searched for them for a week but never found them. The following excerpt describes how she survived alone through the harsh winter.

Axes and spades among the farming implements in the wagon supplied her with the necessary tools, and [by hard work] . . . she [built] in a few weeks, a rude hut of poles and small logs. Stuffing . . . dried grass [between the poles] and banking up the earth around it, she threw over it the wagon-top, which she fastened firmly to stakes driven in the ground, and thus provided a shelter tolerably rain-tight and weather-proof.

[Here] she conveyed the stoves and other contents of the wagon.

The oxen . . . fattened themselves on the sweet grass until the snow fell. She then slaughtered the fattest one, and cutting up the carcass, packed it away for winter's use. Dry logs and limbs of trees, brought together and chopped up with infinite labor, [kept] her in fuel. Although for nearly three months she was almost completely buried in the snow, she managed to keep alive and reasonably comfortable by making a [hole] for the smoke to escape, and digging out fuel from the drift which covered her wood-pile. Her situation was truly forlorn, but still preferable to the risk of being devoured by wolves or mountain lions, which, attracted by the smell of the slaughtered ox, had begun to prowl around her shelter before the great snow fall, but were now unable to reach her beneath the snowy [walls]. She suffered more, however, from the effect of the spring thaw which flooded her hut with water and forced her to shift her quarters to the wagon, which she covered with the cotton top, after removing thither her blankets and provisions . . . For two weeks she was unable to build a fire, subsisting on uncooked Indian meal and raw beef, which she had salted early in the winter.

Late in April, she was found in the last stages of exhaustion, by a party of Indians, who kindly relieved her wants and carried her across the mountains with her household goods . . .

William Fowler, *Woman on the American Frontier* (Hartford: S. S. Scranton and Co., 1877), pp. 450-452.

AMERICA ROLLINS BUTLER–DAILY LIFE OF A FRONTIER WOMAN

Mrs. Butler was a young frontier woman in southern Oregon who, like many such women, kept a diary thinking she would be the only one to read it. In this selection from her 1853 diary, Butler gives us an idea of the pattern of life on the frontier.

Friday, June 3. [1853] Today Oh! horrors, how shall I express it; is the dreaded washing day. Mr. Butler is hoeing corn. John is ditching. Detriall is hoeing. A portion of the company that went out to rescue a white woman has come back. The Indians deny having any with . . . them.

Saturday, June 4. Oh! This is one of the warm days. The heat is almost intolerable in the shade. The men are at work in the field. I bake, iron, darn and various other little chores are accomplished today. Nothing of any particular note today . . .

Monday, June 6. This being the first Monday in June. Consequently is the day of election, the first one ever held in this

County. Much excitement is the result. I am alone all day or a good portion of it. Suffer intolerable with the heat. Cool and pleasant nights . . .

Wednesday, June 8 . . . The day [of] the grand Dedication Ball in Jacksonville. Mr. Butler and I have at last yielded our consent to go . . .

Thursday, June 9. The ball is at last over. I am at home once more. O! what an assemblage of beauty and soft nothings. The Ball was well attended. All the youth and beauty of Jacksonville and the surrounding country were present . . .

Friday, June 10. Second day after the party . . . Have been abed most of the day with headache and toothache. Think if I had the company of some lively female acquaintance I would feel better . . .

Sunday, June 12. This is Sunday, morning. I attend to my domestic duties which are a thousand and one. Arrange my hair and set down with my Bible to read . . .

Saturday, June 18. This is a cool, bright and lovely morning for traveling . . . After completing the arrangement of my house for the morning I commence ironing when the dentist calls to fill a couple of aching teeth. Attempted to extract one but failed after gouging, breaking and digging it below the jaw bone. He give it up as a bad job . . .

Thursday, June 30. Alone all day. Finish a new dress. Wish I had some new book to read to pass off time to some profit or advantage . . . O! dear I am tired of the same dull monotony of time . . .

Saturday, July 2. A pack train today. It is quite warm. I am ironing, mending and baking. Sampson brings the wagon and harness, blows and puffs and usual. I go down to the creek and take a cool bath. I have got a pretty little pet, a young hare but I am fearful it will not eat.

Oscar Winter and Rose Galey, editors, "Mrs Butler's 1853 Diary of Rogue River Valley," *Oregon Historical Quarterly*, XLI (December, 1940), pp. 346-349.

BIDDY MASON, A SUCCESSFUL BLACK PIONEER

Many black men and women came to the West in the nineteenth century, either as slaves or as free persons looking for opportunity. Biddy Mason, who died a rich woman, was brought as a slave to California and received her freedom in 1854. The author of the account that follows describes how Mason became well-known as a woman of wealth and charity.

The subject of this sketch was born in Hancock County, Georgia, [in 1818] and was the most remarkable pioneer of color coming to California. She came under the most trying circumstances . . .

After the Courts of Los Angeles County granted Biddy Mason and her family their freedom, she took her family to the home of Robert Owens in Los Angeles. Then she went in search of work which she readily secured at two dollars and fifty cents per day, as confinement nurse [midwife] . . . The securing of work meant to her the great boon of acquiring not only the money for the support of her dependent family, but also an opportunity of securing a home. With the first money she could save she purchased two lots . . . which today [1919] is the most valuable piece of property in all of beautiful Los Angeles.

Biddy Mason had a splendid sense of the financial value of property and such great hopes for the future of Los Angeles that she continued to buy property and retain it until after the city began to boom, when she sold a forty-foot lot for twelve thousand dollars . . .

Think of this slave woman coming to California in 1851 by ox-team which consisted of three hundred wagons, and, at the end of these wagons, Biddy Mason driving the cattle across the plains, notwithstanding she had her own three little girls, Ellen, Ann and Harriett, to care for en route!

Biddy Mason was a devoted mother. Her most remarkable trait of character was her ability to teach her children and grandchildren the value of money and property . . .

The name of Biddy Mason is reverenced in the City of Los Angeles where her kindness to the poor is fresh in the minds of the public. In an issue of the *Los Angeles Times,* under date of February 12, 1909, . . [was written:] "Biddy Mason was well-known throughout Los Angeles County for her charitable work. She was a frequent visitor to the jail, speaking a word of cheer and leaving some token and a prayerful hope with every prisoner. In the slums of the city she was known as 'Grandma Mason' and did much active service toward uplifting the worst element in Los Angeles . . . During the flood of the early eighties she gave an order to a little grocery store . . . By the terms of this order, all families made homeless by the flood were to be supplied with groceries while Biddy Mason cheerfully paid the bill."

. . . Biddy Mason [died] January 15, 1891.

Delilah Beasley, *The Negro Trail Blazers of California* (Los Angeles: Times Mirror Printing & Binding House, 1919), pp. 109-110.

BETHENIA OWENS-ADAIR, THE FIRST WOMAN DOCTOR IN THE WEST

After teaching for a while, Owens-Adair became a milliner, one of the few businesses considered to be respectable for a woman. But she studied medical books in secret and finally decided to become a doctor, an unheard-of thing for a Western woman. She went east to Philadelphia, where women were admitted to medical school, and in 1871 became the first graduate woman physician in the Far West. Owens-Adair met considerable prejudice when she tried to practice.

On reaching Philadelphia, I matriculated in the Eclectic School of Medicine, and employed a private tutor. I also attended the lectures and clinics in the great Blockly Hospital twice a week, as did all the medical students of the city. In due time, I received my degree, and returned to Roseburg [Oregon] to wind up my [millinery] business which I had left in charge of my sister. A few days after my return, an old man without friends died, and the six physicians who had all attended him at various times, decided to hold an autopsy. At their meeting, Dr. Palmer, who had not forgotten my former "impudence" in using his instrument [while assisting as a nurse], made a motion to invite the new "Philadelphia" doctor to be present. This was carried, and a messenger was dispatched to me with a written invitation. I knew this meant no honor for me, but I said: "Give the doctors my compliments, and say that I will be there in a few minutes." The messenger left, and I followed close behind him. I waited outside until he went in and closed the door. I heard him say, in excited tones: "She said to give you her compliments, and that she'd be here in a minute." Then came a roar of laughter, after which I quietly opened the door and walked in, went forward, and shook hands with Dr. Hoover, who advanced to meet me, saying: "Do you know that the autopsy is on the genital organs?" "No," I answered; "but one part of the human body should be as sacred to the physician as another." Dr. Palmer here stepped back, saying: "I object to a woman's being present at a male autopsy, and if she is allowed to remain, I shall [leave]!" "I came here by written invitation," I said; "and I will leave it to a vote whether I go or stay; but first, I would like to ask Dr. Palmer what is the difference between the attendence of a woman at a male autopsy, and the attendence of a man at a female autopsy?" [The doctors voted her to stay and Dr. Palmer left. There were about forty or fifty spectators.]
    . . . One of the doctors opened an old medicine case, and offered it to me. "You do not want me to do the work, do you?" I asked, in surprise. "Oh, yes, yes, go ahead," he said. I took the case and

complied. The news of what was going on had spread to every house in town, and the excitement was at fever-heat.

When I had at last finished the dissection, the audience [not the doctors] gave me three cheers. As I passed out and down on my way home, the street was lined on both sides with men, women and children, all anxious to get a look at "the woman who dared," to see what sort of a strange . . . being she was. The women were shocked and scandalized! The men were disgusted, but amused . . .

I often jokingly remarked: "I wonder, as I look back now, that I was not tarred and feathered after that autopsy affair: I can assure you it was no laughing matter then to break through the customs, prejudices and established rules of a new country, which is always a risky undertaking, especially if it is done by a woman, whose position is so sharply defined. Only a few years before that date, the students of Jefferson Medical College [in Philadelphia] publicly "rotten-egged" the woman students, as they were leaving Blockly Hospital.

Bethenia Owens-Adair, *Some of Her Life Experiences* (Portland, Oregon: Mann and Beach, 1906), pp. 58-59.

WYOMING–FIRST STATE TO GRANT WOMEN SUFFRAGE, 1869

Esther Morris, the first woman to serve as a justice of the peace, was called "the mother of woman suffrage in Wyoming." The night before the election she invited the two candidates for the Legislature to dinner and made each promise that, if elected, he would introduce a bill giving women the right to vote in Wyoming. Mr. Bright was elected, became President of the Senate, and introduced the bill. It was signed on December 10, 1869.

Female Suffrage

Chapter 31

An act to grant to the Women of Wyoming Territory the Right of Suffrage, and to hold office.

Be it enacted by the Council and House of Representatives of the Territory of Wyoming:

Sec. 1. That every woman of the age of twenty-one years, residing in this territory, may, at every election to be holden [held] under the laws thereof, cast her vote. And her rights to the elective franchise and to hold office shall be the same under the election laws of the territory, as those of electors.

Sec. 2. This act shall take effect and be in force from and after its passage.

Approved: December 10th 1869.

Wyoming Territory Statutes and Laws, 1869 (Cheyenne Public Printer, Tribune Office, 1870), p. 371.

BELLE STARR–OUTLAW

Born Myra Belle Shirley, Belle Starr was the well-educated daughter of upper-class parents who settled in Texas in 1863. After the Civil War she met outlaws from William Quantrill's band and became involved in many robberies and holdups. She was shot in the back in 1889.

A Desperate Woman Killed

Fort Smith, Ark[ansas] Feb. 5—Word has been received from Eufala, Indian Territory, that Belle Starr was killed there Sunday night. Belle was the wife of Cole Younger, and Jim Starr, her second husband, was shot down by the side of Belle less than two years ago.

Belle Starr was the most desperate woman that ever figured on the borders. She married Cole Younger directly after the war, but left him and joined a band of outlaws that operated in the Indian Territory. She had been arrested for murder and robbery a score of times, but always managed to escape.

New York Times, February 6, 1889

WOMEN LACK MANY RIGHTS IN FRONTIER COMMUNITIES

Abigail Duniway became a leading feminist in the Pacific Northwest. Even as a young girl she was made aware of women's inequality. At the birth of her sister, Duniway's mother said:

> Poor baby! She'll be a woman some day. Poor baby!
> A woman's lot is so hard!

Duniway started a newspaper for women in 1871 in Oregon and eventually was to write the Equal Suffrage Proclamation for the state of Oregon in 1912. In the following incident, she shows woman's lack of rights—even in the West.

A woman came to me in great distress, telling me between her sobs that her husband had sold their household furniture and disappeared, and she was left destitute, with five little children . . .

The woman of whom I was speaking dropped upon a chair and

said: "There is a family on a central street that is going away. I could rent their house and keep my family together by taking in boarders; but I haven't any furniture. If I could borrow six hundred dollars on the furniture, I could pay for it in installments, and I thought you might assist me."

I had more obligations of my own than I could carry comfortably, and had to send her away weeping. While I was racking my brain for some way to help her out, a neighbor called on some errand, to whom I related the woman's story. "I'll lend her the money and take a mortgage on her furniture," said my friend, who, though not rich, was known as a benevolent man.

As soon I could . . . I sought the woman in her deserted home, where nothing was left but the weeping children, the family's scanty clothing and a few battered chairs and dishes. To make matters worse, the rent would be due in a few days and the payment would take her last dollar. The memory of the look of relief that came into her face as I related my errand has amply repaid me for every slur or snub and slight that came to me afterwards in pursuit of my public mission. The transfer was soon made; the woman and her children took possession of the furnished home, and a half dozen boarders were installed, creating an income out of which she could supply her table and general operating expenses.

Things were going well with her when her husband returned and took legal possession of everything. He [refused to recognize] the mortgage, which the wife had had no legal right to contract, and there was nothing left for her but the divorce courts. The family was scattered, my philanthropic neighbor lost his money, except what had been paid in two little installments, and the little religious world of Albany [Oregon] went on sighing over the degeneracy of the times that was making divorces easy. In looking backward, it seems strange to me now that I didn't sooner see the need of votes for women.

Abigail Scott Duniway, *Path Breaking* (Portland, Oregon: James, Kerns and Abbott Co., 1914), pp. 22-24.

4

An Era of Reform

Lucy Larcom, one of the best-known of the New England mill girls of the early 1800's, wrote many articles and was politically active. Although she spent long hours in the mill, she had time to think about her own life: "I began to reflect upon life rather seriously for a girl of 12 or 13," she wrote, "What was I here for? What could I make of myself? Must I submit to be carried along with the current, and do just what everybody else did? No; I knew I should not do that . . ." And she, along with many other women in the first part of the nineteenth century, made lives for themselves that helped to change traditional ideas of women's proper role.

Lucy Larcom's job as a mill worker was in sharp contrast with the role of the "ideal" woman of the early 1800's. After the American Revolution many Americans became more prosperous. As life became more stable in the East, women were expected to remain home, dress well, act properly, and in general to reflect their husband's position in society.

The Role of the "Lady"

Women were expected to be "ladies." Girls of the period were taught that "graceful and dignified retirement" was the proper role for a

This illustration from a fashion magazine showed Americans what the "lady" should look like.

"true woman." Women were judged by their religious devotion, submissiveness, purity, and attention to their home and family. Girls read articles in popular magazines, such as *Godey's Lady's Book,* which taught them: "Sit not with another in a place that is too narrow; read not out of the same book, let not your eagerness to see anything induce you to place your head close to another person's." Girls who did not follow these rules were threatened with horrible deaths, illustrated often in stories of the period.

The British writer Harriet Martineau described the idea of "the lady" with disgust in her book *Society in America:*

> While woman's intellect is confined, her morals crushed, her health ruined, her weakness encouraged and her strength punished, she is told that her lot is cast in the paradise of women: and there is no country in the world where there is so much boasting of the "chivalrous" treatment she enjoys . . . her husband's hair stands on end at the idea of her working . . . . In short, indulgence is given her as a substitute for justice.

As time went on, more and more women began to agree with Martineau that their treatment lacked justice. They decided to ignore the ideal of the lady and become active in the developing society. Some of these women became the leaders of the social reform movements that developed during the years before the Civil War as concern for human welfare increased.

Education

Between the end of the American Revolution and the outbreak of the Civil War, women could be found working to break down the barriers to their sex's participation in society. They also provided leadership for reform in health care, treatment of prisoners, education, work, and the abolition of slavery.

One of the most significant of their activities was the development of educational opportunities for women. In colonial America, the education of girls was not generally considered a matter for community concern. Girls were taught in the morning before the boys came, or during vacations, if at all.

In the Jacksonian era, there was great emphasis on democracy. Leaders encouraged males to get an education in order to be more responsible voters. Since women could not vote, education for girls continued to be ignored. Some women worked to change this condition, however. Emma Willard believed that women should be educated. She established a school that would train girls to teach as well as to handle their homes competently. Willard's curriculum included natural philosophy, mathematics, English writing and lit-

Emma Willard.

erature, history, geography, languages, art and music, and "domestic sciences." In 1819 she spoke before the New York State Legislature in an attempt to obtain a grant of tax monies for education, but she was not successful. Willard continued her efforts and in 1821, with the financial support of Troy, New York, was able to open the Troy Female Seminary, which provided a high school education for girls.

Willard also encouraged the knowledge of and use of the body, and included gymnastics and a course in physiology in the curriculum. In fact, visitors were so shocked to see the girls studying the human circulatory system that Willard was forced to cover parts of the human body with heavy paper in the texts used.

Catherine Beecher was an outstanding teacher-trainer. She revised courses of study, stressing specialization in teaching and physical education. Beecher believed women's proper place was the home, but she also felt they should be well educated for this role. In November 1837 Mary Lyon opened Mt. Holyoke Female Seminary in a red brick building in South Hadley, Massachusetts. The school boasted of a curriculum equal to that of the best men's colleges of the time. Before the creation of Mt. Holyoke, if a woman wished higher education, she had to go to Oberlin College in Ohio. Early in 1837 it had become the first coeducational college in the nation. Several of the outstanding female leaders of the century were educated at Oberlin, which was also the first college to admit black students.

Occasionally, a rare woman received a superior education. Margaret Fuller's father, who wanted to show that she was superior to any boy, taught her languages and the classics. She was a brilliant woman and a leading Boston scholar. Fuller edited a literary journal, *The Dial,* and in 1845 became the first female reporter on the New York *Tribune.* Tragically she, her husband, and child were drowned in a shipwreck in 1850.

Black children had almost no opportunity for formal education in the United States until after the Civil War, but there were some black women and white women before the war who tried to change this. Myrtilla Miner, a white woman who faced fierce opposition, started the first school to train young black women as teachers in Washington, D.C., in 1851. Earlier, Prudence Crandall, a Quaker, had accepted a black girl named Sarah Harris into her school. This caused a great protest, which led Crandall to close that school and to open one for blacks in Canterbury, Connecticut. The townspeople passed laws to close the school and attacked it, once by placing manure in her well. Eventually, fearful of the safety of the children, Crandall closed the school.

Tight corsets were a symbol of the restrictive lives many women led. Amelia Bloomer's costume provided greater comfort and mobility for the women who wore it. However, the costume was ridiculed and its wearers were considered to be unladylike.

A "BLOOMER" (in *Leap Year*).—"Say! oh, say, Dearest, will you be mine?"

Although faced with great opposition—Emma Willard was told "they will be educating the cows next"—opportunities for women to educate themselves increased greatly during the first half of the nineteenth century.

Health

Included in the new curriculum of most of the women's schools were courses in physical exercise. Visitors to America in the early 1800's were horrified at the poor state of women's health. Women were continually ill, especially those of the middle-class. This was partly due to the influence of the ideal of the "lady" who was fragile and fainted easily. It was also due to poor health habits, which included almost no bathing. Ignorance contributed to the problem as did prudery, which made it an ordeal for a woman to be examined by a male doctor.

Dress patterns also had a great deal to do with women's health problems. The corset, pulled tight to create a stylishly small waist, also restricted breathing. Occasionally women actually had a rib removed to bow to fashion's demands. A description of the procedure followed by the lady in dressing in the 1840's illustrates the health problems created by dress. In the winter, the woman would first put on a flannel petticoat, then a crinoline, then a calico skirt, a wheel of horsehair, and then a starched white embroidered muslin petticoat. By 1860 the skirts were ten yards in circumference!

Dress reform was attempted in the years before the Civil War. Elizabeth Smith Miller became annoyed with the current fashions which she found inconvenient when gardening and doing housework. She designed a costume which she called the "short dress." It consisted of a skirt worn about four inches below the knee and a pantaloon-type trouser to the ankle. When Amelia Bloomer described the costume in her new paper *The Lily,* she was swamped with letters requesting information and patterns. People began to call the costume "bloomers." Although most feminist leaders stopped wearing it because they felt it distracted from other issues, Amelia Bloomer and others continued to wear it at home.

Health problems facing American women were also recognized by Elizabeth Blackwell. Because there were no women doctors, she decided to become one. In colonial times, women had acted as doctors, especially during the birth of babies. As educational opportunities for men grew, women with no formal training were forced out of these medical jobs. Elizabeth Blackwell was considered to be either mad or evil because she wanted to go to medical school. Medical schools refused to admit her, except for one in Geneva, New York. This school never expected her to attend, but she did.

She successfully completed her education, and in 1849 became the first woman to graduate in medicine in the United States. Blackwell had to go to Paris to get her first practical experience and was not accepted as a colleague by other doctors when she returned to America. This forced her to open a clinic of her own with her sister Emily, who had also become a doctor. The New York Infirmary for Women and Children aided needy patients and provided a place where women like Blackwell could get medical experience. Her work helped to improve women's health and to open medicine and other professions to females.

Other attempts to reform women's health practices were made in this period by persons such as Mary Sargeant Nichols. In 1832 she began giving women the popular "coldwater" treatment as therapy for their various ailments. Nichols became the first woman to lecture on anatomy, physiology, and hygiene. (Her husband took all of her earnings from these lectures.) She and others believed health reforms would give women more freedom.

Women also began fighting for temperance, an end to the use of alcohol. They felt the use of liquor was bad for the health and well-being of women and men. Although Americans today may look back upon those who fought for an end to the use of alcohol and see them as ludicrous, in the early nineteenth century intemperance in a man was a tragedy for a woman, since all of the family's money was controlled by the man. The temperance movement did not reach full power until the late 1800's, even though Amelia Bloomer and her contemporaries fought for temperance before the Civil War.

Women also turned their attention to improving the lives and health of unfortunate members of society. The best known of these reformers was Dorothea Lynde Dix. In 1841 this frail Bostonian became too ill to continue her job as a schoolteacher. Friends suggested that she occupy herself by teaching Sunday school for prisoners in a local jail. There she was appalled to find the mentally ill imprisoned with criminals, and she decided to bring these conditions to public attention. Dix traveled throughout Massachusetts, Rhode Island, New York, and many other states investigating conditions and preparing reports to the legislatures. Her work led to the building of the first mental hospital in New Jersey. Dix's influence can be seen by the fact that in 1843 there were only 13 mental hospitals in the United States, but by 1880 there were 123.

Maria Mitchell, the famous astronomer, was the only woman elected to the American Academy of Arts and Sciences until 1943. To this day women in scientific fields are the exception rather than the rule.

Journalism and Science

The activity of women in professional areas such as teaching and medicine as well as in the reform movements of temperance and mental health, was accompanied by other breakthroughs. In 1840 at least 17 magazines were published, and women often contributed to them. Best known was *Godey's Lady's Book,* edited by Sarah Josepha Hale. Women became active in newspaper writing. Jane Croly, known as "Jennie June," wrote one of the first women's columns in a city paper and was probably the first woman to syndicate her material. Anne Royall, a controversial figure because of her outspokenness, edited a newspaper for 23 years and supported reform causes.

At the same time women were beginning to write about their part in building America. Elizabeth Ellet found that none of the books she read described women's role in United States history, and so she researched that history by reading old letters and by talking with descendants of leading women. In 1848 she published *The Women of the American Revolution* and in 1852 she described the American woman of the West. Ellet was the first American women's historian.

In 1847, Maria Mitchell, an astronomer from Nantucket, Massachusetts, discovered a comet that was named for her. She had become interested in astronomy because she lived in a whaling community where the stars were important for navigation and because her father, who was also an astronomer, encouraged her. The year

The growth of factories changed the lives of many women. One wrote, "we are very busily engaged during the day, but then we have the evening to ourselves." The idealized conditions shown here deteriorated during the 1840's.

after she discovered the comet, Mitchell was elected to the American Academy of Arts and Sciences. This unusual scientist was the first female to become a member of that group.

Factories

A gap began to develop between middle-class women, who were involved in reform work and professional activities, and working-class women, who had to work to survive. In the early part of the nineteenth century, many women became part of the rapid industrialization of the nation. The first textile mill was completed in 1823. From the first, women outnumbered men in the mills. Although they could also work at domestic labor and at teaching, mill work was much more attractive to young women at that time. As millworker Lucy Larcom wrote:

> Country girls were naturally independent, and the feeling that at this new work the few hours they had of every-day leisure were entirely their own was a satisfaction to them. They preferred it to going out as hired help. It was like a young man's pleasure in entering upon business for himself.

New England women were drawn to the mills for several reasons besides the leisure time. Hard work had always been essential in farm communities, but farms were often unprofitable. At the mills women could earn $2 a week, which seemed high because money was rare on the farm. (This was, however, one-half to one-third of what men were paid.) Thus a desire for independence and income, along with an acceptance of hard labor, brought thousands of young women to the milltowns in the first half of the century.

In the towns, women lived in carefully chaperoned boarding-houses. Although their leisure time was limited to only two hours a day, they took part in many activities outside of the mills. These young workers studied and went to lectures, were active in religious affairs, and in Lowell, Massachusetts, even started a world-famous magazine called *The Lowell Offering*. Its editor was a mill worker named Harriet Farley. Many of the workers smuggled reading material onto the job, although it was against regulations.

All was not peaceful, however. Low wages and long hours caused discontent. In 1824 a strike by women workers took place in Pawtucket, Rhode Island. Another strike was recorded in Lowell, Massachusetts, in 1836 where the marchers sang:

Women led the protest during the 1860 shoemakers' strike in Lynn, Massachusetts. Women had organized unions among seamstresses, umbrella sewers, and clothing and textile workers. They protested low wages, long hours, and inhumane working conditions.

Oh, isn't it a pity, such a pretty girl as I,
Should be sent to the factory to pine away and die?

Strikes and protests began to occur more frequently after this, as factory owners cut wages and increased working hours. Sarah Bagley, a fiery mill worker, became more critical of conditions in Lowell and organized workers to protest. Through the formation of the Lowell Female Labor Reform Association, she collected signatures on a petition to limit the working day to ten hours. This was presented to the Massachusetts Legislature in 1845, but the petition was rejected. These were some of the earliest attempts at labor reform in the United States.

As conditions grew worse after 1840, more and more people looked down upon women who worked in the mills. In spite of this, industrialization, with all of its evils, provided a means by which women could support themselves and their families and become independent.

Summary

The first half of the nineteenth century was of great importance in the history of the American woman. The idea of the "lady" was still popular, but changes were occurring in women's lives. Although they were not supposed to work, many did. Educational opportunities were fought for and won. Prejudice against women in the professions was attacked. Women helped to make America aware of social evils. Each time a woman became involved in reform or fought to be allowed to do what she wanted, she increased opportunities for all women and further destroyed the myth of the "lady".

By the 1840's, most of the energy of women reformers became focused on abolition and women's rights. In the face of these explosive issues, the appeal of temperance, education, and labor reforms declined.

LITTLE WOMEN

Louisa May Alcott received her education primarily from her father, Amos Bronson Alcott, a leading reformer of the period before the Civil War. At the age of sixteen she began to write for publication. In 1868 she wrote the first volume of *Little Women*, her enormously successful book that described her own family life. In this selection, Amy, Meg, Jo, and Beth discuss their views of the female role.

"Christmas won't be Christmas without any presents," grumbled Jo, lying on the rug.

"It's so dreadful to be poor!" sighed Meg, looking down at her old dress.

"I don't think it's fair for some girls to have plenty of pretty things, and other girls nothing at all," added little Amy, with an injured sniff.

"We've got father and mother and each other," said Beth contentedly, from her corner.

The four young faces on which the firelight shone brightened at the cheerful words, but darkened again as Jo said sadly,—

"We haven't got father, and shall not have him for a long time." She didn't say "perhaps never," but each silently added it, thinking of father far away, where the fighting was. [Civil War].

Nobody spoke for a minute; then Meg said in an altered tone,—

"You know the reason mother proposed not having any presents this Christmas was because it is going to be a hard winter for everyone; and she thinks we ought not to spend money for pleasure, when our men are suffering so in the army. We can't do much, but we can make our little sacrifices, and ought to do it gladly. But I am afraid I don't;" and Meg shook her head, as she thought regretfully of all the pretty things she wanted.

"But I don't think the little we should spend would do any good. We've each got a dollar, and the army wouldn't be much helped by our giving that. I agree not to expect anything from mother or you, but I do want to buy Uninde and Sintram for myself; I've wanted it *so* long," said Jo, who was a bookworm.

"I planned to spend mine in new music," said Beth, with a little sigh, which no one heard but the hearth-brush and kettle-holder.

"I shall get a nice box of Farber's drawing-pencils; I really need them," said Amy decidedly.

"Mother didn't say anything about our money, and she won't wish us to give up everything. Let's each buy what we want, and have a little fun; I'm sure we work hard enough to earn it," cried Jo, examining the heels of her shoes in a gentlemanly manner.

"I know *I* do—teaching those tiresome children nearly all day, when I'm longing to enjoy myself at home," began Meg, in the complaining tone again.

"You don't have half such a hard time as I do," said Jo. "How would you like to be shut up for hours with a nervous, fussy old lady, who keeps you trotting, is never satisfied, and worries you till you're ready to fly out of the window or cry?"

"It's naughty to fret; but I do think washing dishes and keeping things tidy is the worst work in the world. It makes me cross; and my hands get so stiff, I can't practice well at all;" and Beth looked at her rough hands with a sigh that anyone could hear that time.

"I don't believe any of you suffer as I do," cried Amy; "for you don't have to go to school with impertinent girls, who plague you if you don't know your lessons, and laugh at your dresses, and label your father if he isn't rich, and insult you when your nose isn't nice."

"If you mean *libel*, I'd say so, and not talk about *labels*, as if papa was a pickle-bottle," advised Jo, laughing.

"I know what I mean, and you needn't be *statirical* about it. It's proper to use good words, and improve your *vocabilary*," returned Amy, with dignity.

"Don't peck at one another, children. Don't you wish we had the money papa lost when we were little, Jo? Dear me! how happy and good we'd be, if we had no worries!" said Meg, who could remember better times.

"You said, the other day, you thought we were a deal happier than the King children, for they were fighting and fretting all the time, in spite of their money."

"So I did, Beth. Well, I think we are; for, though we do have to work, we make fun for ourselves, and are a pretty jolly set, as Jo would say."

"Jo does use such slang words" observed Amy, with a reproving look at the long figure stretched on the rug. Jo immediately sat up, put her hands in her pockets, and began to whistle.

"Don't, Jo; it's so boyish!"

"That's why I do it."

"I detest rude, unlady-like girls!"

"I hate affected, niminy-piminy chits!"

" 'Birds in their little nests agree,' " sang Beth, the peacemaker, with such a funny face that both sharp voices softened to a laugh, and the "pecking" ended for that time.

"Really, girls, you are both to be blamed," said Meg, beginning to lecture in her elder-sisterly fashion. "You are old enough to leave off boyish tricks, and to behave better, Josephine. It didn't matter so much when you were a little girl; but now you are so tall, and turn up your hair, you should remember that you are a young lady."

"I'm not! and if turning up my hair makes me one, I'll wear it in two tails till I'm twenty," cried Jo, pulling off her net, and shaking down a chestnut mane. "I hate to think I've got to grow up and be Miss March, and wear long gowns, and look as prim as a China aster! It's bad enough to be a girl, anyway, when I like boys' games and work and manners! I can't get over my disappointment in not being a boy; and it's worse than ever now, for I'm dying to go and fight with Papa, and I can only stay at home and knit, like a poky old woman!" And Jo shook the blue army-sock till the needles rattled like castanets, and her ball bounded across the room.

"Poor Jo! It's too bad, but it can't be helped; so you must try to be contented with making your name boyish, and playing brother to us girls," said Beth, stroking the rough head at her knee with a hand that all the dishwashing and dusting in the world could not make ungentle in its touch.

"As for you, Amy," continued Meg, "you are altogether too particular and prim. Your airs are funny now; but you'll grow up an affected little goose, if you don't take care. I like your nice manners and refined ways of speaking, when you don't try to be elegant; but your absurd words are as bad as Jo's slang."

"If Jo is a tomboy and Amy a goose, what am I, please?" asked Beth, ready to share the lecture.

"You're a dear, and nothing else," answered Meg warmly; and no one contradicted her, for the "Mouse" was the pet of the family.

Louisa M. Alcott, *Little Women* (Boston: Roberts Bros., 1886), pp. 7-10.

EMMA WILLARD–EDUCATOR

Emma Willard, who realized that women were denied adequate educational opportunities, wanted schools to provide women with a wide variety of skills and subjects. In her 1819 speech to the New York Legislature she encouraged the establishment of a school which would teach music, geography, science, domestic instruction, and many other subjects. Here she defends her belief that improved education would be beneficial for women and society.

Benefits of Providing for Female Education

1. Females, by having their understandings cultivated, their reasoning powers developed and strengthened, may be expected to act more from the dictates of reason, and less from those of fashion and caprice.

2. With minds thus strengthened they would be taught systems of morality, enforced by the sanctions of religion; and they might be expected to acquire juster and more enlarged views of their duty . . .

3. This plan of education, offers all that can be done to preserve female youth from a contempt of useful labor. The pupils would become accustomed to it . . . and it is to be hoped . . . that they might in future life, regard it as respectable.

To this it may be added, that if housewifery could be raised to a regular art, and taught upon philosophical principles, it would become a higher and more interesting occupation . . .

5. By being enlightened in moral philosophy, and in that, which teaches the operations of the mind, females would be enabled to perceive the nature and extent, of that influence, which they possess over their children, and the obligation, which this lays them under, to watch the formation of their characters with increasing vigilance . . .

Emma Willard, *Address to the Public; Particularly to the Members of the Legislature of New York* . . . (Middlebury, 1819), pp. 55-57.

MARGARET FULLER–INTELLECTUAL AND FEMINIST

Margaret Fuller's rigorous education influenced both her concept of herself as an intellectual and her dissatisfaction with the current status of women. In the following imaginary dialogue, Fuller points out the conflicts between women and men.

"Is it not enough," cries the irritated trader, "that you have done all you could to break up the national union, and thus destroy the prosperity of our country, but now you must be trying to break up family union, to take my wife away from the cradle and the kitchen-hearth to vote at polls, and preach from a pulpit? Of course, if she does such things, she cannot attend to those of her own sphere. She is happy enough as she is. She has more leisure than I have, every means of improvement, every indulgence."

"Have you asked her whether she was satisfied with these *indulgences*?"

"No, but I know she is. She is too amiable to desire what would make me unhappy, and too judicious to wish to step beyond the sphere of her sex. I will never consent to have our peace disturbed by any such discussions."

" 'Consent—you?' It is not consent from you that is in question—it is assent from your wife."

"Am not I the head of my house?"

"You are not the head of your wife. God has given her a mind of her own."

"I am the head and she the heart."

"God grant you play true to one another, then! I suppose I am to be grateful that you did not say she was only the hand. If the head represses no natural pulse of the heart, there can be no question as to you giving your consent."

In the following description Fuller explained the purposes for which a woman should be educated.

. . . What Woman needs is not as a woman to act or rule, but as a nature to grow, as an intellect to discern, as a soul to live freely and unimpeded, to unfold such powers as were given her when we left our common home . . .

I was talking on this subject with Miranda, a woman, who, if any in the world could, might speak without heat and bitterness of the position of her sex. Her father was a man who cherished no sentimental reverence for WOMAN, but a firm belief in the equality of the sexes. She was his eldest child, and came to him at an age when he needed a companion. From the time she could speak and go alone, he addressed her not as a plaything, but as a living mind . . . He respected his child, however, too much to be an indulgent parent. He called on her for clear judgement, for courage, for honor and fidelity; in short, for such virtues as he knew. In so far as he possessed the keys to the wonders of this universe, he allowed free use of them to her, and, by the incentive of a high expectation, he forbade, so far as possible, that she should let the privilege lie idle.

Thus this child was early led to feel herself a child of the spirit. She took her place easily, not only in the world of organized being, but in the world of mind . . . With men and women her relations were noble, — affectionate without passion, intellectual without coldness. The world was free to her, and she lived freely in it. Outward adversity came, and inward conflict; but that faith and self-respect had early been awakened which must always lead, at last, to an outward serenity and an inward peace.

Margaret Fuller Ossoli, *Women in the 19th Century and Kindred Papers* (Boston: J.P. Jewett and Company, 1855), pp. 28-29, 38-39.

FANNIE JACKSON COPPIN BECOMES A PROMINENT EDUCATOR

Fannie Jackson Coppin was born a slave, but as a child she was purchased by her aunt and sent to live in Massachusetts. There she worked in a place where she could go to school and secure the equivalent of an elementary school education. With the help of the African Methodist Episcopal Church, Coppin was able to attend Oberlin College in 1860. She did well and went on to hold a teaching job, eventually becoming the principal of the Female Department at the Institute for Colored Youth in Philadelphia. She describes her education at Oberlin.

My aunt in Washington still helped me and I was able to pay my way to Oberlin . . .Oberlin was then the only College in the United States where colored students were permitted to study. The faculty did not forbid a woman to take the gentlemen's course, but they did not advise it. There was plenty of Latin and Greek in it, and as much mathematics as one could shoulder . . . It was custom in Oberlin that forty students from the junior and senior classes were employed to teach the preparatory classes. As it was now time for the juniors to begin their work, the Faculty informed me that it was their purpose to give me a class, but I was to distinctly understand that if the pupils rebelled against my teaching, they did not intend to force it. Fortunately for my training at the normal school, and my own dear love of teaching, though there was a little surprise on the faces of some when they came into the class, and saw the teacher, there were no signs of rebellion. The class went on increasing in numbers until it had to be divided, and I was given both divisions . . .

When I was within a year of graduation, an application came from a Friends school in Philadelphia, for a colored woman who could teach Greek, Latin and higher mathematics. The answer returned was: "We have the woman, but you must wait a year for her."

. . . I never rose to recite in my classes at Oberlin but I felt that I had the honor of the whole African race upon my shoulders. I felt that, should I fail, it would be ascribed to the fact that I was colored.

Fannie Jackson Coppin, *Reminiscences of School Life* (Philadelphia: African Methodist Episcopal Book Concern, 1913), pp. 12, 15.

ELIZABETH BLACKWELL OPENS THE MEDICAL PROFESSION TO WOMEN

Elizabeth Blackwell overcame many conflicts in order to achieve success as the first graduate of her sex in the medical profession. She became a doctor in 1848. In these excerpts from her autobiography, she talks about the forces which led her to study medicine.

. . . My brothers were engaged in business, my sisters variously occupied, the family life was full and active . . . But I soon felt the want of a more engrossing pursuit than the study of music, German, and metaphysics, and the ordinary interests that social life presented.

It was at this time that the suggestion of studying medicine was first presented to me, by a lady friend. This friend finally died of a painful disease, the delicate nature of which made the methods of treatment a constant suffering to her. She once said to me: "You are fond of study, have health and leisure; why not study medicine? If I could have been treated by a lady doctor, my worst sufferings would have been spared me." But I at once repudiated the suggestion as an impossible one, saying that I hated everything connected with the body, and could not bear the sight of a medical book.

This was so true, that I had been always foolishly ashamed of any form of illness. When attacked many years before by intermittent fever, I desperately tried to walk off the deadly chill; and when unable to do so, shut myself up alone in a dark room till the stage of the fever was over, with a feeling that such subjection to disease was contemptible. As a school-girl I had tried to harden the body by sleeping on the floor at night, and even passing a couple of days without food, with the foolish notion of thus subduing one's physical nature . . . and the very thought of dwelling on the physical structure of the body and its various ailments filled me with disgust.

So I resolutely tried for weeks to put the idea suggested by my friend away; but it constantly recurred to me.

. . . At this time I had not the slightest idea of how to become a physician, or of the course of study necessary for this purpose. As the idea seemed to gain force, however, I wrote to and consulted with several physicians, known to my family, in various parts of the country, as to the possibility of a lady becoming a doctor.

The answers I received were curiously unanimous. They all replied to the effect that the idea was a good one, but that it was impossible to accomplish it; that there was no way of obtaining such an education for a woman; . . . and that, in short, the idea, though a valuable one, was impossible of execution.

This verdict, however, no matter from how great an authority, was rather an encouragement than otherwise to a young and active person who needed an absorbing occupation.

If an idea, I reasoned, were really a valuable one, there must be some way of realizing it. The idea of winning a doctor's degree gradually assumed the aspect of a great moral struggle, and the moral fight possessed immense attraction for me.

The moral aspect of the subject was increased by a circumstance which made a very strong impression on me. There was at that time a certain Madame Restell flourishing in New York. This person was a noted abortionist, and known all over the country. She was a woman of great ability, and defended her course in the public papers. She made a large fortune, drove a fine carriage, had a pew in a fashionable church, and though often arrested, was always bailed out by her patrons. She was known distinctively as a "female physician," a term exclusively applied at that time to those women who carried on her vile occupation.

. . . That the honorable term "female physician" should be exclusively applied to those women who carried on this shocking trade seemed to me to be a horror. It was an utter degradation of what might and should become a noble position for women.

Elizabeth Blackwell, *Pioneer Work in Opening the Medical Profession to Women* (London: J.M. Dent & Sons, 1895), pp. 26-30.

DOROTHEA DIX FIGHTS TO CHANGE THE TREATMENT OF THE INSANE

Dorothea Dix found little to interest her or occupy her time until March 1841, when she was asked to teach a Sunday school class for the women in the East Cambridge jail. She was shocked to find that the insane, who suffered terribly from mistreatment and neglect, were mixed in with criminals. Correcting these conditions became Dix's mission in life.

. . . about two years [ago] leisure afforded opportunity and duty prompted me to visit several prisons and almshouses in the vicinity of this metropolis. I found near Boston, in the jails and asylums for the poor, a numerous class brought into unsuitable connection with criminals and the general mass of paupers. I refer to idiots and insane persons, dwelling in circumstances not only adverse to their own physical and moral improvement, but productive of extreme disadvantages to all other persons brought into association with them. I applied myself diligently to trace the causes of these evils, and sought to supply remedies . . . I shall be obliged to speak with great plainness, and to reveal many things revolting to the taste, and from which my woman's nature shrinks with particular sensitiveness. But truth is the highest consideration. *I tell what I have seen*—painful and shocking as the details often are—that from them you might feel more deeply the imperative obligation which lies upon you [the legislature] to prevent the possibility of a repetition or continuance of such outrages upon humanity . . .

I come to present the strong claims of suffering humanity. I come to place before the Legislature of Massachusetts the condition of the miserable, the desolute, the outcast. I come as the advocate of helpless, forgotten, insane, and idiotic men and woman; . . .

I proceed, gentlemen, briefly to call your attention to the *present* state of insane persons confined within this Commonwealth, in *cages, closets, cellars, stalls, pens! Chained, naked, beaten with rods,* and *lashed* into obedience . . .

It is the Commonwealth, not its integral parts, that is accountable for most of the abuses which have lately and do still exist. I repeat it, it is defective legislation which perpetuates and multiplies these abuses. In illustration of my subject, I offer the following extracts from my Note-book and Journal:—

Springfield. In the jail, one lunatic woman, furiously mad, a State pauper, improperly situated, both in regard to the prisoners, the keepers and herself . . . [Another woman's] appeals for employment and companionship are most touching, but the mistress replied "She had no time to attend to her." . . .

Concord. A woman from the hospital in a cage in the almshouse. In the jail several, decently cared for in general but not properly placed in a prison . . .

Lincoln. A woman in a cage.

Medford. One idiotic subject chained, and one in a close stall for seventeen years . . .

Dorothea Dix, "Memorial to the Legislature of Massachusetts, 1843," *Old South Leaflets,* Vol. VI, No. 148, pp. 1-4.

GODEY'S LADY'S BOOK

Sarah Josepha Hale was the editor of *Godey's Lady's Book*, "the only periodical in the Republic, devoted solely to the mental, moral and religious improvement of WOMEN." Typical article titles give us a feeling of what was published by many of the best women writers of the period: "Preparations for Pleasure," "The Bonnie Wife," "Women at 21," "Female Accomplishments," "The Young Wife." *Godey's Lady's Book* was as popular as women's magazines are today, and provided similar advice, as the following article shows.

"Matrimony"

"Is she engaged?"—Is he paying attention to any one?"—"When will they be married?" Such are the questions, which are invariably heard wherever there is a gathering together of "grown up children" of the present day. Matrimony, love and courtship, form the standing subjects of conversation . . . Mothers talk to their daughters of their chances of matrimony; and fathers reckon up in the presence of their children, the amount of Bank Stock, or the acres of landed property, which are respectively held by their different visitors, neighbors or acquaintances; and having ascertained to a mathematical certainty, the wealthiest of the number, invariably recommend him or her as a prize worth seeking after. The first—we had almost said—the only, definite idea which a young woman just entering upon her teens can boast of, is that she *must* be married—some time or other—to somebody or other—married well, if she can—poorly if she must—but at all events married she must be . . .

Why should the young and beautiful so soon learn to fix her thoughts with an all-engrossing interest upon this subject—to speculate and devise plans for what is usually termed "marrying well,"—which, being interpreted, signifies marrying a large estate—a handsome house—without much regard to the person or the intellect necessarily appended to these desirable commodities? And what is marriage after all!—A leap in the dark—a launching out upon an untried ocean . . .

Marriage too often takes place before the parties have been able fully to understand each other—before the guarded reserve . . . of courtship [has] passed away and given place to the frank impulses of nature and feeling, . . .

If not for money, marry for love. Aye—and starve for it too— . . . Love is a very good thing in its proper place.—It will do very well—to talk of, especially in the [dawdling] hour of a moonlight evening, when the perfect stars are looking down from above . . Love sounds well in theory—it is beautiful in practice—it reads well in romance—it is the soul of poetry. Love is a blessed thing in the halls of affluence—or even of competence—but it is the mortal enemy of poverty . . .

Call money if you please the "root of all evil." In the present state of society, it is the very mainspring of existence,— . . . Love, without it, is but a beautiful delusion. It can neither boil the pot, nor pay for its savory contents. It cannot look unconcerned in the face of a dun, or escape the visitation of the Sheriff. It cannot shorten the long face of the doctor by the prompt payment of his longer bill. It cannot move the sympathy of the landlord, or reconcile the lawyer to the loss of his fee. It is an old, but we fear a true saying, "When Poverty comes in at the door Love goes out at the window."

Godey's Lady's Book, September, 1831, pp. 174-175.

LIFE IN THE MILLS

The Female Labor Reform Association was organized in Lowell, Massachusetts during the 1840's, because it was evident that conditions in the mill towns were not as good as they had originally seemed to be. Sarah Bagley aided in organizing a petition campaign in 1845 which had as its purpose the legislation of a ten-hour work day. The following testimony from hearings before the Massachusetts legislature describes some of the working conditions in factories.

. . . The petitioners declare that they are confined "from 13 to 14 hours per day in unhealthy apartments," and are thereby "hastening through pain, disease and privation, down to a premature grave." They therefore ask the Legislature "to pass a law providing that ten hours shall constitute a day's work," and that no corporation or private citizen "shall be allowed, except in cases of emergency, to employ one set of hands more than ten hours per day." . . .

The whole number of names on the several petitions is 2,139, of which 1,151 are from Lowell. A very large proportion of the Lowell petitioners are females. Nearly one half of the Andover [another mill town] are females. The petition from Fall River is signed exclusively by males.

. . . On the 13th of February, the Committee held a session to hear the petitioners from the city of Lowell. Six of the female and three of the male petitioners were present, and gave in their testimony.

The first petitioner who testified was *Eliza R. Hemmingway.* She had worked 2 years and 9 months in the Lowell Factories; 2 years in the Middlesex, and 9 months in the Hamilton Corporations. Her employment is weaving,—works by the piece . . . She is now at work in the Middlesex mills and attends one loom. Her wages average from $16-$23 a month exclusive of board [good for the period]. She complained of the hours for labor being too many, and the time for meals too limited. In the summer season, the work is commenced at 5 o'clock, A.M., and continued till 7 o'clock, P.M., with half an hour for breakfast and three quarters of an hour for dinner. During eight months of the year, but half an hour is allowed for dinner. The air in the room she considered not to be wholesome. There were 293 small lamps and 61 large lamps lighted in the room in which she worked, when evening work is required. These lamps are also lighted sometimes in the morning. About 130 females, 11 men, and 12 children (between the ages of 11 and 14) work in the room with her . . . she thinks that there is no day when there are less than six of the females out of the mill, from sickness. Has known as many as thirty. She, herself, is out quite often, on account of sickness . . . She thought there was a general desire among the females to work but ten hours, regardless of pay . . .

[The Legislative Committee examined the mills and reported that the health of the operatives and their working conditions were good.]

. . . we have come to the conclusion *unanimously,* that legislation is not necessary at the present time, . . .

The Committee do not wish to be understood as conveying the impression, that there are no abuses in the present system of labor; we think there are abuses; . . . We think it would be better if the hours for labor were less,—if more time was allowed for meals, if more attention was paid to ventilation . . . We acknowledge all this, but we say, the remedy is not with us. We look for it in the progressive improvement of art and science, in a higher appreciation of man's destiny, in a less love for money, and in a more ardent love for social happiness and intellectual superiority . . .

Massachusetts General Court Legislative Documents, #50, 1845, pp. 1-3, 15, 16.

A LITERARY OUTLET FOR YOUNG WORKING WOMEN

The Lowell Offering was a magazine written by women who worked in New England mills. Most of these "Lowell girls" worked more than twelve hours a day. The magazine included fiction, poetry, letters about health, tales of home life, women's rights, fashion, and articles about prejudice against labor. Typical were such titles as, "A Christmas Tale," "Ada, the Factory Maid," "A Manual Labor School," "Beauty," and "Life's Changes." Often the Lowell girls defended their right to work.

Dignity of Labor

From whence originated the idea, that it was derogatory to a lady's dignity, or a blot upon the female character, to labor? and who was the first to say, sneeringly, 'Oh, she *works* for a living?' Surely, such ideas and expressions ought not to grow on republican soil. The time has been, when ladies of the first rank were accustomed to busy themselves in domestic employment.

Homer [ancient Greek writer] tells us of princesses who used to draw water from the springs, and wash with their own hands the finest of the linen of their respective families . . . And in later times, the wife of George the Third, of England, has been represented as spending a whole evening in hemming pocket-handkerchiefs, while her daughter Mary sat in the corner, darning stockings.

Few American fortunes will support a woman who is above the calls of her family; and a man of sense, in choosing a companion to jog with him through all the up-hills and down-hills of life, would sooner choose one who *had* to work for a living, than one who thought it beneath her to soil her pretty hands with manual labor, although she possessed her thousands. To be able to earn one's own living by laboring with the hands, should be reckoned among female accomplishments; and I hope the time is not far distant when none of my countrywomen will be ashamed to have it known that they are better versed in useful, than they are in ornamental accomplishments.

A New Society

It was Saturday night. The toils of the week were at an end; and, seated at the table with my book, I was feasting upon the treasures of knowledge which it contained. One by one my companions had left me, until I was alone. How long I continued to read I know not; but I had closed my book, and sat ruminating upon the many changes and events which are continually taking place in this transitory world of ours. My reverie was disturbed by the opening of the door, and a little boy entered the room, who, handed me a paper, retired without speaking. I unfolded the paper, and the first article which caught my eye was headed, "Annual Meeting of the Society for the Promotion of Industry, Virtue, and Knowledge." It read as follows: 'At the annual meeting of this society, the following resolutions were unanimously adopted:

"1. Resolved, That every father of a family who neglects to give his daughters the same advantages for an education which he gives his sons, shall be expelled from this society, and be considered a heathen."

"2. Resolved, That no member of this society shall exact more than eight hours of labor, out of every twenty-four, of any person in his or her employment."

"3. Resolved, That, as the laborer is worthy of his hire, the price for labor shall be sufficient to enable the working-people to pay a proper attention to scientific and literary pursuits."

"4. Resolved, That the wages of females shall be equal to the wages of males, that they may be enabled to maintain proper independence of character, and virtuous deportment."

"5. Resolved, That no young gentleman of this society shall be allowed to be of age, or to transact business for himself, until he shall have a good knowledge of the English language, understand book-keeping, both by single and double entry, and be capable of transacting all town business."

"6. Resolved, That no young lady belonging to this society shall be considered marriageable, who does not understand how to manage the affairs of the kitchen, and who does not, each month, write at least enough to fill one page . . . "

"7. Resolved, That we will not patronize the writings of any person who does not spend at least three hours in each day, when health will permit, either in manual labor, or in some employment which will be a public benefit, and which shall not appertain to literary pursuits."

"8. Resolved, That each member of this society shall spend three hours in each day in the cultivation of the mental faculties, or forfeit membership, extraordinaires excepted."

"9. Resolved, That industry, virtue and knowledge, (not wealth and titles,) shall be the standard of respectability for this society."

I stopped at the ninth resolution, to ponder upon what I had read; and I thought it was remarkably strange that I had not before heard of this society. There was a gentle tap at the door, and a gentleman entered the room, with a modest request for subscribers to a new periodical which was about to be issued from the press. I showed him what I had been reading. He glanced his eyes upon it, and exclaimed, "Oh happy America! Thrice happy land of Freedom! Thy example shall yet free all nations from the galling chains of mental bondage; and teach to earth's remotest ends, in what true happiness consists!"

By reading the remainder of the article, I learned that this society, and its auxiliaries, already numbered more than two-thirds of the population of the United States, and was rapidly increasing; but the date puzzled me extremely; it was April 1, 1860 . . .

The Lowell Offering, A Repository of Original Articles (Lowell, Massachusetts: Powers and Bagley), Vol. I (1840-1841), p. 191-192, Vol. II (1841-1842), p. 192.

"WOMEN HAVE LEAPED FROM THEIR SPHERES."

The extensive public activity of women in reform movements caused considerable concern among those people who wished women to remain in their traditional roles. Reverend Doctor Nehemiah Adams, a traditionalist, voiced his objections in a sermon. They were answered by reformer Maria Weston Chapman in a satirical poem which she signed "The Lords of Creation."

[Rev. Dr. Nehemiah Adams' ideas:]

We invite your attention to the dangers which at present seem to threaten the female character with wide-spread and permanent injury.

The appropriate duties and influence of woman are clearly stated in the New Testament . . .

We appreciate the [everyday] prayers and efforts of woman in advancing the cause of religion at home and abroad . . . But when she assumes the place and tone of man as a public reformer, our care and protection of her seem unnecessary; we put ourselves in self-defense against her; she yields the power which God has given her for her protection, and her character becomes unnatural . . .

[Maria Weston Chapman's answer:]

"The Times That Try Men's Souls"

Confusion has seized us, and all things go wrong,
 The women have leaped from "their spheres,"
And, instead of fixed stars, shoot as comets along,
 And are setting the world by the ears!
In courses erratic they're wheeling through space,
In brainless confusion and meaningless chase.

In vain do our knowing ones try to compute
 Their return to the orbit designed;
They're glanced at a moment, then onward they shoot,
 And are neither "to hold nor to bind;"
So freely they move in their chosen ellipse,
The "Lords of Creation" do fear an eclipse.

They've taken a notion to speak for themselves,
 And are wielding the tongue and the pen;
They've mounted the rostrum; the termagent* elves,
 And—oh horrid!—are talking to men!
With faces unblanched in our presence they come
To harangue us, they say, in behalf of the dumb.

They insist on their right to petition and pray,
 That St. Paul, in Corinthians, has given them rules
For appearing in public; despite what those say
 Whom we've trained to instruct them in schools;
But vain such instructions, if women may scan
And quote texts of Scripture to favor their plan . . .

Lords of Creation

*termagent—violent, brawling woman

E.C. Stanton, S.B. Anthony, M.J. Gage, editors, *The History of Woman Suffrage* (New York: Fowler and Wells, 1881), Vol. I, pp. 81, 82-83.

5

Abolition and Woman's Rights

There are no men's or women's rights;
there are human rights.

Before the Civil War, this idea, which seems very simple to us, was the most controversial idea one could express. Southern abolitionist Angelina Grimké, who made the above statement, knew that both the fight against slavery and the fight for woman's rights were necessary struggles for equality.

Abolition

The American antislavery movement had its beginnings with the publication of William Lloyd Garrison's *Liberator* in 1831. Garrison was the foremost abolitionist leader of his time. He believed that American society, North as well as South, was immoral, with slavery the worst of its sins. There had been antislavery movements before, but after 1830 abolitionists became more aggressive and pressed for an immediate end to slavery.

Many women joined the abolitionist movement. In Philadelphia in 1833 three women attended the formation of the American Anti-Slavery Society. Soon after, the Philadelphia Female Anti-Slavery Society was formed by 20 concerned women. Many

Lucretia Mott (center) possessed great moral and physical courage. This strength allowed her to withstand the jeers and abuse she received from both antifeminists and supporters of slavery.

similar societies were founded as Northern women became more aware of the horrible life of American slaves.

One of the outstanding leaders of the antislavery movement was Lucretia Mott. She was a Quaker minister, and since the Quakers believed in equality for women, she had been able to develop her talents as a speaker and leader. For 40 years she was the president of the Philadelphia Female Anti-Slavery Society. Gentle and motherly, she was also brave and determined.

The courage of antislavery women was demonstrated by an incident in Boston in 1835. William Lloyd Garrison was scheduled to speak to the female antislavery society. An enraged group of citizens surrounded the hall and threatened the safety of those inside. The mayor of Boston refused to take any action and objected to the presence of black women. He suggested that they be sent away. The white and black women walked out of the hall, hand in hand. They walked through the mob with their heads held high. The mob turned on Garrison and dragged him through the streets on the end of a rope. The publicity from this incident encouraged other women to join the movement.

Interest in abolition grew. In 1833 the antislavery leader Lydia Maria Child took the unusual step of publishing a book entitled *An Appeal in Favor of That Class of Americans Called Africans*. Its arguments in favor of abolition impressed people, and her knowledgeable discussion surprised many who assumed that women could not write intelligently. Through the 1840's Child served as editor of the *National Anti-Slavery Standard,* a Philadelphia newspaper.

Woman's Rights

The issue of woman's rights did not concern the abolition movement until the appearance of Sarah and Angelina Grimké. These sisters, who were raised on a plantation in South Carolina, had seen slavery firsthand. It upset them so much that they left the South and became active abolitionists. They began to lecture in New England in the 1830's and drew large audiences. Although people were interested in their views, the Grimkés attracted attention because they were women and it was rare to find women lecturing in public. Even though they were fearful and shy, the Grimkés found themselves at the center of a large, concerned following.

Until this time, most of the women who disapproved of slavery were not concerned with their own inequality. However, when

Elizabeth Cady Stanton received an excellent formal education which was further developed by the hours she spent in her father's judicial office. Listening to the problems of women who came to him, Elizabeth Cady Stanton became acutely aware of the lack of rights of the women of her time.

Angelina and Sarah Grimké were confronted by people who were against women speaking in public, they began to think about their rights as women. Thus, the two movements, abolition and woman's rights, became linked.

The Congregational clergy of Massachusetts became alarmed at the popularity of the Grimkés and issued the famous Pastoral Letter which, among other things, stated that "the power of woman is in her dependence, flowing from the consciousness of that weakness which God has given her for protection . . . . But when she assumes the place and tone of man as a public reformer, our care and protection of her seem unnecessary. . . ."

To the Grimké sisters and their friends it became important to show that Biblical arguments used against women speaking in public were the same as those used against Negro equality. These women felt that both movements were founded to fight similar inequalities.

There were three main attitudes toward this controversy. Theodore Weld, Angelina's husband, and Lydia Maria Child felt that women in the antislavery movement should exercise but not defend their right to speak. They felt that the very fact that women were speaking would further their cause.

William Lloyd Garrison, on the other hand, repeatedly pointed out that women had become involved in the abolitionist movement by their own choice. Although he was not a champion of woman's rights, he was a champion of freedom for all. If a woman was prepared to speak and to serve on committees to further the cause of equality of blacks, Garrison was prepared to defend her, not as a woman but as an individual.

Third, Angelina Grimké explained that "all human beings have the same rights because they are all moral beings. Sex has no more to do with rights than does color . . . and by extension the white person should not have rights to which the black man is not entitled. . . . Whatsoever it is morally right for a man to do, it is morally right for a woman to do."

Thus the sisters from the South were thrown into a controversy that was to continue for a century. Although some abolitionists were able to go along with human rights for all, others were not.

Seneca Falls

In 1840 a World Anti-Slavery Convention was held in London. The events of this convention further convinced abolitionist women that they were treated less equally than abolitionist men. The convention was attended by a number of American women and men, among

As a young girl in Poland, Ernestine Rose was betrothed to a man considerably older than she. She made history by disputing her arranged marriage before the Polish High Tribunal and winning her case. After immigrating to America, Ernestine Rose worked actively for the woman's rights movement.

them Lucretia Mott and Elizabeth Cady Stanton. After much debate, the group ruled that only male delegates could be seated on the main floor of the convention and that the women present should sit quietly in the balcony. Lucretia Mott and Elizabeth Cady Stanton were angered and upset by this action and decided that when they returned to the United States they would call a meeting about the rights of women. This meeting did not take place for eight years, however.

When Elizabeth Stanton and her husband Henry, a radical abolitionist, returned from London, they moved to Seneca Falls, New York. Henry Stanton became active in law and politics, and his wife stayed home caring for their seven children. She explained later, "I now fully understood the practical difficulties most women had to contend with in the isolated household." Shortly after, she, Lucretia Mott, who was visiting nearby, Jane Hunt, Martha Wright (Mrs. Mott's sister), and Mary Ann McClintock, all of them Quakers, decided to call a meeting. An announcement appeared in the July 14, 1848, issue of the *Seneca County Courier.*

On July 19, 1848, over 300 persons appeared for the Seneca Falls Convention, which was held in a small chapel in the town. Forty men demanded to be included even though the advertisement had excluded men on the first day of the convention. The meeting was chaired by James Mott, Lucretia Mott's husband, because none of the women felt able to run it. On this day Elizabeth Cady Stanton made her first speech and was to continue speaking for her cause for 50 years because she felt that "the time had come for the question of woman's wrongs to be laid before the public . . . that woman herself must do this work; for woman alone can understand the height, the depth, the length and the breadth of her degradation."

At this convention the Declaration of Sentiments, patterned after the Declaration of Independence, was presented. In it the women wrote that

> all men and women are created equal; that they are endowed by their Creator with certain inalienable rights, that among these are·life, liberty, and the pursuit of happiness . . . . The history of mankind is a history of repeated injuries . . . on the part of man toward woman, having in direct object the establishment of an absolute tyranny over her. To prove this, let facts be submitted to a candid world.

A number of resolutions were passed at this meeting. The most controversial of all the issues was the demand for the vote, which was suggested by Elizabeth Cady Stanton. Many of the women attending felt that this was not an important issue. The resolution was barely passed and only with the help of Frederick Douglass, the famous black orator and ex-slave. Little did Elizabeth Cady Stanton know that it would take 72 years to win the right to vote.

The Seneca Falls Declaration of Sentiments put into words many of the feelings of abolitionists and other women and became the starting point of the American woman's rights movement. As a result of this modest beginning, women from many walks of life were able, probably for the first time, to understand that they were not alone—other females felt oppressed by the circumstances of their lives. A woman's rights convention was held every year from 1850 to 1860 with the exception of 1857.

Issues of the Movement

Why were these meetings held? Was there anything to do but talk? Could needed reforms occur without the vote? Most women active in the movement were more interested in property reform, control of earnings, guardianship of children, educational and job oppor-tunities, and legal status than they were in the vote. The conventions discussed such questions as: what status did a married woman have in relation to her property? when was divorce possible? what was her relationship to her church? These were the questions to be solved, and helped to form the basic ideas of the woman's rights movement.

Between 1848 and 1860 the woman's movement pressed state

Harriet Tubman believed that God had chosen her to help her people. Determined to escape from slavery, she said, "I had reasoned this out in my mind, there was two things I had a right to, liberty and death. If I could not have one I would have the other, for no man should take me alive." Tubman (left) is shown with some slaves she helped to escape.

legislatures to change laws that would improve women's status. In 1848 New York State passed the Married Woman's Property Act. The act stated that any property belonging to the woman before her marriage or acquired during her marriage could not be taken away from her. This gave women some control over their property. Ernestine Rose, a rabbi's daughter from Poland, collected hundreds of signatures on petitions that led to the passage of this act. Other reforms in New York during this period included a woman's right to collect her own wages, to own property and collect rent for it, as well as to sell it, to sue in court, and also to have joint guardianship of her children with her husband. Other states began to pass similar laws as well.

In the 1850's unusual, strong women such as Harriet Tubman, Sojourner Truth, and Lucy Stone gained prominence. By their actions they helped to strengthen both movements, the abolition of slavery and the gaining of woman's rights.

Harriet Tubman was born a slave. When she was a child, she bravely tried to help a fellow slave and was hit over the head by her master. As a result of this blow, she had fainting spells throughout her life. Tubman eventually escaped from her master and went North. Even though she was free, she returned time and time again to the South to lead slaves to safety through the Underground Railroad. She was determined never to lose anyone. If a slave became afraid and refused to go on, she would hold a pistol to his or her head and insist that this slave go on. Tubman was revered and called "the Moses of her people."

Another extraordinary woman of the period, Lucy Stone, graduated from Oberlin College, which was noted for its antislavery beliefs. She lectured for the American Anti-Slavery Society and as she became more concerned with woman's rights, she began to speak on both subjects. Stone became a famous orator and leader of the movement. When she married Henry Blackwell in 1855, they drew up a contract that protected her rights, and she took the radical step of keeping her maiden name. Today in the United States the Lucy

Isabella Baumfree chose the name Sojourner Truth and traveled around the country speaking out on abolition and woman's rights.

Stone League is still fighting to encourage women to keep their maiden names.

Perhaps better than anyone else, Sojourner Truth bridges abolition and woman's rights. An ex-slave, in 1827 she became active in the antislavery struggle. In 1851 she went to a woman's rights convention and despite fears that she would hurt the cause because she was black, she was allowed to speak. Her eloquent words impressed on those who listened the need for equality for all; man and woman, black and white.

> The man over there says women need to be helped into carriages and lifted over ditches and to have the best place everywhere. Nobody ever helps me into carriages or over puddles, or gives me the best place—and ain't I a woman?

Summary

The two reform movements, abolition and woman's rights, were unified by a common concern for equality. When women felt discriminated against in the antislavery movement, they began to turn their attention to their own need for equal treatment. The struggle for the death of slavery ended with the emancipation of blacks after the Civil War. The woman's rights issues were put aside in the face of this terrible struggle and were reconsidered only at the war's end.

FANNY KEMBLE DESCRIBES ABUSED FEMALE SLAVES

Fanny Kemble was a British actress who became popular in America. In 1834 she married Pierce Butler and soon discovered that he was the owner of a Georgia plantation with over 700 slaves. Kemble's antislavery thinking preoccupied her life after her marriage and helped to cause her eventual divorce. The following description was written during her stay on the plantation in 1838 and 1839.

Before closing this letter [she is writing to a friend], I have a mind to transcribe to you the entries for today recorded in a sort of a daybook, where I put down very [briefly] the number of people who visit me, their petitions and ailments, and also such special particulars concerning them as seem to me worth recording. You will see how miserable the physical condition of many of these poor creatures is; and their physical condition, it is insisted by those who uphold this evil system, is the only part of it which is prosperous, happy, and compares well with that of Northern laborers. Judge from the details I now send you; and never forget, while reading them, that the people on this plantation are well off, and consider themselves well off, in comparison with the slaves on some of the neighboring estates.

Fanny has had six children; all dead but one. She came to beg to have her work in the field lightened.

Nanny has had three children; two of them are dead. She came to implore that the rule of sending them into the field three weeks after their confinement might be altered.

Leah, Caesar's wife, has had six children; three are dead.

Sophy, Lewis's wife, came to beg for some old linen. She is suffering fearfully; has had ten children; five of them are dead. The principal favor she asked was a piece of meat, which I gave her.

. . . *Sarah*, Stephen's wife; this woman's case and history were alike deplorable. She had had four miscarriages, had brought seven children into the world, five of whom are dead, and was again with child. She complained of dreadful pains in the back, and an internal tumor which swells with the exertion of working in the fields; probably, I think, she is ruptured. She told me she had once been mad and had run into the woods, where she contrived to elude discovery for some time, but was at last tracked and brought back, when she was tied up by the arms, and heavy logs fastened to her feet, and was severly flogged . . .

. . . There was hardly one of these women, as you will see by the details I have noted of their ailments, who might not have been a candidate for a bed in a hospital, and they had come to me after working all day in the fields . . .

. . . Another of my visitors had a still more dismal story to tell; her name was Die; she had had sixteen children, fourteen of whom were dead; she had had four miscarriages: one had been caused with falling down with a very heavy burden on her head, and one from having her arms strained up to be lashed. I asked her what she meant by having her arms tied up. She said their hands were first tied together, sometimes by the wrists, and sometimes, which was worse, by the thumbs, and they were then drawn up to a tree or post, so as almost to swing them off the ground, and then their clothes rolled around their waist, and a man with a cowhide stands and stripes them. I give you the woman's words. She did not speak of this as of anything strange, unusual, or especially horrid and abominable; and when I said: "Did they do that to you when you were with child?" she simply replied: "Yes, missis." And to all this I listen—I, an Englishwoman, the wife of the man who owns these wretches, and I cannot say: "That thing shall not be done again; that cruel shame and villainy shall never be known here again." . . .

Frances Anne Kemble, *Journal of a Residence on a Georgia Plantation, in 1838-1839* (New York: Harper and Bros., 1863), pp. 229-231, 240-241.

THE BREAKUP OF SLAVE FAMILIES

One of the most popular American novels was the antislavery story, **Uncle Tom's Cabin**. It was written by Harriet Beecher Stowe, a Northern woman whose home was often a refuge for frightened fugitive slaves. The following excerpt from **Uncle Tom's Cabin** shows the common practice of separating slave mothers from their children through sale. Haley, a slave trader, is admiring a child who belongs to Mr. Shelby. Mr. Shelby owes Haley money.

[Shelby has asked the boy to perform some songs and dances.]

"Hurrah! bravo! what a young 'un!" said Haley; "that chap 's a case, I'll promise. Tell you what," said he, suddenly clapping his hand on Mr. Shelby's shoulder, "fling in that chap, and I'll settle the business—I will. Come, now, if that ain't doing the thing up about the rightest!"

At this moment, the door was pushed gently open, and a young quadroon [of white and black ancestry] woman, apparently about twenty-five, entered the room.

There needed only a glance from the child to her, to identify her as its mother . . .

"Well, Eliza?" said her master, as she stopped and looked hesitatingly at him.

"I was looking for Harry, please, sir;" and the boy bounded toward her . . .

[Haley wants to buy the woman as well as the boy.]

"I tell you, Haley, this must not be spoken of; I say no, and I mean no," said Shelby, decidedly.

"Well, you'll let me have the boy, though," said the trader; "you must own I've come down pretty handsomely for him."

"What on earth can you want with the child?" said Shelby.

"Why, I've got a friend that's going into this yer branch of the business—wants to buy up handsome boys to raise for the market. Fancy articles, entirely—sell for waiters, and so on, to rich 'uns, that can pay for handsome 'uns. It sets off one of yer great places—a real handsome boy to open door, wait, and tend. They fetch a good sum; and this little devil is such a comical, musical concern, he's just the article."

"I would rather not sell him," said Mr. Shelby, thoughtfully; "the fact is, sir, I'm a humane man, and I hate to take the boy from his mother, sir."

"O, you do?—La! yes—something of that ar natur. I understand, perfectly. It is mighty onpleasant getting on with women, sometimes. I al'ays hates these yer screachin', screamin' times. They are *mighty* onpleasant; but, as I manages business, I generally avoids 'em, sir. Now, what if you get the girl off for a day, or a week, or so; then the thing's done quietly,—all over before she comes home. Your wife might get her some ear-rings, or a new gown, or some such [things], to make up with her."

"I'm afraid not."

"Lor bless ye, yes! These critters an't like white folks, you know; they gets over things, only manage right. Now, they say," said Haley, assuming a candid and confidential air, "that this kind o' trade is hardening to the feelings; but I never found it so. Fact is, I never could do things up the way some fellers manage the business. I've seen 'em as would pull a woman's child out of her arms, and set him up to sell, and she screechin' like mad all the time;—very bad policy—damages the article—makes 'em quite unfit for service, sometimes. I knew a real handsome gal once, in Orleans, as was entirely ruined by this sort o' handling. The fellow that was trading for her didn't want her baby; and she was one of your real high sort, when her blood was up. I tell you, she squeezed up her child in her arms, and talked, and went on real awful. It kinder makes my blood run cold to think on 't; and when they carried off the child, and locked her up, she jest went ravin' mad, and died in a week. Clear waste, sir, of a thousand dollars, just for want of management,—there's where 't is. It's always best to do the humane thing, sir; that's been *my* experience." And the trader leaned back in his chair, and folded his arm, with an air of virtuous decision, apparently considering himself an abolitionist.

[Mr. Shelby tells Haley he will consider what to do. He explains to his wife later that he has decided to sell Eliza's son. Suspecting this decision, Eliza hides in a closet and listens to the Shelbys' conversation.]

When the voices died into silence, she rose and crept stealthily away. Pale, shivering, with rigid features and compressed lips, she looked an entirely altered being from the soft and timid creature she had been hitherto. She moved cautiously along the entry, paused one moment at her mistress' door, and raised her hands in mute appeal to Heaven, and then turned and glided into her own room . . . there, on the bed, lay her slumbering boy, his long curls falling negligently around his unconscious face, his rosy mouth half open, his little fat hands thrown out over the bed-clothes, and a smile spread like a sunbeam over his whole face.

"Poor boy! poor fellow!" said Eliza; "they have sold you! but your mother will save you yet!" . . .

[She writes a note to her mistress, packs and wakes the child.]

"Hush, Harry," she said; "musn't speak loud, or they will hear us. A wicked man was coming to take little Harry away from his mother, and carry him 'way off in the dark; but mother won't let him—she's going to put on her little boy's cap and coat, and run off with him, so the ugly man can't catch him . . ."

Harriet Beecher Stowe, *Uncle Tom's Cabin* (Boston: J.P. Jewett and Company, 1852), pp. 17-20, 60-61.

SARAH GRIMKÉ WRITES TO HER SISTER ABOUT THE RIGHTS OF WOMEN

The Grimké sisters, although southern, joined the antislavery movement in the 1830's. They realized that their rights as women were also being called into question by American society. In the following letters, Sarah Grimké expresses her feelings about her rights as a woman and her shame over the treatment of blacks.

Concord, 9th month, 6th, 1837

My Dear Sister:

There are few things which present greater obstacles to the improvement and elevation of woman to her appropriate sphere of usefulness and duty, than the laws which have been enacted to destroy her independence, and crush her individuality; laws which, although they are framed for her government, she has had no voice in establishing, and which rob her of some of her *essential rights*. Woman has had no political existence. With the single exception of presenting a petition to the legislative body, she is a cipher in the nation; or, if not actually so in representative governments, she is only counted, like the slaves of the South, to swell the number of law-makers who form decrees for her government, with little reference to her benefit, except so far as her good may promote their own . . .

. . . That the laws which have generally been adopted in the United States, for the government of women, have been framed almost entirely for the exclusive benefit of men, and with a design to oppress women, by depriving them of all control over their property, is too [evident] to be denied . . .

Thine in the bonds of womanhood,
Sarah M. Grimké

Brookline, 1837

My Dear Sister:

. . . There is another class of women in this country, to whom I cannot refer, without feelings of the deepest shame and sorrow. I allude to our female slaves. Our southern cities are 'welmed' beneath a tide of pollution; the virtue of female slaves is wholly at the mercy of irresponsible tyrants, and women are bought and sold in our slave markets, to gratify the brutal lust of those who bear the name of Christians. In our slave states, if amid all her degradation and ignorance, a woman desires to preserve her virtue [untouched], she is either bribed or whipped into compliance, or if she dares resist her seducer, her life by the laws of slave states may be, and has actually been sacrificed to the fury of disappointed passion. Where such laws do not exist, the power which is necessarily vested in the master over his property, leaves the defenseless slave entirely at his mercy, and the sufferings of some females on this account, both physical and mental, are intense.

. . . Can any American woman look at these scenes of shocking licentiousness and cruelty, and fold her hands in apathy, and say, 'I have nothing to dó with slavery?' *She cannot and be guiltless* . . . .

Thine in the bonds of womanhood,
Sarah M. Grimké

Sarah Grimké, *Letters on the Equality of the Sexes* (Boston: Isaac Knapp, 1838), pp. 74, 81, 51-52, 54.

WORLD'S ANTI-SLAVERY CONVENTION, 1840

The conflict which developed over the seating of women delegates at the Anti-Slavery Convention held in London in 1840 encouraged the beginning of the woman's rights movement in the United States. Elizabeth Cady Stanton, one of the participants in the London meeting, describes these events.

. . . The question of woman's right to speak, vote and serve on committees, not only [caused] the division in the ranks of the American Anti-Slavery Society, in 1840, but it disturbed the peace of the World's Anti-Slavery Convention, held that same year in London. The call for that Convention invited delegates from all Anti-Slavery organizations. Accordingly several American societies saw fit to send women, as delegates, to represent them . . . But after going three thousand miles to attend a World's Convention, it was discovered that women formed no part of the constituent elements of the moral world. In summoning the friends of the slave from all parts of the two hemispheres to meet in London, John Bull [the typical Englishman] never dreamed that woman, too, would answer to his call. Imagine then the commotion in the conservative anti-slavery circles in England, when it was known that half a dozen of those terrible women who had spoken [many times], voted on men and measures, prayed and petitioned against slavery, women who had been mobbed, ridiculed by the press, and denounced by the [religious leaders], who had been the cause of setting all American Abolitionists by the ears, and split their ranks [apart], were on their way to England . . .
[A debate began at the convention over whether the women should be seated as delegates.]
. . . The vote was taken, and the women excluded as delegates of the Convention, by an overwhelming majority.
George Thompson*: 'I hope, as the question is now decided, that Mr. Phillips will give us the assurance that we shall proceed with one heart and one mind.'
Mr. Phillips* replied: 'I have no doubt of it. There is no unpleasant feeling in our minds. I have no doubt the women will sit with as much interest behind the bar [a separate section] as though [they had been seated as regular delegates.] All we asked was an expression of opinion, and, having obtained it, we shall now act with the utmost cordiality.'
Would there have been no unpleasant feelings in Wendell Phillips' mind, had Frederick Douglass [a famous black abolitionist] and Robert Purvis [a former slave and an abolitionist] been refused their

*both had supported the seating of women

seats in a convention of reformers under similar circumstances? And, had *they* listened one entire day to debates on their peculiar fitness for plantation life, and unfitness for the forum and public assemblies, and been rejected as delegates on the grounds of color, could Wendell Phillips have so far mistaken their real feeings, and been so insensible to the insults offered them, as to have told a convention of men who had just trampled on their most sacred rights, that "they would no doubt sit with as much interest behind the bar, as in the convention"? . . . The fact is important to mention, . . . to show that it is almost impossible for the most liberal of men to understand what liberty means for women . . .

William Lloyd Garrison, having been delayed at sea, arrived too late to take part in the debates. Learning on his arrival that the women had been rejected as delegates, he declined to take his seat in the Convention; and, through all those interesting discussions on a subject so near his heart, lasting ten days, he remained a silent spectator in the gallery . . .

As Lucretia Mott and Elizabeth Cady Stanton wended their way arm in arm down Great Queen Street that night, reviewing the exciting scenes of the day, they agreed to hold a woman's rights convention on their return to America, as the men to whom they had just listened had [shown] their great need of some education on that question . . .

The movement for woman's suffrage, both in England and America, may be dated from this World's Anti-Slavery Convention.

E.C. Stanton, S.B. Anthony, M.J. Gage, editors, *The History of Woman Suffrage* (New York: Fowler and Wells, 1881), Vol. I, pp. 53-54, 60-62.

SENECA FALLS DECLARATION OF SENTIMENTS

The Seneca Falls Convention of 1848 marked the official beginning of the woman's rights movement. It was there that women demanded their "inalienable rights." The following advertisement, in the Seneca County Courier, July 14, 1848, was issued by Lucretia Mott, Elizabeth Cady Stanton, Mary Ann McClintock, and Martha Wright.

Seneca Falls Convention

WOMAN'S RIGHTS CONVENTION—A Convention to discuss the social, civil, and religious condition and rights of woman, will be held in the Wesleyan Chapel, at Seneca Falls, New York, on Wednesday and Thursday, the 19th and 20th of July, current; commencing at 10 o'clock A.M. During the first day the meeting will be exclusively for women, who are earnestly invited to attend. The public generally are invited to be present on the second day, when Lucretia Mott, of Philadelphia, and other ladies and gentlemen, will address the convention.

E.C. Stanton, S.B. Anthony, M.J. Gage, editors, *The History of Woman Suffrage* (New York: Fowler and Wells, 1881), Vol. I, p. 67.

At the Convention, the Declaration of Sentiments was presented by Elizabeth Cady Stanton. It was discussed and unanimously adopted by the group.

Declaration of Sentiments

When, in the course of human events, it becomes necessary for one portion of the family of man to assume among the people of the earth a position different from that which they have hitherto occupied, but one to which the laws of nature and of nature's God entitle them, a decent respect to the opinions of mankind requires that they should declare the causes that impel them to such a course.

We hold these truths to be self-evident: that all men and women are created equal; that they are endowed by their Creator with certain inalienable rights, that among these are life, liberty, and the pursuit of happiness; that to secure these rights governments are instituted, deriving their just powers from the consent of the governed. Whenever any form of government becomes destructive of these ends, it is the right of those who suffer from it to refuse allegiance to it, and to insist upon the institution of a new government, laying its foundation on such principles, and organizing its powers in such form as to them shall seem most likely to effect their safety and happiness. Prudence, indeed, will dictate that governments long established should not be changed for light and transient causes; and accordingly, all experience hath shown that mankind are more disposed to suffer, while evils are sufferable, than to right themselves by abolishing the forms to which they were accustomed. But when a long train of abuses and usurpations, pursuing invariably the same object evinces a design to reduce them under absolute despotism, it is their duty to throw off such government, and to provide new guards for their future security. Such has been the patient sufferance of the women under this government, and such is now the necessity which constrains them to demand the equal station to which they are entitled.

The history of mankind is a history of repeated injuries and usurpations on the part of man toward woman, having in direct object the establishment of an absolute tyranny over her. To prove this, let facts be submitted to a candid world.

He has never permitted her to exercise her inalienable right to the elective franchise.

He has compelled her to submit to laws, in the formation of which she had no voice.

He has withheld from her the rights which are given to the most ignorant and degraded men—both natives and foreigners.

Having deprived her of this first right of a citizen, the elective franchise, thereby leaving her without representation in the halls of legislation, he has oppressed her on all sides.

He has made her, if married, in the eye of the law, civilly dead.

He has taken from her all right in property, even to the wages she earns.

He has made her, morally, an irresponsible being, as she can commit many crimes with impunity, provided they be done in the presence of her husband. In the covenant of marriage, she is compelled to promise obedience to her husband, he becoming, to all intents and purposes, her master—the law giving him power to deprive her of her liberty, and to administer chastisement.

He has so framed the laws of divorce, as to what shall be the proper causes of divorce; in case of separation, to whom the guardianship of the children shall be given; as to be wholly regardless of the happiness of woman—the law, in all cases, going upon a false supposition of the supremacy of man, and giving all power into his hands.

After depriving her of all rights as a married woman, if single and the owner of property, he has taxed her to support a government which recognizes her only when her property can be made profitable to it.

He has monopolized nearly all the profitable employments, and from those she is permitted to follow, she receives but a scanty remuneration.

He closes against her all the avenues to wealth and distinction, which he considers most honorable to himself. As a teacher of theology, medicine, or law, she is not known.

He has denied her the facilities for obtaining a thorough education—all colleges being closed against her.

He allows her in Church, as well as State, but a subordinate position, claiming Apostolic authority for her exclusion from the ministry, and, with some exceptions, from any public participation in the affairs of the Church.

He has created a false public sentiment, by giving to the world a different code of morals for men and women, by which moral delinquencies which exclude women from society, are not only tolerated but deemed of little account in man.

He has usurped the prerogative of Jehovah himself, claiming it as his right to assign for her a sphere of action, when that belongs to her conscience and to her God.

He has endeavored, in every way that he could, to destroy her confidence in her own powers, to lessen her self-respect, and to make her willing to lead a dependent and abject life.

Now, in view of this entire disfranchisement of one-half the people of this country, their social and religious degradation,—in view of the unjust laws above mentioned, and because women do feel themselves aggrieved, oppressed, and fraudulently deprived of their most sacred rights, we insist that they have immediate admission to all the rights and privileges which belong to them as citizens of the United States.

In entering upon the great work before us, we anticipate no small amount of misconception, misrepresentation, and ridicule; but we shall use every instrumentality within our powers to effect our object. We shall employ agents, circulate tracts, petition the state and national legislatures, and endeavor to enlist the pulpit and the press in our behalf. We hope this Convention will be followed by a series of Conventions, embracing every part of the country.

Firmly relying upon the final triumph of the Right and the True, we do this day affix our signatures to this declaration.

> Lucretia Mott
> Harriet Cady Eaton
> Margaret Pryor
> Elizabeth Cady Stanton
> Eunice Newton Foote
> Mary Ann McClintock

Report of the Woman's Rights Convention Held at Seneca Falls, N.Y. July 19 and 20th, 1848. (Rochester, N.Y.: John Dick, Publisher, 1848), pp. 5-8.

ERNESTINE ROSE RECALLS HER EXPERIENCES

In this letter to Susan B. Anthony, one of the founders of the suffrage movement, feminist Ernestine Rose explains the role she played in getting the married woman's property bill through the New York State Legislature in 1848. The bill opened the way for many other advancements of married women.

London, January 9, 1877

My Dear Miss Anthony:

. . . I sent the first petition to the New York Legislature to give a married woman the right to hold real estate in her own name, in the winter of 1836 and '37, to which after a good deal of trouble I obtained five signatures. Some of the ladies said the gentlemen would laugh at them; others, that they had rights enough; and the men said the women had too many rights already. Woman at that time had not learned to know that she had any rights except those that man in his generosity allowed her; both have learned something since that time which they will never forget. I continued sending petitions with increased numbers of signatures until 1848 and '49, when the Legislature enacted the law which granted to woman the right to keep what was her own. But no sooner did it become legal than all the women said, "Oh! That is right! We ought always to have had that."

During the eleven years from 1837 to 1848, I addressed the New York Legislature five times and since 1848 I can not say positively, but a good many times; you know all that better than any one else.

Your affectionate friend,
Ernestine L. Rose

E.C. Stanton, S.B. Anthony, M.J. Gage, editors, *The History of Woman Suffrage* (New York: Fowler and Wells, 1881), Vol. I, pp. 98-100.

PROPERTY RIGHTS FOR WOMEN

The first property act specifically for the protection of married women was passed in Mississippi in 1839. The following excerpts are from two similar acts passed by the New York State Legislature in 1848 and 1860. Both were prompted by pressures which Susan B. Anthony, Elizabeth Cady Stanton, and others had put on the state government. Each bill added to the rights that married women received.

AN ACT FOR THE MORE EFFECTUAL PROTECTION OF THE PROPERTY OF MARRIED WOMEN.
Passed April 7, 1848

The People of the State of New York, represented in Senate and Assembly do enact as follows:

1. The real and personal property of any female who may hereafter marry, and which she shall own at the time of marriage, and the rents, issues and profits thereof shall not be subject to the disposal of her husband, nor be liable for his debts, and shall continue her sole and separate property, as if she were a single female.

2. The real and personal property, and the rents, issues and profits thereof of any female now married shall not be subject to the disposal of her husband; but shall be her sole and separate property as if she

were a single female except so far as the same may be liable for the debts of her husband heretofore contracted.

3. It shall be lawful for any married female to receive, by gift, grant, devise or bequest, from any person other than her husband and hold to her sole and separate use, as if she were a single female, real and personal property, and the rents, issues and profits thereof, and the same shall not be subject to the disposal of her husband, nor be liable for his debts.

4. All contracts between persons in contemplation of marriage shall remain in full force after such marriage takes place.

AN ACT CONCERNING THE RIGHTS AND LIABILITIES OF HUSBAND AND WIFE

Passed March 20, 1860

The People of the State of New-York, represented in Senate and Assembly, do enact as follows:

1. The property, both real and personal, which any married woman now owns, as her sole and separate property; that which comes to her by descent, devise, bequest, gift or grant; that which she acquires by her trade, business, labor or services, carried on or performed on her sole or separate account; that which a woman married in this state owns at the time of her marriage, and the rents, issues and proceeds of all such property, shall, notwithstanding her marriage, be and remain her sole and separate property, and may be used, collected and invested by her in her own name, and shall not be subject to the interference or control of her husband, or liable for his debts, except such debts as may have been contracted for the support of herself or her children, by her as his agent.

2. A married woman may bargain, sell, assign and transfer her separate personal property . . .

3. Any married woman possessed of real estate as her separate property, may bargain, sell and transfer such property, and enter into any contract in reference to the same, but no such conveyance or contract shall be valid without the assent, in writing, of her husband, except as herein after provided.

4. [County court may grant power to any married woman to (transfer) property.]

5. [Court to determine whether notice shall be given.]

6. If it shall satisfactorily appear to such court, upon such application, that the husband of such applicant has wilfully

abandoned his said wife, and lives separate and apart from her, or that he is insane, or imprisoned as a convict in any state prison, or that he is an habitual drunkard, or that he is in any way disabled from making a contract, or that he refuses to give his consent, without good cause therefore, then such court shall cause an order to be entered upon its records, authorizing such married woman to sell and [transfer] her real estate, or contract in regard thereto without the assent of her husband, with the same effect as though such [transference] or contract had been made with his assent.

7. [Married women may sue and be sued.]

8. [No bargain of a married woman carrying on trade shall be binding on her husband.]

9. Every married woman is hereby constituted and declared to be the joint guardian of her children, with her husband, with equal powers, rights and duties in regard to them, with the husband.

10. At the decease of husband or wife, leaving no minor child or children, the survivor shall hold, possess and enjoy a life estate in one-third of all the real estate of which the husband or wife died seised.

11. At the decease of the husband or wife, [without a will], leaving minor child or children, the survivor shall hold, possess and enjoy all the real estate of . . . the husband or wife . . ., and all the rents, issues and profits thereof during the minority of the youngest child, and one-third thereof during his or her natural life.

Laws of New York State, 71st Session, 1848, N.Y. Page 307.

Laws of New York State, 83rd Session, 1860, N.Y. pages 157-159.

A NEW MARRIAGE CONTRACT

At the marriage of Lucy Stone and Henry Blackwell in 1855, two reform movement leaders, the following marriage contract was read. They had written this as a protest against the loss of indentity of married women, which was the legal condition of women in the United States.

While acknowledging our mutual affection by publicly assuming the relationship of husband and wife . . . this act on our part implies no [approval] of, nor promise of voluntary obedience to such of the present laws of marriage, as refuse to recognize the wife as an independent, rational being, while they confer upon the husband an injurious and unnatural superiority . . . We protest especially against the laws which give to the husband:

1. The custody of the wife's person.
2. The exclusive control and guardianship of their children.
3. The sole ownership of her personal [property], and use of her real estate, unless previously settled upon, . . .
4. The absolute right to the product of her industry.
5. Also against laws which give to the widower so much larger and more permanent an interest in the property of his deceased wife, than they give to the widow in that of the deceased husband.
6. Finally, against the whole system by which the 'legal existence of the wife is suspended during marriage,' so that in most states, she neither has a legal part in the choice of her residence, nor can she make a will, nor sue or be sued in her own name, nor inherit property.

E.C. Stanton, S.B. Anthony, M.J. Gage, editors, *The History of Woman Suffrage* (New York: Fowler and Wells, 1881), Vol. I, pp. 260-261.

SOJOURNER TRUTH SPEAKS BEFORE A WOMAN'S RIGHTS CONVENTION

At the Ohio Woman's Rights Convention in 1851 Sojourner Truth, a former slave, rose to speak. From her lips came a plea to all women to get the world "right side up again" by fighting for equal rights. Her speech had an enormous impact on the audience.

The leaders of the movement trembled on seeing a tall, gaunt black woman in a gray dress and white turban, [topped] with an uncouth sun-bonnet, march deliberately into the church, walk with the air of a queen up the aisle, and take her seat upon the pulpit steps. A buzz [of disapproval] was heard all over the house, and there fell on the listening ear, "An abolition affair!" "Woman's rights and niggers!" "I told you so!" "Go it, darkey!"
[The meeting continued.]

Again and again, timorous and trembling ones came to me [Frances Gage] and said, with earnestness, "Don't let her speak, Mrs. Gage, it will ruin us. Every newspaper in the land will have our cause mixed up with abolition and niggers, and we shall be utterly denounced." My only answer was, "We shall see when the time comes."
[The second day begins.]

There were very few women in those days who dared to "speak in meeting"; and the [ministers who opposed equal rights] were seemingly getting the better of us, while the boys in the galleries and the sneerers among the pews, were hugely enjoying [the discomfort], as they supposed, of the "strong-minded." Some of the tender-skinned friends were on the point of losing dignity, and the atmosphere [suggested] a storm. When, slowly from her seat in the corner rose Sojourner Truth, who, till now, had scarcely lifted her head. "Don't let her speak!" gasped half dozen in my ear. She moved slowly and solemnly to the front, laid her old bonnet at her feet, and turned her great speaking eyes to me. There was a hissing sound of [disapproval] above and below. I rose and announced "Sojourner Truth," and begged the audience to keep silence a few moments.

The tumult subsided at once, and every eye was fixed on this almost Amazon form, which stood nearly six feet high, head erect, and eyes piercing the upper air like one in a dream. At her first word there was a profound hush. She spoke in deep tones, which, though not loud, reached every ear in the house, and away through the throng at the doors and windows.

"Well, children, where there is so much racket there must be something out of kilter. I think that between the niggers of the South and the women of the North, all talking about rights, the white men will be in a fix pretty soon. But what's all this here talking about?

That man over there says that women need to be helped into carriages, and lifted over ditches, and to have the best place everywhere. Nobody ever helps me into carriages, or over mud-puddles, or gives me any best place!" And raising herself to her full height, and her voice to a pitch like rolling thunder, she asked "And ain't I a woman? Look at me! Look at my arm! . . . I have ploughed and planted and gathered into barns, and no man could head me! And ain't I a woman? I could work as much and eat as much as a man—when I could get it—and bear the lash as well! And ain't I a woman? I have born thirteen children and seen them most all sold off to slavery, and when I cried out with my mother's grief, none but Jesus heard me! And ain't I a woman?

. . . If my cup won't hold but a pint and yours holds a quart, wouldn't you be mean not to let me have my little half-measure full . . . ?

Then that little man in black there, [a minister] he says women can't have as much rights as men, 'cause Christ wasn't a woman! Where did your Christ come from? . . . From God and a woman! Man had nothing to do with Him . . .

. . . If the first woman God ever made was strong enough to turn the world upside down all alone, these women together . . . ought to be able to turn it back again, and get it right side up again! And now they is asking to do it, the men better let them . . . Obliged to you for hearing on me, and now old Sojourner hasn't got nothing more to say."

Amid roars of applause, she returned to her corner, leaving more than one of us with streaming eyes, and hearts beating with gratitude.

E.C. Stanton, S.B. Anthony, M.J. Gage, editors, *The History of Woman Suffrage* (New York: Fowler and Wells, 1881), Vol. I, pp. 115-116.

6

The Civil War and Reconstruction

Brave in emergency, strategic in plan,
Nursing the wounded, leading in the van,
Devoted, patriotic, trusted, tried,—
In war's red glare stands woman glorified!

The "red glare" of the Civil War forced most Americans to turn their attention to war-related activities. Concern for social reforms and the woman's rights movement gave way to a determination by all to win the war for their side. In spite of this, the Civil War and Reconstruction period broadened the opportunities for women to participate in American society.

The creation of the Confederacy divided American women into Northerners and Southerners. They performed similar tasks on both sides. Women fought as soldiers, nursed the wounded, ran hospitals, taught children and adults, spied, raised money, and worked in government service.

Participation in Support Activities

In June of 1861 the Union Secretary of War, Simon Cameron, created the Sanitary Commission. Although its leader was a man, the commission was run and supported by women, and it served to

118

Many groups organized nursing services to treat the sick and wounded during the Civil War. A Sister of Charity offers comfort to a soldier.

coordinate the work of thousands of local societies in the North. The commission supplied nurses to hospitals, upgraded sanitation and hygiene, shipped food, clothing, and medicine to hospitalized soldiers, and maintained hospital ships and convalescent homes.

One of the most famous of the Sanitary Commission leaders was Mary Livermore. When the Civil War began, she hired a housekeeper and a governess for her family and left to join the Sanitary Commission in Chicago. By 1862 she and another patriotic woman, Jane Hoge, became the leaders of the Chicago office. Livermore traveled, lectured, and eventually established over 3,000 local societies devoted to aiding the Union soldiers. When, in 1863, she resolved to fight scurvy in the army, she led in the collection of 18,000 bushels of vegetables and 61,000 pounds of dried fruit and provided for their transport. Livermore was also responsible for the Sanitary Fair of Chicago, a hugely successful money-raising project.

The Confederacy did not have a centrally organized relief program. One reason was that the loyalty of most people in the South was to an individual state, so state societies were common. Confederate women provided home manufactures and helped to set up medical facilities at home and at the front. When the war broke out, there was no Confederate medical service, and women such as Juliet Hopkins organized state services. Hopkins headed the Alabama service, and although her husband was given the title of

Alabama hospital agent, she had the actual responsibilities. Her work was so important that her picture was placed on Alabama's currency.

Cultural differences between the North and South created differences in the ways in which Northern and Southern women participated in the war. Confederate women did not have a tradition of working outside the home, and the South had only 10 percent of the nation's industry. Thus there were very few trained women workers. Women who did choose to serve outside the home were often ridiculed. Lack of women workers created a severe problem for the Confederacy throughout the war.

Early in the war Kate Cumming, who lived in Alabama, volunteered to help in Confederate hospitals. Her family refused to give her permission for this work because they felt it was not suitable for a "refined lady." She rebelled, however, and in 1862 Cumming and 40 other volunteers left for Mississippi. Although a law passed in that year gave approval for women to work in Confederate hospitals, prejudice against these women was very strong. Even in the years of greatest need, the actual job of nursing was left largely to men, either specially recruited for the job or soldiers convalescing from war injuries.

Although there was some prejudice in the North as well, many hundreds of women served as nurses and hospital administrators during the Civil War. At the beginning of the war the United States

As in every war throughout history, women followed the soldiers and provided support services for them.

*In the chaotic begin-
nings of the Civil War,
Clara Barton resource-
fully accumulated band-
ages, food, and medi-
cine for the wounded.*

Army had no general hospital and no trained staff. Elizabeth Blackwell, America's first woman doctor, knew about Florence Nightingale's work in Europe and decided to organize a force of trained nurses to aid the North. In 1861 Blackwell called a meeting that formed a Central Relief Committee. Within three days, 100 women had been chosen to be trained as nurses. This program and others like it aided the North greatly during the war, in contrast to the limited supply of Southern women nurses.

Physicians in the North were usually men; in the South they were always men. Dr. Mary Walker worked as a Union doctor; it took her three years to get an appointment and she encountered tremendous hostility from the male doctors. When she was captured by the Confederacy, she was considered to be such an unusual sight that crowds jammed the streets to see her.

As the war dragged on, female nurses moved from the hospitals to the battlefields, setting up field hospitals and scraping for supplies. Most famous of these women was outspoken Mary Bickerdyke, who became an administrator of a hospital in Illinois. She began to work on the battlefields among the wounded. Known as "Mother Bicker-dyke" she cared for the soldiers as if they were "her boys."

Another woman who served at the front was the "Angel of the Battlefield," Clara Barton. At the Battle of Antietam she nursed soldiers while bullets whizzed by her. Her greatest contribution came later, however, when she trained nurses and organized the American Red Cross.

Sarah Edmonds was a Union spy. Disguised as a black youth, Edmonds worked behind the Confederate lines.

Military Activities of Women

Exciting work was done by unusually brave Northern and Southern women. Being a spy was dangerous, and in addition such women were considered to be of dubious moral character. Rose Greenhow and Belle Boyd were well-known Confederate spies and both served time in federal jail after being discovered. Loreta Velasquez was one of the most famous Confederate women, although historians doubt that some of the experiences which she wrote about really happened. She claimed to have served as a soldier, spy, and railroad conductor. She described how, as a secret agent for the South, she ran blockades to supply the South with needed goods.

The North also had its spies. Harriet Tubman served the Union Army as a spy and scout, and often received valuable information from other blacks. A freed black woman, Mary Elizabeth Bowser, worked with her former mistress, Elizabeth Van Lew, in transmitting information to the Union leaders. Bowser was placed by Van Lew as a servant in the home of the President of the Confederacy, Jefferson

Davis, where she "pretended to be a bit dull" and obtained much information.

Most unusual were the fighting women—women who disguised as men fought in the armies, often undiscovered. Probably more than 400 women served their cause in this way. Because they were regarded by everyone as having low morals, they received little notice. Sarah Edmonds served for two years with the Union Army as "Franklin Thompson" and fought in the Battle of Bull Run. She served as a mail carrier and a spy. Eventually in 1884 she received a pension of $12 a month.

Anna Ella Carroll became a controversial postwar figure. She claimed that she had been the strategist who had suggested to Lincoln the use of the Tennessee River in a Union military plan. This information had won a battle that resulted in a decisive Union victory. In 1870 Carroll demanded credit from Congress for her plan, but it was denied. Some historians believe that Lincoln was unwilling to credit a woman for such an important contribution.

Most women chose to help the war effort through nursing, collecting supplies, and raising money rather than spying or soldiering. The activities of unusual women like Tubman and Edmonds, however, served to change the traditional stereotypes about all women.

Expansion of Professional Opportunities for Women

Women served the Union and the Confederacy in ways other than direct military activities. Few women had served in government positions before the Civil War. Francis Spinner, who was appointed United States Treasurer in 1861, began the practice of hiring women to fill many jobs in his department. In spite of opposition, Spinner stuck to his beliefs, and women government workers became a regular part of Washington life after the war.

Because many men were at the front, women were often hired to take their places in the jobs they had left. Desperate communities hired women as teachers because they were available and willing to work for less money than men. This development was especially important in the South. Women who had worked in the South before the war were usually pitied because working was considered to be unladylike. But the shortage of men changed this attitude. In an attempt to keep Northern abolitionist women from teaching in the South, Southern women taught freed black children.

Many Northern women did go South to teach the newly-liberated slaves, however. A project was started to educate the blacks who had been abandoned by their masters on the coastal islands off Georgia

This New England woman was one of many Northern women who came to the South to teach freed blacks. A class might contain both a young child and a great grandmother. One Tennessee official reported that black parents would "starve themselves, and go without clothes in order to send their children to school."

and South Carolina. Laura Towne, Martha Schofield, and Frances Gage were several of the dedicated teachers who went South to prove that emancipation could work. Charlotte Forten, the daughter of a prominent Northern black businessman, was also part of this project. Her writings describe the difficult conditions under which these teachers worked and the success they achieved.

Problems of Reconstruction

At the close of the war many women had to rebuild their lives. Almost every Southern woman had been impoverished by the war. Many had been refugees, moving from town to town to escape Northern armies. To make ends meet they worked at household industries, often while holding other jobs. Because the men had been away, women had had to assume complete responsibility for the home. Families had been torn apart—brothers had fought against one another and women's loyalty was often divided. Southern women had endured great hardships as a result of the war.

The effects of the Civil War and the years of Reconstruction differed according to where the women lived. Northern women did not have to face a complete change in their way of life and an army of occupation as did Southern women. The Northerners lost jobs to returning men, attempted unsuccessfully to get compensation for war work, and generally faced worsening labor conditions. But Southern women had to recover and reconstruct shattered lives.

One writer who described the Southern countryside said that it "looked for many miles like a broad black streak of ruin and desolation." While the President and Congress—all men—argued about Reconstruction policies, women were selling their personal possessions and attempting to return to homes they had abandoned. Children worked; one North Carolina woman hitched herself to a plow driven by her 11-year-old son and farmed in that way. Women who had had slaves to care for their needs were now forced to support themselves and care for all aspects of their home.

The contrast between reality and ideals is evident in the difference between the actual lives of Vicksburg women, who had lived in caves during the war and eaten rats to survive, and this proclamation by a trade group in South Carolina made in 1867:

> ... the true mission of women [is] to elevate, to refine, to improve mankind. . . . The domestic circle, the school, the hospital, the bedside of suffering—these are the true spheres of woman. It is her mission to make home happy.

The reality and the ideal were still apart.

For black women, freed from slavery, conditions were as bad as or worse than before. Although some were educated, most black women had no education or property and only limited experience. Some women remained on their former owners' plantations, some received help from private organizations, and some were cared for by the Freedmen's Bureau. The bureau was created by Congress in 1865, largely due to the pressure of Josephine Griffing, whose goal was to care for the former slaves. She worked throughout her life to help freed women and men succeed in their new lives.

The newly freed black woman suffered greatly. In addition to economic hardships, the Ku Klux Klan terrorized black families throughout the South during Reconstruction. Homes were burned, black men were lynched, and sexual abuse of black women was common. Prominent black women helped as best they could, but conditions worsened.

Perhaps the most bitter experience of the war for women as a group was the failure to get Congress to grant female suffrage when granting suffrage to black males. During the war, feminists such as Elizabeth Cady Stanton had put aside their fight for woman's rights in order to work for the preservation of the Union. They organized the National Woman's Loyal League to collect signatures in support of the Thirteenth Amendment ending slavery. They succeeded in collecting more than 400,000 signatures.

Yet, when the vote was discussed, both black leaders and white leaders agreed that it was the "Negro's Hour." This angered Stanton and many others who had worked for abolition. The Fourteenth Amendment, which gave the vote to black males, was the first part of the Constitution specifically to include the word "male." This was a great defeat for feminists. The fear of pressuring for two unpopular causes at one time resulted in the postponement of female suffrage for more than 50 years.

Summary

The years of the Civil War and Reconstruction had a great influence on the history of the American woman. Many women had assumed new responsibilities, and many found that working outside the home had become a necessity. Government work, teaching, and nursing were opened to women. Some of the shock at the sight of women working began to disappear, especially in the South. Women speakers became common during the war, and this helped to open the way for greater participation by females in political life. Perhaps most significant, however, was the development of national organizations such as the Sanitary Commission and the National Woman's Loyal League. The ability of women to organize helped to bring about many of the changes in American society that took place in the 50 years following the Civil War.

ABRAHAM LINCOLN ASKS WOMEN TO AID THE UNION EFFORT

In 1861, at the beginning of the Civil War, Abraham Lincoln asked the women of the North to help take care of the sick and wounded soldiers. The Sanitary Commission was established to oversee this responsibility. The medical and support services Union women provided answered the need that the President expressed in this letter.

To the Loyal Women of America:

Treasury Building, Washington
October 1, 1861

Countrywomen:

You are called upon to help take care of our sick and wounded soldiers and sailors.

It is true that government undertakes their care, but all experience, in every other country as well as our own, shows that government alone cannot completely provide for the humane treatment of those for whom the duty of providing, as well as possible, is acknowledged. Even at this period of the war, and with a much smaller proportion of sick and wounded than is to be expected, there is much suffering, and dear lives are daily lost because government cannot put the right thing in the right place at the right time. No other government has ever provided as well for its soldiers, so soon after the breaking out of war of this magnitude, and yet it remains true that there is much suffering, and that death unnecessarily occurs from the imperfectness of the government's arrangements . . . [in spite of difficulties of government agents] . . . humanity to the sick, must to a certain extent, be sacrificed, under government, to the purpose of securing the utmost possible strength and efficiency to the military force. . . .

. . . Hence, an intermediate agency becomes necessary, which, without taking any of the duties of the regular agents of government out of their hands, can, nevertheless, offer to them means of administering to the wants of the sick and wounded much beyond what could be obtained within the arbitrary limits of supply established by government . . .

The Sanitary Commission, a volunteer and unpaid bureau of the War Department of the government, constitutes such an agency.

. . . For the means of administering to the needs of the sick and wounded, the Commission relies upon gift offerings of their own handiwork from the loyal women of the land. It receives not one dollar from government . . .

It is, therefore, suggested that societies be at once formed in every neighborhood where they are not already established, and that existing societies of suitable organization, as Dorcas Societies, Sewing Societies, Reading Clubs and Sociables, devote themselves, for a time, to the sacred service of their country; that energetic and respectable committees be appointed to call from house to house, and store to store, to obtain contributions . . .

Every woman in the country can, at the least, knit a pair of woolen stockings, or, if not, can purchase them . . .

The Sanitary Commission is doing a work of great humanity, and of direct practical value to the nation, in this time of its trial. It is entitled to the gratitude and confidence of the people, and I trust it will be generously supported. There is no agency through which voluntary offerings of patriotism can be more effectively made.

Abraham Lincoln

Washington. September 30, 1861

"Report Concerning the Woman's Central Association of Relief at New York," *United States Sanitary Commission*, #32 (New York: 1861), pp. 35-39.

HOSPITAL WORK AND WOMAN'S DELICACY

During the Civil War there was a question as to whether or not women could handle sickness and death in the military hospitals. Many people argued that this responsibility was not a proper one for females. Phoebe Pember, a Confederate hospital administrator, argued that aiding suffering soldiers would, in fact, improve the character of the women who attempted it, without hurting their "delicacy and purity."

There is one subject connected with hospitals on which a few words should be said—the distasteful one that a woman must lose a certain amount of delicacy and reticence in filling any office in them. How can this be? There is no unpleasant exposure under proper arrangements, and even if there be, the circumstances which surround a wounded man, far from friends and home, suffering in a holy cause and dependent upon a woman for help, care and sympathy, hallow and clear the atmosphere in which she labors. That woman must indeed be hard and gross who lets one material thought lessen her efficiency. In the midst of suffering and death, hoping with those almost beyond hope in this world; praying by the bedside of the lonely and heart-stricken; closing the eyes of boys hardly old enough to realize man's sorrow, much less suffer by man's fierce hate, a woman must soar beyond the conventional modesty considered correct under different circumstances.

If the ordeal does not chasten and purify her nature, if the contemplation of suffering and endurance does not make her wiser and better, and if the daily fire through which she passes does not draw from her nature the sweet fragrance of benevolence, charity, and love,—then, indeed, a hospital has been no fit place for her.

Phoebe Pember, "Hospital Work and Women's Delicacy," in J.L. Underwood, *The Women of the Confederacy* (New York: Neale Publishing Co., 1906), p. 107.

A FORMER SLAVE HELPS TO FIGHT THE CIVIL WAR

Susie King Taylor won her freedom from slavery during the Civil War. She then served as a laundress, teacher, and nurse in a black regiment and afterward wrote an account of her experiences. Her support work during the time of battle shows the various abilities that made American women valuable to the war effort.

About 4 o'clock, July 2 [1864], the charge was made. The firing could be plainly heard in camp. I hastened down to the landing and remained there until eight o'clock that morning. When the wounded arrived, or rather began to arrive, the first one brought in was Samuel Anderson of our company. He was badly wounded. Then others of our boys, some with their legs off, arm gone, foot off, and wounds of all kinds imaginable. They had to wade through creeks and marshes, as they were discovered by the enemy and shelled very badly. A number of the men were lost, some got fastened in the mud and had to cut off the legs of their pants, to free themselves. The 103rd New York suffered the most [a white regiment], as their men were very badly wounded.

My work now began. I gave my assistance to try to alleviate their sufferings. I asked the doctor at the hospital what I could get for them to eat. They wanted soup, but that I could not get; but I had a few cans of condensed milk and some turtle eggs, so I thought I would try to make some custard. I had doubts as to my success, for cooking with turtle eggs was something new to me, but the adage has it, "Nothing ventured, nothing done," so I made a venture and the result was a very delicious custard. This I carried to the men, who enjoyed it very much. My services were given at all times for the comfort of these men. I was on hand to assist whenever needed. I was enrolled as company laundress, but I did very little of it, because I was always busy doing other things through camp, and was employed all the time doing something for the officers and comrades . . .

Susie King Taylor, *Reminiscences of My Life in Camp* (Boston: Published by the author, 1902), pp. 34-35.

ROSE GREENHOW SPIES FOR THE CONFEDERACY

Before the Civil War, Rose Greenhow strongly supported the expansion of slavery in the nation. When war broke out, information she gathered as a member of an espionage ring aided the Confederates in the Battle of Bull Run. In the following excerpt, Greenhow describes her arrest in August 1861.

. . . on Friday, August 23, 1861, as I was entering my own door, on returning from a promenade, I was arrested by two men, one in citizen's dress, and the other in the fatigue dress of an officer of the United States Army [North] . . . They followed close upon my footsteps.

I had stopped to enquire after the sick children of one of my neighbors, on the opposite side of the street. From several persons on the side-walk at the time, *en passant*, I derived some valuable information; amongst other things, it was told me that a guard had been stationed around my house throughout the night, and that I had been followed during my promenade . . . This caused me to observe more closely the two men who had followed, and who walked with an air of conscious authority past my house to the end of the pavement, where they stood surveying me.

I continued my conversation apparently without noticing them, remarking rapidly to one of our humble agents who passed, "Those men will probably arrest me. Wait at Corcoran's Corner, and see if I raise my handkerchief to my face, give information of it!" The person to whom this order was given went whistling along. I then put a very important note into my mouth, which I destroyed; and turned, and walked leisurely across the street, and ascended my own steps.

A few moments after, and before I could open the door, the two men above described rapidly ascended also, and asked, with some confusion of manner, "Is this Mrs. Greenhow?" I answered, "Yes." They still hesitated; whereupon I said, "Who are you, and what do you want?" "I come to arrest you." "By what authority?" The man Allen, or Pinkerton (for he had several aliases), said, "By sufficient authority." "Let me see your warrant." He mumbled something about verbal authority from the War and State Departments, and then both stationed themselves upon either side of me, and followed into the house. I rapidly glanced my eye to see that my signal had been understood [the handkerchief], and remarked quietly, "I have no power to resist you; but had I been inside of my house, I would have killed one of you before I had submitted to this illegal process." . . .

Rose Greenhow, *My Imprisonment and the First Year of Abolition Rule at Washington* (London: R. Bentley, 1863), pp. 52-54.

SARAH EDMONDS–NURSE AND SPY

It is estimated that more than 400 women fought for the North disguised as men. One of them was Sarah Emma Edmonds, who served for two years in the Union army. Edmonds, who used the name Franklin Thompson, fought in the Battle of Bull Run and in the campaign of 1862. After the war, she decided to tell her story and claim a pension. But it was not until 1884 that the government granted her $12 a month.

. . . I did not enjoy taking care of the sick and wounded as I once did, but I longed to go forth and do, as a noble chaplain did at the Battle of Pittsburg Landing. He picked up the musket and cartridge-box of a wounded soldier, stepped into the front rank, and took deliberate aim at one rebel after another until he had fired 60 rounds of cartridge; and as he sent a messenger of death to each heart he also sent up the following brief prayer: "May God have mercy upon your miserable soul."

. . . It is true I was becoming dissatisfied with my situation as nurse, and was determined to leave the hospital.

. . . Chaplain B told me that he knew of a situation he could get for me if I had sufficient moral courage to undertake its duties; . . .

That morning a detachment of the 37th New York had been sent out as scouts, and had returned bringing in several prisoners, who stated that one of the Federal spies had been captured at Richmond and was to be executed . . . Now it was necessary for that vacancy to be supplied . . ., it was a situation of great danger and vast responsibility, and this was the one which Mr. B could procure for me. But was I capable of filling it with honor to myself and advantage to the Federal government? . . . I did consider it thoroughly, and made up my mind to accept it with all its fearful responsibilities . . .

My name was sent to headquarters, and I was soon summoned to appear there myself . . . . I was questioned, and cross-questioned with regard to my views of the rebellion and my motive in wishing to engage in so perilous an undertaking. My views were freely given, my object briefly stated, and I had passed trial number one.

Next I was examined with regard to my knowledge of the use of firearms, and in that department I sustained my character in a manner worthy of a veteran. Then I was again cross-questioned but this time by a new committee of military stars. Next came a phrenological* examination, and finding that my organs of secretiveness, combativeness, etc., were largely developed, the oath of allegiance was administered, . . .

*phrenological—the practice of feeling the shape of the head in order to understand someone's personality.

S. Emma Edmonds, *Nurse and Spy in Union Army* (Hartford: W.S. Williams & Co., 1864), pp. 101, 104-106.

JOURNALISTS PRAISE WOMEN'S PARTICIPATION IN THE WAR

During the Civil War newspapers often published editorials describing, criticizing, and praising the work of women in the war effort. This magazine article encourages its readers to recognize the services of America's "unknown heroines."

Unknown Heroines

While the soldiers fight and fall, and their names are hailed and remembered with lasting sorrow and gratitude, let us not forget that there are other heroes whose devotion is not less, and heroines who, forsaking home, and friends, and all the bright promises of life, devote themselves silently to the work of helping and educating the unfortunates whom the war has committed to our charity, and who fall unknown and unnamed, except by the few hearts which have followed them with sympathy and admiration.

Miss MARY E. SHEFFIELD, of Norwich, Connecticut, died lately, at Memphis, of disease contracted in her self-sacrificing labors as a teacher of the National Freedman's Relief Association. Her work was performed with unfaltering fidelity among the poorest and most friendless of her fellow-creatures. Her measure of human duty was not the applause of spectators, but the suffering of her brethren, and the true sorrow at her loss is in the hearts of those who have love to give and nothing more.

The war has developed a national character that was not suspected. By fire and steel and terrible contest the young men of the country have been cast into soldiers and heroes. But few know how constant and unreserved are the offers for a service that has no outward glory or even mention from the sisters of these young men all over the land. Wherever the army has opened a path, they have walked in it. Angels of mercy, and peace, and enlightenment, they follow the advancing lines of bayonets. Their work is little heeded; their names are unrecorded; but there is a book of life in which these names are deathless; for these women early heard and obeyed the divine whisper, "Whoso doeth it unto the least of these my little ones, doeth it unto me."

Harper's Weekly, July 2, 1864, pp. 418-419.

A YOUNG GIRL AT GETTYSBURG, 1863

The Battle of Gettysburg lasted three days. Tillie Pierce, a young girl living in Gettysburg at the time, recalls how she and her family tried to get to a safe place and their experiences during the fighting.

It began to look as though we were getting into new dangers at every step, instead of getting away from them.

We went into the house and after waiting a short time, [a] soldier came to us saying:

"Now I have a chance for you. There is a wagon coming down the road and I will try to get them to make room for you."

The wagon was already quite full, but the soldier insisted and prevailed. We fully appreciated his kindness, and as he helped us on the wagon we thanked him very much.

But what a ride! I shall never forget it. The mud was almost up to the hubs of the wheels, and underneath the mud were rocks. The wagon had no springs, and as the driver was anxious to put the greatest distance between himself and the battle in the least time possible, the jolting and bumping were brought out to perfection.

At last we reached Mr. Weikert's and we were gladly welcomed to their home.

It was not long after our arrival, until the Union artillery came hurrying by. It was indeed a thrilling sight. How the men impelled their horses! How the officers urged the men as they all flew past toward the sound of the battle! Now the road is getting all cut up; they take to the fields, and all is an anxious, eager hurry! Shouting, lashing the horses, cheering the men, they all rush madly on.

Suddenly we behold an explosion; it is that of a caisson [chest of ammunition]. We see a man thrown high in the air and come down in a wheat field close by. He is picked up and carried into the house. As they pass by I see his eyes are blown out and his whole person seems to be one black mass. The first words I hear him say as the poor fellow is borne past me, are:

"Oh dear! I forgot to read my Bible today! What will my poor wife and children say?"

I saw the soldiers carry him up stairs; they laid him upon a bed and wrapped him in cotton. How I pitied that poor man! How terribly the scenes of war were being irresistibly portrayed before my vision.

After the artillery had passed, infantry began coming. I soon saw that these men were very thirsty and would go to the spring which is on the north side of the house.

I was not long in learning what I could do. Obtaining a bucket, I hastened to the spring, and there, with others, carried water to the moving column until the spring was empty. We then went to the pump standing on the south side of the house, and supplied water from it. Thus we continued giving water to our tired soldiers until night came on, when we sought rest indoors.

It was toward the close of the afternoon of this day that some of the wounded from the field of battle began to arrive where I was staying. They reported hard fighting, many wounded and killed, and were afraid our troops would be defeated and perhaps routed.

The first wounded soldier whom I met had his thumb tied up. This I thought was dreadful, and told him so.

"Oh," said he, "this is nothing; you'll see worse than this before long."

"Oh! I hope not," I innocently replied.

Tillie Pierce Alleman, *At Gettysburg or What a Girl Saw and Heard of the Battle* (New York: W. Lake Borland, 1889), pp. 40-43.

A YANKEE RAID

Elizabeth Jane Beach, a Southern housewife, was the victim of a Union raid on New Albany, Mississippi in 1864. In a letter to her parents she related how the Yankees took everything from her family—the chickens, bread, cooking utensils, vegetables. Most Southerners suffered this type of deprivation.

New Albany, Miss.
July 29th, 1864

Dear Father and Mother

I am seated once more to write to you all . . . I can't begin to tell you what they done to other people, it would take so long but will try and tell you how they treated us, they came . . . like ants, all over the house up stairs and down, in every hole and corner, searching and peeping every where, carried off every Irish potato, beet, onion, [and] beans, even took time to pick pans of beans, took my pillow cases to put them in, took towels, one new table cloth, all my knives but three, some of my dishes and every pan they could find. Took my shears, Asa's [her husband] hatchet. Tore my house all to pieces, it would take me a week to mess it up like they did, pulled all our dirty clothes out of the closets, and examined them. Took all Asa's clothes they could find. Worked here all day. I reckon two hundred had been upstairs looked around and came down. I followed after them, until I was nearly broke down, scared nearly to death for fear they would find my things that were hid for I knew that was my all, provision clothes, bed-clothes, blankets and every thing was in there, after awhile about a dozen of the infantry came in, and upstairs they went to searching all about, commenced looking under the floor. I had a few things hid under there, they commenced pulling them out, pulled out medicine, tobacco, cards and other little things, but did not seem to want anything but the tobacco. After awhile one rascal went up in the corner and in stooping to put his hand under the floor, put it against the planks, and they slipped a little. He pulled them off, and says, "By George, boys here is the place." They just ripped the planks off and in they went. One says, "Run down and guard the door, don't let another fellow come up. We'll divide the things amongst us." I had in there meat, flour, sugar, coffee, molasses, lard and salt, all of Asa's good clothes, Sarah's, mine and the children's. We all had new shoes in there that we had not worn, in a pillowcase. They pulled them all out and looked at them. I stood over them and as they would pull out the shoes and clothes, I would grab them and tell them that they could not have them, but every time they came to anything of Asa's they would take it. . . . They left me nothing to eat at all. Took every solitary thing I had, except one jar of lard and my salt. There was not even a grain of corn on the place to make hominy after they were gone, and we had enough of everything to last us till Christmas. I hated their taking my chickens and groceries worse than anything else. I knew we could get meat and bread as soon as they left, but the other things cannot be replaced without sending to Memphis, and we have no cotton . . . .

Your affectionate daughter,
E.J. Beach

Elizabeth Jane Beach, "The Yankees in New Albany," *Journal of Mississippi History,* II (January, 1940), pp. 42-48.

WOMEN EDUCATE THE FREED SLAVES DURING THE WAR

Charlotte Forten had been brought up in the North in a prominent black family. Along with many others who had worked for abolition, she participated in a project to educate freed blacks. Forten traveled south to the Sea Islands off the coast of Georgia and South Carolina where this project was established. She later wrote several magazine articles describing the school she helped to organize.

The first day at school was rather trying. Most of my children were very small, and consequently restless. Some were too young to learn the alphabet. These little ones were brought to school because the older children—in whose care their parents leave them while at work—could not come without them. We were therefore willing to have them come, although they seemed to have discovered the secret of perpetual motion, and tried one's patience sadly. But after some days of positive, though not severe treatment, order was brought out of chaos, and I found but little difficulty in managing and quieting the tiniest and most restless spirits. I never before saw children so eager to learn, although I had several years' experience in New-England schools. Coming to school is a constant delight and recreation to them. They come here as other children go to play. The older ones, during the summer, work in the fields from early morning until eleven or twelve o'clock, and then come into school, after their hard toil in the hot sun, as bright and as anxious to learn as ever . . .

They are willing to make many sacrifices that their children may attend school. One old woman, who had a large family of children and grandchildren, came regularly to school in the winter, and took her seat among the little ones. She was at least sixty years old. Another woman—who had one of the best faces I ever saw—came daily, and brought her baby in her arms.

Charlotte Forten, "Life on the Sea Islands," *Atlantic Monthly*, XIII (May and June, 1864), pp. 591, 667.

ELIZABETH KECKLEY AIDS THE FREED SLAVES

Elizabeth Keckley, a former slave, founded an association to aid freed slaves who were coming north during the Civil War. She travelled extensively to raise money and publicize her work. Here she explains how the association began.

In the summer of 1862, freedmen began to flock into Washington from Maryland and Virginia. They came with a great hope in their hearts, and with all their worldly goods on their backs. Fresh from the bonds of slavery, fresh from the benighted regions of the plantations, they came to the Capitol looking for liberty, and many of them not knowing it when they found it. Many good friends reached forth kind hands, but the North is not warm and impulsive. For one kind word spoken, two harsh ones were uttered; there was something repelling in the atmosphere, and the bright joyous dreams of freedom to the slave faded—were sadly altered, in the presence of that stern, practical mother, reality . . .

One fair summer evening I was walking the streets of Washington, accompanied by a friend, when a band of music was heard in the distance. We wondered what it could mean, and curiosity prompted us to find out its meaning. We quickened our steps, and discovered that it came from the house of Mrs. Farnham. The yard was brilliantly lighted, ladies and gentlemen were moving about, and the band was playing some of its sweetest airs. We approached the sentinel on duty at the gate, and asked what was going on. He told us that it was a festival given for the benefit of the sick and wounded soldiers in the city. This suggested an idea to me. If the white people can give festivals to raise funds for the relief of suffering soldiers, why should not the well-to-do colored people go to work to do something for the benefit of the suffering blacks? I could not rest. The thought was ever present with me, and the next Sunday I made a suggestion in the colored church, that a society of colored people be formed to labor for the benefit of the unfortunate freedmen. The idea proved popular, and in two weeks "The Contraband Relief Association" was organized, with forty working members.

Elizabeth Keckley, *Behind the Scenes or Thirty Years a Slave and Four Years in the White House* (New York: G.W. Carleton & Co., 1868), pp. 111-114.

THE KU KLUX KLAN TERRORIZES BLACK WOMEN DURING RECONSTRUCTION

The Ku Klux Klan was formed after the Civil War to restore white supremacy in the South. It used force and violence to terrorize black people and their white supporters. An example of their methods is shown in the following testimony given during hearings about the Klan in 1871.

Testimony of Harriet Simril

Harriet Simril (colored) was called as a witness for the prosecution and being duly sworn testified as follows:

Q. Who is your husband? A. Sam Simmons.

Q. Where do you live? A. At Clay Hill in York county [South Carolina].

Q. How long have you lived there? A. A good many years.

Q. Has your husband lived there a good many years? A. Yes, sir.

Q. Did he vote at the last election? A. Yes, sir.

Q. Do you know what politics he is? A. He is a radical [Reconstructionist].

Q. Did the Ku Klux [Klan] ever visit your house? A. Yes, sir; I think along in the spring . . .

Q. Have they been there more than once? A. Yes, sir; they came on him three times [her husband].

Q. Now tell the jury what they did each time. A. The first time they came my old man was at home; they hollered out "open the door," and he got up and opened the door; they asked him what he had in his hand, he told them the door pin; they told him to come out and he came out; these two men that came in, they came in and wanted me to make up a light; the light wasn't made up very good and they struck matches to a pine stick, and looked about to see if they could

see anything. They never said anything, and these young men walked up and they took my old man out after so long—and they wanted him to join the Democratic ticket; and after that they went a piece above the house and hit him about five cuts with the cowhide.
Q. Do you know whether he promised to be a Democrat or not? *A*. He told them he would rather quit all politics if that was the way they was going to do to him.
Q. What did they do to you? *A*. That is the second time they came. They came back after the first time on Sunday night after my old man again, and this time the crowd was bigger . . . They called for him and I told them he wasn't here . . . They asked me where was my old man? I told them I couldn't tell; when he went away he didn't tell me where he was going. They searched about in the house a long time, and stayed with me an hour that time . . .
Q. What did they do to you? *A*. Well, they were spitting in my face and throwing dirt in my eyes, and when they made me blind they bursted open my cupboard. I had five pies in my cupboard, and they eat all my pies up, and then took two pieces of meat . . . and after a while they took me out of doors and told me all they wanted was my old man to join the Democratic ticket . . . and after they had got me out of doors they dragged me into the big road and they ravished [raped] me out there.
Q. How many of them? *A*. There was three.
Q. One right after another? *A*. Yes, sir.
Q. Threw you down on the ground? *A*. Yes, sir, they throwed me down . . .
Q. What was your condition when they left you? How did you feel? *A*. After they got done with me I had no sense for a long time. I laid there, I don't know how long . . .
Q. Have the Ku Klux [Klan] ever come to you again? *A*. . . . They came . . . but I was never inside the house . . .
Q. Did they burn your house down? *A*. Yes, sir; I don't know who burned it down but . . . I went to my house and it was in ashes . . .

The Great Ku Klux Trials, Official Report of the Proceedings Before U.S. Circuit Court, Held at Columbia S.C., November term, 1871. (South Carolina, 1872), pp. 152-153.

MARY SURRATT IS HANGED AS A CONSPIRATOR

In 1865 Mary Surratt was convicted of participating in a plot to assassinate Abraham Lincoln. She was hanged with four others, although she claimed to be innocent. It appears from later evidence that she was indeed innocent and was a victim of the fear and divisiveness the war had created. The following is an account of her hanging which took place on July 7, 1865. Surratt was the first American woman to be executed for a crime against the government.

End of the Assassins

The conspirators have gone to their long home, the swift hand of justice has smitten them, and they stand before the judgement seat . . .

Mrs. Surratt's friends have been constant and faithful. They have manipulated presses and created public sentiment. The papers received here to-day were singularly unanimous in the supposition that the President would commute the sentence of Mrs. Surratt to imprisonment for life. Such a sentiment found no echo here. It was well known that the counsel, family and friends of the culprit were determined to make every exertion, to strain every nerve in a strong pull and tug at the tender heart of the President in her behalf. She was a woman, and a sick woman at that . . . [But] woman as she was, she knew her business well; sick as she was she had strength sufficient for her fearful purpose, and stern as the sentence was, the justice was absolute, the execution certain. We have heared many express the desire that the woman's life might be spared, and its weary hours passed in the quiet of the prison, but no one who knew the President and his unmoveable nature supposed for an instant that the sentence would be changed . . .

[People had come for many miles and spent a great deal of money to witness the execution.]

. . . As the night [before the execution] wore on Mrs. Surratt, who had been removed from the larger room where she has been confined since her illness, began to toss uneasily on her narrow bed. She was really ill and the kind offices of the physician were fequently needed. Conscious of the approach of day, she betook herself again to the preparation of her soul for its infinite journey. She rallied mentally and physically and determined evidently to bear and brave the scaffold . . .

Seemingly convinced of the utter hopelessness of her situation . . . Mrs. Surratt rose from her bed and again betook herself to her devotional exercises. It may seem strange that this woman, who was proven to know all about the projected assassination, who kept open house for the scoundrels who planned and the villains who did the deed, who insisted that she had never seen and never knew Payne [a conspirator] and who said, when informed of her sentence, "I had no hand in the murder of the President," should seem so calm and consistent in her preparation for death . . .

[The conspirators are taken to the scaffold.]

The scaffold was so arranged so that the four condemned could be hung at the same time . . .

Mrs. Surratt was attended by two soldiers, Her waist and ankles were in irons; she was attired in a plain black alpacca dress, with black bonnet and thin veil. Her face could easily be seen. She gazed up at the horrid instrument of death, and her lips were moving rapidly as in prayer. She was assisted up on the scaffold and seated in a chair near the drop. She gazed upon the noose, which dangled in the wind before her face, and again her lips moved as if in prayer . . .

The limbs of each of the prisoners were now pinioned. The caps were drawn over their heads, Mrs. Surratt exclaiming in a faint voice, "Don't let me, fall; hold on!" . . .

The bodies fell simultaneously, and swayed backward and forward for a few minutes. Mrs. Surratt appeared to suffer very little . . .

New York Times, July 8, 1865.

THE LEGEND OF BARBARA FRIETCHIE

The story of Barbara Frietchie is familiar to many American school children. She was ninety-six in 1862 when the Confederate Army passed through her home town in Maryland. She is supposed to have displayed the Union flag which was fired upon by the Confederate troops. She caught the falling flag and continued to wave it. There is much doubt about the truth of the story, but one of the best known poems of American history was written about it by John Greenleaf Whittier.

Barbara Frietchie

Up from the meadows rich with corn,
Clear in the cool September morn,

The clustered spires of Frederick stand
Green-walled by the hills of Maryland.

Round about them orchards sweep,
Apple and peach trees fruited deep,

Fair as the garden of the Lord
To the eyes of the famished rebel horde,

On that pleasant morn of the early fall
When Lee marched over the mountain-wall;

Over the mountains winding down,
Horse and foot, into Frederick town.

Forty flags with their silver stars,
Forty flags with their crimson bars,

Flapped in the morning wind: the sun
Of noon looked down, and saw not one.

Up rose old Barbara Frietchie then,
Bowed with her fourscore years and ten;

Bravest of all in Frederick town,
She took up the flag the men hauled down;

In her attic window the staff she set,
To show that one heart was loyal yet.

Up the street came the rebel tread,
Stonewall Jackson riding ahead.

Under his slouched hat left and right
He glanced; the old flag met his sight.

"Halt!"—the dust-brown ranks stood fast,
"Fire!"—out blazed the rifle-blast.

It shivered the window, pane and sash;
It rent the banner with seam and gash.

Quick as it fell, from the broken staff
Dame Barbara snatched the silken scarf.

She leaned far out on the window-sill,
And shook it forth with a royal will.

"Shoot, if you must, this old gray head,
But spare your country's flag," she said.

A shade of sadness, a blush of shame,
Over the face of the leader came;

The nobler nature within him stirred
To life at that woman's deed and word;

"Who touches a hair of yon gray head
Dies like a dog! March on!" he said.

All day long through Frederick street
Sounded the tread of marching feet:

All day long that free flag tost
Over the heads of the rebel host.

Ever its torn folds rose and fell
On the loyal winds that loved it well;

And through the hill-gaps sunset light
Shone over it with a warm good-night.

Barbara Frietchie's work is o'er,
And the Rebel rides on his raids no more.

Honor to her! and let a tear
Fall, for her sake, on Stonewall's bier.

Over Barbara Frietchie's grave,
Flag of Freedom and Union, wave!

Peace and order and beauty draw
Round thy symbol of light and law;

And ever the stars above look down
On thy stars below in Frederick town!

The Writings of John Greenleaf Whittier (Boston: Houghton Mifflin Co., 1888), Vol. III, pp. 245-248.

7
Reform and the Progressive Era

In 1893 social reformer Florence Kelley was appointed the chief factory inspector in Illinois. Her bureau uncovered sickening conditions in the Chicago slaughterhouses:

> Some of the children are boys who cut up the animals as soon as the hide is removed, little butchers working directly in the slaughterhouse, at the most revolting part of the labor performed in the stockyards. These children stand, ankle deep, in water used for the purpose of carrying off blood and refuse into the drains; they breathe air so sickening that a man not accustomed to it can stay in the place but a few minutes; and their work is the most brutalizing that can be devised.

The beef processed in such slaughterhouses was then shipped to local butcher shops in America's new and expanding cities. The conditions Kelley observed could be found in many areas of American production. Industrial development had become the dominant force in the life of the nation.

As the growth of industry led to deteriorating working conditions, many people demanded new controls to end abuses. Extensive social, economic, and political changes occurred in America after the Civil War as a result of the efforts of reformers like Kelley.

Millions of immigrants came to the United States to gain political, economic, and religious freedom. They accepted the most undesirable and lowest-paying jobs in order to achieve the American dream for themselves and their children.

Changing Conditions

As factories demanded workers, more and more people moved to the cities. Many of these workers were women. In 1870 female workers made up 15 percent of the labor force, and by 1900, 20 percent. Often these women worked in sweatshops, toiling 14 or 15 hours a day, earning as little as a few cents an hour. Conditions such as these illustrate the worst effects of industrialization on women.

The growth of industry created a tremendous need for cheap labor—a need that was filled by the millions of poor, unskilled, and uneducated immigrants who came to the United States after the Civil War. An immigrant woman generally had the choice of working in the home of a well-to-do woman or joining thousands of other immigrant women in industry. Such an immigrant was Sadie Kanstoroom who arrived in New York City from Palestine at the turn of the century. As a child of 12 she went to work in the rapidly growing textile industry, employed at first in a garter factory and then in a lace firm. Industrialization, immigration, and the response to these conditions shaped her life and those of other Americans of the era.

The backbreaking work of factory women helped to liberate, rather than oppress, another group of American women. Many middle-class women were freed from much of the time-consuming job of running a home by the products that industry provided. Such developments as canned and packaged goods, modern plumbing, and the sewing machine reduced the amount of time that had to be spent on housework, and many women found leisure time for education and other outside interests. Middle-class women also benefitted from immigration, which provided inexpensive domestic labor to free them even further from their homes. Advances in medical knowledge and practice increased life expectancy for mothers and resulted in a decrease in infant mortality.

Women Organize

The women who found themselves with leisure time in the late 1800's had a tradition of organization that guided their lives. In the earliest American communities, women had organized churches, social activities, and schools. When the Civil War came, organizations such as the Sanitary Commission provided the first major opportunity for national contact among women. So when industrialization moved production from the home to the factory, leisured women continued their tradition of organizing.

The temperance movement had started in the 1840's, but met with little success. In the 1870's the movement was rejuvenated by a crusading zeal that spread from the Middle West throughout the nation. Thousands of saloons were closed. Frances Willard, the dynamic leader of the temperance movement for many years, described her first experience with the antiliquor crusade as inspiring. She joined a group of women in Pittsburgh who entered a saloon:

> The tall, stately lady who led us placed her Bible on the bar and read a psalm . . . Then we sang "Rock of Ages" as I thought I had never sung it before . . . This was my Crusade baptism. The next day I went on to the West and within a week had been made president of the Chicago W.C.T.U.

The Women's Christian Temperance Union (WCTU) was formed in 1874, and by 1880 Frances Willard was the national president. Though its main concern was an end to the use of liquor, Willard involved the organization in many causes, including the growing suffrage movement. Hers was the most powerful and influential women's organization for many years. Sometimes the WCTU took

Carry Nation, with hatchet and Bible, became a symbol of the temperance movement.

direct, violent action. Carry Nation, a hatchet-wielding eccentric, worked for temperance as a result of her unhappy marriage to an alcoholic. Her saloon smashings became famous although her actions embarrassed other WCTU members and were not typical of temperance women.

In 1868 the New York Press Club held a dinner for Charles Dickens. Women could not get tickets to this dinner, and one who was turned down was the well-known journalist Jane ("Jennie June") Croly. Her response to this incident was to organize a woman's club that would manage its own affairs without male help and would create a "bond of fellowship" among women. She called her club Sorosis. Among the club's aims, said Alice Cary, who was the presiding officer at the first meeting, was a proposal to

> teach women to think for themselves, and get their opinions at first hand, not so much because it is their right as because it is their duty.

By 1869 Sorosis had 83 members, including, it was noted proudly, six artists, 22 authors, one historian, 11 poets, nine teachers, and two physicians. The formation of this club is generally regarded as the beginning of the women's club movement in the United States. In 1890 clubs from 17 states formed the General Federation of Women's Clubs, which, by World War I, claimed over a million members.

Women joined clubs throughout the nation for many reasons: to make social contacts, for self-improvement, to help end their boredom, and out of a desire to improve their communities. The clubs provided all of these opportunities while giving thousands of women practice in making public speeches, preparing reports, dealing with strangers, and working with municipal governments.

Because the federation did not seat black women, they formed their own organizations. Black women had often been involved in church work and secret societies designed to give aid to the needy. The black woman's club movement dates from July 1895, when the first national conference was held in Boston. The meeting was a response to a letter published in a newspaper in Missouri describing the American black woman as immoral and lacking in character. Angrily, black leaders called their forces together to educate the country. The National Association of Colored Women was formed in 1895, to bring together clubs from various communities. Josephine St. Pierre Ruffin, Mary Church Terrell, the first president, and other prominent women worked to make it possible for "many bright, colored women to enjoy the fellowship and helpfulness of many of the best organizations of American women." Mary Terrell would remain an outstanding spokeswoman for black women until her death in 1954.

Education

American women were becoming better educated. In 1890, 2,500 women had received college degrees, and by 1910, 8,437 women had achieved this goal. They graduated from Vassar College, which had opened its doors in 1865, Wellesley, and Smith, which opened in 1875, and the Harvard Annex (later to be called Radcliffe) which admitted its first students in 1882. Similar educational opportunities developed in the South. Mississippi chartered the first state-supported college for women in 1884, and two years later H. Sophie Newcomb College was opened in Louisiana.

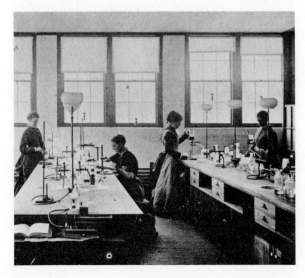

A science laboratory at the Massachusetts Institute of Technology. Until 1885 women and men were not allowed to work together in the same laboratory.

Female college graduates were constantly trying to disprove the idea that educated women were less womanly as a result of their education. This was hard to do because surveys showed that college women married later, if at all (50 percent did not marry), and they had fewer children than noncollege-educated women. Jane Addams, a major social reformer of the period and herself unmarried, wrote that in her era women who wished to work professionally after graduating from college were forced to choose between a family and a career.

Social Reform

Jane Addams was one of a group of women and men who dedicated their lives to helping correct the inequalities caused by the growth of big business, large cities, and steady immigration. These people pressured both local and federal governments to pass reform legislation to improve the lives of all Americans. Theodore Roosevelt, who was President from 1900 to 1908, believed that no class of people should have special privileges in a democracy. He said, "I stand for a square deal. The labor unions . . . the corporations . . . all the citi-

Jane Addams, founder of Hull House.

zens shall have a square deal." Addams, Roosevelt, and others who worked for these goals during the years from 1890 to 1913 were part of a movement called Progressivism.

One of Jane Addams' major concerns was the dehumanizing effect of vice, corruption, and disease on the urban poor. In 1887, while in England, she had become aware of the severe poverty of the poor in the English slums. She vowed that when she returned to America she would work to aid Americans in similar conditions. By opening Hull-House in 1889 in the slums of Chicago, Addams hoped to accomplish two goals. First, Hull-House would provide social services and social-action programs for the poor immigrant slum dwellers. Addams also hoped to give leisured middle-class women like herself useful work and enable them to "share the lives of the poor." This life was described by Addams:

> Unsanitary housing, poisonous sewage, contaminated water, infant mortality, the spread of contagion, adulterated food, impure milk, smoke-laden air, ill-ventilated factories, dangerous occupations, juvenile crime, unwholesome crowding, prostitution and drunkenness are the enemies which the modern city must face and overcome would it survive.

Within five years Hull-House had a day nursery, gym, dispensary, sewing classes, and a boarding house for working women, and was pressuring for legislative reform. Hull-House had also become the training ground for a notable group of women who themselves became reform leaders of the period.

Other settlements, following the lead of Hull-House, were founded in American cities. Janie Porter Barrett, a black social welfare leader in Virginia, founded the Locust Street Social Settlement in Hampton, Virginia in 1890, the first one in that state and one of the first for blacks in the United States. There she offered instruction in child care, gardening, livestock care, cooking, and sewing.

Barrett's activities were necessary because most of the Progressive reforms ignored the special problems of black people. Some black women were professionally successful, but the vast majority suffered under the burden of double discrimination, as women and as blacks.

The years from 1890 to 1920 were the years of Jim Crow laws so strict that blacks in many places had to step off the sidewalk when whites appeared or risk beatings and death. Black women, believed many white Americans, could not remain married because they lacked morality. As a result of this type of thinking black women were often sexually abused by white men.

"Here is a woman. In the Old Country she had lived much of her life, done most of her work outdoors. In America, the flat confines her.... There is no place and she has not room to turn about.... Everything is in poor repair, the rain comes through the ceilings, the wind blows dirt through the cracks in the wall."

The Uprooted,
Oscar Handlin

An indication of the suffering of black people during those years was the lynching of thousands of black women and men by mobs, often for no reason at all but on "general principles." Ida Wells-Barnett spent much of her life conducting a one-women crusade against lynching; traveling, speaking, and writing numerous articles and books. And although the number of lynchings decreased, the burden of double discrimination remained. In spite of their efforts settlement houses and other social services did little to help blacks live an easier life.

Reformers, whether trained at the settlement or following its example, attacked a wide variety of urban problems. In 1899, after working at Hull-House to abolish child labor and limit women's working hours, Florence Kelley became the head of the National Consumers' League. A forceful and dynamic leader, Kelley supported action for better working conditions, consumer protection, and an end to child labor. Kelley started a "white label" campaign, giving employers who met the league's requirements a label for goods to encourage consumers to buy their products. The league lobbied for shorter hours and higher wages and attempted to organize consumer pressure for this end.

Louis Brandeis, who was later to become a United States Supreme Court Justice, served as counsel for the league which was a leader in the fight to have maximum hours laws declared constitutional. The effort was successful when, in 1908, in the case of *Muller v. Oregon*, the United States Supreme Court declared a maximum-hour law for women to be constitutional. This was the beginning of the history of protective legislation in the United States.

Other women fought individually to improve the lives of American mothers and children. Their names are too numerous to list, but some representative examples should show the wide range of interests of the period.

Grace Hoadley Dodge in New York helped to form an association of working girls' societies which, by 1890, had become a national association. She worked to obtain vocational training for young people in the public schools, and this interest in education led to her appointment in 1886 to the New York City Board of Education. Dodge was a leader in the founding of Columbia University Teachers College. A vocational high school in New York City bears Dodge's name in honor of her work in these fields.

Sara Josephine Baker's work in New York in the summer of 1908 reduced infant mortality dramatically. She traveled from house to house instructing poverty-stricken women in child care. Baker's work earned her the directorship of the Division of Child Hygiene in New York, the world's first public health agency devoted to children's health.

Albion Fellows Bacon's life was changed when her children contracted scarlet fever. She believed that poor school children had unknowingly carried the disease which her children caught. This belief led her to volunteer to work in the slums of Evansville, Indiana. Appalled by the conditions she found, Bacon started a long battle to improve the tenements that housed the poor. In 1913 her work, which included addressing the Indiana legislature, was successful in obtaining state regulation of housing in Indiana.

The actions of reformers were not designed to create a feminist revolution, nor were they even directly related to changing the role American women played in society. The reformers' work was considered by most Americans to be within the proper sphere of woman's activities. If "woman's place was in the home," women who worked for society's betterment explained that their concerns were related to the home and an expansion of their traditional domestic concerns. One Progressive male wrote that the woman's place was indeed in the home.

> But to-day would she serve the home she must go beyond the house. No longer is the home compassed by four walls. Many of its most important duties lie now involved in the bigger family of the city and State.

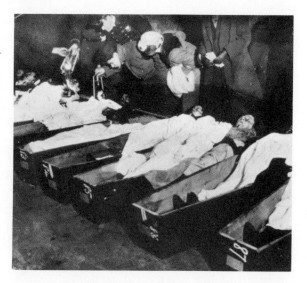

146 bodies were found in the charred ruins of the 1911 Triangle Shirt Waist Company fire. The company had ignored safety precautions and had kept fire exits locked. Many of the young women workers jumped to their deaths on the streets below. This tragedy called attention to dangerous working conditions and fanned the flames of reform.

Women were working for the downtrodden, the poor, and the young, and they were protective, hardworking, and compassionate—characteristics that were acceptable for women in the United States.

Labor Reform

The attempt to unionize female workers was a struggle that sometimes involved women in activities less traditionally feminine than settlement house work or club activities. In 1900 there were about 5 million working women in the United States, but few were organized into unions. Working conditions were often horrible. Laundresses, for example, toiled stripped to the waist in temperatures over 100°; girls making matches received little pay and their jawbones rotted from the chemicals with which they worked. Children worked alongside their mothers for many hours at a time. Women earned one-half as much as men on the average. Yet women were not unionized because most of them were unskilled and thus ignored by the American Federation of Labor. Also, many women hoped to escape work through marriage and thus saw their work as temporary. They were not interested in unionization.

In 1903 a coalition of working-class and middle-class women, led by Margaret Dreier Robins, formed the National Women's Trade Union League. Its purpose was to improve conditions of work, and it followed the Progressive tactics of investigation, education, and persuasion.

The league also actively supported strikes, including the strike of garment workers in New York in 1909. Most of the strikers were Jewish immigrant girls between the ages of 16 and 25. They were attacked, arrested, and generally mistreated on the picket lines. The middle-class and upper-class women who supported this strike and other labor union activities were brought into direct contact with the labor movement and working women. Since unions were regarded with suspicion and fear by many Americans, women who were involved in union activities were often regarded with less approval than club or settlement women.

Radicalism and Woman's Rights

Other women turned to communism, socialism, and anarchy to effect rapid change in American society. Emma Goldman, who was Russian-born, emigrated to America in 1885. Like so many others, she worked for $2.50 a week in a clothing factory in Rochester, New York. Conditions in that factory led her to become an anarchist and, labeled as "Red Emma," she began to speak at rallies, encouraging the use of violence to change conditions. She spent the year 1893 in jail because she had spoken at a New York City rally and told the unemployed listeners to take bread from the wealthy and privileged. In 1919 she was deported to Russia, but not before she had spoken across the country on anarchy, birth control, and the "new woman."

Less radical than Emma Goldman, but also less accepted than club or settlement women, was Mary Harris Jones. To the miners for whom she labored she was better known as "Mother Jones." Born in 1830, she emigrated from Ireland, married, and had four children. After her family died in a yellow-fever epidemic, she worked as a dressmaker. Jones, like Goldman, became resentful of employers' treatment of workers and by her fiftieth year she had become a labor organizer and agitator. Mother Jones traveled around the country, serving as an organizer and educator of workers, especially coal miners. In 1912 she was sentenced to prison for a 20-year term after being convicted of a conspiracy to commit murder. She was soon freed, however, because of labor pressure. Her advice to women who had watched her 50-year career was, "No matter what your fight, don't be ladylike!"

By the end of the Progressive era women had deeply involved themselves in helping other people to overcome oppressive conditions created by immigration and industrialization. The principles of protective legislation, a just minimum wage, an end to child labor, and a general feeling of social obligation for community betterment were all established largely due to the efforts of middle-class and working-class women.

Charlotte Perkins Gilman published *Women and Economics* in 1899. She argued that it was necessary for women to be economically independent. Gilman supported the idea of cooperative families where household duties would be performed by a professional staff. This would free women to combine working and raising a family. Gilman and her ideas were well-known and she was considered radical in her time, as indeed she was. The adoption of her ideas would have created a revolution both in women's role and in the pattern of family life. After suffrage was won, her ideas were largely forgotten.

Many of the Progressive women considered themselves "emancipated." However, the term "emancipated woman" triggered the stereotype of a believer in free love or in the destruction of the family. Victoria Woodhull, an eccentric feminist, furthered that stereotype and helped to confuse many people's ideas about the feminist movement. Her weekly magazine discussed and supported suffrage, free love, and sexual freedom for women. The latter two subjects were extremely unusual for a woman of the 1870's to talk about publicly. Woodhall was the first woman to run for President of the United States. Her platform consisted of her own unusual ideas. Although such ideas were meant to be regarded seriously, she was made fun of. Woodhull hurt the woman's movement in America for many years, as "equality for women" and "free love" became associated in people's minds.

Summary

By the time World War I broke out, women were deeply involved in the social, political, and economic life of the nation. Industry depended upon their labor. They worked in a variety of ways to improve their communities. Some women, such as Gilman and Woodhull, had attempted to open social discussion in order to change radically the male-female relationship. Even politics, traditionally and legally closed to women, found it was not immune. Women could not vote, but Addams and Kelley showed that women's influence could still be felt as they exerted pressure for and won passage of a variety of reform laws.

A number of the feminist leaders believed that the vote for women would give them real power to change conditions. They felt that the vote would give women greater influence over legislators and legislation. Others, however, felt that the vote was not too important an issue. In spite of this lack of unity, the vote came to be seen as a symbol of justice and power, and suffrage became the major goal of the woman's movement.

CARRY NATION WRECKS SALOONS IN HER WORK
FOR TEMPERANCE

Beginning in 1880, Kansas was "dry" —that is, no liquor could be sold legally. But the law was not enforced, and in 1899 Carry Nation took it upon herself to stop the sale of liquor in that state. Entering saloons, she smashed bottles and furniture with rocks or her famous hatchet. Although her methods were not accepted by many temperance workers, and were often used to ridicule the whole temperance movement, Carry Nation became well known.

[She discovers that liquor is being sold in Kiowa, in Barber county, Kansas and decides to deal with it herself. The officials wouldn't listen to her.]

... When I found I could effect nothing through the officials, I was sad, indeed. I saw that Kansas homes, hearts and souls were to be sacrificed. I had lost all the hopes of my young life through drink [her husband was an alcoholic], I saw the terrible results that would befall others. I felt that I had rather die than see the saloons come back into Kansas. I felt desperate. I took this to God daily, feeling that He only, could rescue ... I was awakened by a voice which seemed to be speaking in my heart, these words, "GO TO KIOWA," and my hands were lifted and thrown down and the words, "I'LL STAND BY YOU." ... I was impressed with a great inspiration, the interpretation was very plain, it was this: "Take something in your hands, and throw at these places in Kiowa and smash them." ... Note this reader, that I did not think of smashing, God told me to do it. I was a busy home keeper, did all my house work, was superintendent of two Sunday schools, one in the country, was jail evangelist, and president of the W.C.T.U. and kept open house for all of God's people, where all the Christian workers were welcome to abide at my house. When no one was looking I walked out into the yard and picked up brick bats and rocks, and hid them under my kitchen apron, took them in my room, wrapped them in newspapers. I did this until I got quite a lot ...

[She travels to Kiowa]

... I got to Kiowa at half past eight, stayed all night. Next morning I had my horse hitched and drove to the first dive kept by a Mr. Dobson, whose brother was then sheriff of the county. I stacked up these smashers [rocks, etc] on my left arm, all I could hold. They looked like packages wrapped in paper. I stood before the counter and said: "Mr. Dobson, I told you last spring to close this place. You did not do it, now I have come down with another warning, get out of the way, I do not want to strike you, but I am going to break this place up." I threw as hard, and as fast as I could, smashing mirrors and bottles and glasses and it was astonishing how quickly this was done. These men seemed terrified, threw up their hands and backed up in the corner. My strength was that of a giant. I felt invincible. God was certainly standing by me.

. . . I broke up three of these dives that day, broke the windows on the outside to prove that the man who rents his house is a partner also with the man who sells . . . I smashed five saloons with rocks, before I ever took a hatchet . . .

Carry A. Nation, *The Use and Need of the Life of Carry A. Nation* (Topeka: F.M. Steves & Sons, 1908), pp. 129-130, 133-134.

THE BLACK WOMAN'S CLUB MOVEMENT

The first national conference of black women was held in Boston in July 1895. This meeting, which began the club movement among black women, was triggered by a letter to a newspaper describing the black women of America as deficient in character and virtue. Fannie Barrier Williams, a founder of the woman's club movement, describes its background.

The negro as an "alien" race, as a "problem," as an "industrial factor," as "ex-slaves," as "ignorant" etc., are well known and instantly recognized; but colored women as mothers, as home-makers, as the center and source of the social life of the race have received little or no attention. These women have been left to grope their way unassisted toward . . . the badges of race respectability. They have had no special teachers to instruct them. No conventions of distinguished women of the more favored race have met to consider their peculiar needs. There has been no fixed public opinion to which they could appeal; no protection against the libelous attacks upon their characters, and no chivalry generous enough to guarantee their safety against man's inhumanity to woman. Certain it is that colored women have been the least known, and the most ill-favored class of women in this country . . .

In considering the social advancement of these women, it is important to keep in mind the point from which progress began, and the fact that they have been mainly self-taught in all those precious things that make for social order, purity and character. They have gradually become conscious of the fact that progress includes a great deal more than what is generally meant by the terms culture, education and contact.

The club movement among colored women reaches into the sub-social condition of the entire race. Among white women clubs mean the forward movement of the best women in the interest of the best womanhood. Among colored women the club is the effort of the few competent in behalf of the many incompetent; that is to say that the club is only one of many means for the social uplift of a race. . .

The consciousness of being fully free has not yet come to the great masses of the colored women of this country. The emancipation of the mind and spirit of the race could not be accomplished by legislation. More time, more patience, more suffering and more charity are still needed to complete the work of emancipation.

The training which first enabled colored women to organize and successfully carry on club work was originally obtained in church work . . . The meaning of unity of effort for the common good, the development of social sympathies grew into woman's consciousness through the privileges of church work.

Still another school of preparation for colored women has been their secret societies. "The ritual of these secret societies is not without a certain social value." They demand a higher order of intelligence than is required for church membership. Care for the sick, provisions for the decent burial of the [poor] dead, the care of orphans and the enlarging sense of sisterhood all contributed to the development of the very conditions of heart that qualify women for the more inclusive work of those social reforms that are the aim of women's clubs. The churches and secret societies have helped to make colored women acquainted with the general social condition of the race and the possibilities of social improvement.

With this training the more intelligent women of the race could not fail to follow the example and be inspired by the larger club movement of the white women. The need of social reconstruction became more apparent as they studied the results of women's organizations. Better homes, better schools, better protection for girls of [little] home training, better sanitary conditions, better opportunities for competent young women to gain employment, and the need of being better known to the American people appealed to the conscience of progressive colored women from many communities.

. . . While the National Federation of Woman's Clubs has served as a guide and inspiration to colored women, the club movement among them is something deeper than a mere imitation of white women. It is nothing less than the organized anxiety of women who have become intelligent enough to recognize their own low social condition and strong enough to initiate the forces of reform.

Fannie Barrier Williams (and Booker T. Washington), *A New Negro for a New Century* (Chicago: American Publishing House, 1900), pp. 379-384.

EDUCATED WORKING WOMEN DESCRIBE THEIR EXPERIENCES

In 1895 the state of Massachusetts published the results of an investigation of college-educated working women and men. The women were asked to submit facts and opinions about their work and their working problems. Many of them expressed anger at discrimination they encountered.

Opinions of Employés

1. "Men oftener than women have to support others. In spite of this I cannot see why a man should be paid $200 [annually] more than I am paid to do the same work when he does it no better, and that is what was proposed to me at one time, with the distinct statement on the part of the principal and trustees that my work was 'perfectly satisfactory in every way.' A married man solely because he is married has sometimes been paid more than one unmarried."

2. "When I came here, for less salary than I had been receiving, it was distinctly understood that if I did good work I should receive the full salary. The second year I was given $1,500, not long after $1,800, and after much protest on my part (for my work has been for the whole eleven years heavier—much heavier—than that of any other department except Chemistry), the salary was made $2,000; and I am distinctly given to understand that being a *woman* I need not hope for any more."

3. "There are not enough women, qualified to compete with men in the higher lines of teaching and supervision, to command the same confidence in them as a class."

4. "Women, as a class, have not as much confidence in themselves as men. In my opinion if women would give sufficient time to necessary preparation, in their chosen line of work, fully to equip themselves for that work and, at the same time, cultivate confidence in themselves, their ability, and their profession, they would, like men, be able to meet the question of wages with the words:—'I ask no more than I am worth but I believe myself to be worth all that I ask. Kindly give me a trial.' . . ."

5. "I fear I am not a fair representative of *office* workingwomen, at least my sympathies are not all with them. I do not think they are, as a class, as good workers as men, and if I had an office under my charge, I would put in almost all men clerks even at higher salaries, for I verily believe that I could get more and better work from them, with less complaints, than from women. . . "

Horace G. Wadlin, "Compensation in Certain Occupations of Graduates of Colleges for Women," *25th Annual Report of Mass. Bureau of Statistics of Labor* (Boston: Wright & Potter, 1895), pp. 28, 29-30, 31, 32, 33.

A PROGRESSIVE REFORMER IN ACTION

Jane Addams was an outstanding reformer of the Progressive era. In the following excerpt from her autobiographical description, *Twenty Years at Hull-House*, she recalls many of the things the settlement provided for its community of working people.

I. First Days at Hull-House

The dozens of younger children who from the first came to Hull-House were organized into groups which were not quite classes and not quite clubs. The value of these groups consisted almost entirely in arousing a higher imagination and in giving the children the opportunity which they could not have in the crowded schools, for initiative and for independent social relationships. The public schools then contained little hand work of any sort, so that naturally any instruction which we provided for the children took the direction of this supplementary work. But it required a constant effort that the pressure of poverty itself should not defeat the educational aim. The Italian girls in the sewing classes would count that day lost when they could not carry home a garment, and the insistence that it should be neatly made seemed a super-refinement to those in dire need of clothing . . .

In spite of these flourishing clubs for children early established at Hull-House, and the fact that our first organized undertaking was a kindergarten, we were very insistent that the Settlement should not be primarily for the children, and that it was absurd to suppose that grown people would not respond to opportunities for education and social life. Our enthusiastic kindergartner herself demonstrated this with an old woman of ninety, who, because she was left alone all day while her daughter cooked in a restaurant, had formed such a persistent habit of picking the plaster off the walls that one landlord after another refused to have her for a tenant. It required but a few weeks' time to teach her to make large paper chains, and gradually she was content to do it all day, and in the end took quite as much pleasure in adorning the walls as she had formerly taken in demolishing them . . . To [help] life for a woman of ninety was an unfailing [rejection] of the statement that the Settlement was designed for the young . . .

In those early days we were often asked why we had come to live on Halsted Street when we could afford to live somewhere else. I remember one man who used to shake his head and say it was "the strangest thing he had met in his experience," but who was finally convinced that it was "not strange but natural." In time it came to seem natural to all of us that the Settlement should be there. If it is natural to feed the hungry and care for the sick, it is certainly natural to give pleasure to the young, comfort to the aged, and to minister to the deep-seated craving for social intercourse that all men feel. Whoever does it is rewarded by something which, if not gratitude, is at least spontaneous and vital and lacks that irksome sense of obligation with which a substantial benefit is too often acknowledged . . .

II. Pioneer Labor Legislation in Illinois

Our very first Christmas at Hull-House, when we as yet knew nothing of child labor, a number of little girls refused the candy which was offered them as part of the Christmas good cheer, saying simply that they "worked in a candy factory and could not bear the sight of it." We discovered that for six weeks they had worked from seven in the morning until nine at night and they were exhausted as well as [full]. The sharp consciousness of stern economic conditions was thus thrust upon us in the midst of the season of good will.

During the same winter three boys from a Hull-House club were injured at one machine in a neighboring factory for lack of a guard which would have cost but a few dollars. When the injury of one of these boys resulted in his death, we felt quite sure that the owners of the factory would share our horror and remorse, and that they would do everything possible to prevent the recurrence of such a tragedy. To our surprise they did nothing whatever, and I made my first acquaintance then with those pathetic documents signed by parents of working children, that they will make no claim for damages resulting from "carelessness."

The visits we made in the neighborhood constantly discovered women sewing upon sweatshop work, and often they were assisted by incredibly small children. I remember a litte girl of four who pulled out basting threads hour after hour, sitting on a stool at the feet of her Bohemian mother, a little bunch of human misery. But even for that there was no legal [help] for the only child labor law in Illinois, with any provision for enforcement, had been secured by the coal-miner's unions, and was confined to children employed in mines.

We learned to know many families in which the working children contributed to the support of their parents, not only because they spoke English better than the older immigrants and were willing to take lower wages, but because their parents gradually found it easier to live upon their earnings. A South Italian peasant who has picked olives and packed oranges from his toddling babyhood, cannot see at once the difference between the outdoor healthy work which he has performed in the varying seasons, and the long hours of monotonous factory life which his child encounters when he goes to work in Chicago. . . . it became evident that we must add carefully collected information to our general impression of neighborhood conditions if we would make it of any genuine value.

There was at that time no statistical information on Chicago industrial conditions, and Mrs. Florence Kelley, an early resident of Hull-House, suggested to the Illinois State Bureau of Labor that they investigate the sweating system in Chicago with its attendant child labor. The head of the Bureau adopted this suggestion and engaged Mrs. Kelley to make the investigation. When the report was presented to the Illinois Legislature, a special committee was appointed to look into the Chicago conditions . . .

As a result of its investigations, this committee recommended to the Legislature the provisions which afterwards became those of the first factory law of Illinois, regulating the sanitary conditions of the sweatshop and fixing fourteen as the age at which a child might be employed. Before the passage of the law could be secured, it was necessary to appeal to all elements of the community, and a little group of us addressed the open meetings of trade-unions and of benefit societies, church organizations, and social clubs literally every evening for three months . . . The Hull-House residents that winter had their first experience in lobbying . . .

Jane Addams, *Twenty Years at Hull-House* (New York: Macmillan Co., 1910), pp. 105, 106-107, 109, 198-202. Reprinted with permission of Macmillan Publishing Co., Inc.

A BLACK WOMAN DESCRIBES PREJUDICE IN THE NATION'S CAPITAL

Mary Church Terrell, an outstanding black leader in the late nineteenth and early twentieth centuries, worked in the black club movement as well as in suffrage organizations. She traveled widely as a representative of black women here and abroad. Yet, prejudice was inescapable in her life as well as in those of the people she represented. Here she describes her experiences in Washington, D.C.

For fifteen years I have resided in Washington, and while it was far from being a paradise for colored people when I first touched these shores it has been doing its level best ever since to make conditions for us intolerable. As a colored woman I might enter Washington any night, a stranger in a strange land, and walk miles without finding a place to lay my head. Unless I happened to know colored people who live here or ran across a chance acquaintance who could recommend a colored boarding-house to me, I should be obliged to spend the entire night wandering about . . .

As a colored woman I may walk from the Capitol to the White House, ravenously hungry and abundantly supplied with money with which to purchase a meal, without finding a single restaurant in which I would be permitted to take a morsel of food, if it was patronized by white people, unless I were willing to sit behind a screen. As a colored woman I cannot visit the tomb of the Father of this country which owes its very existence to the love of freedom in the human heart and which stands for equal opportunity to all, without being forced to sit in the Jim Crow section of an electric car which starts from the very heart of the city—midway between the Capitol and the White House. If I refuse thus to be humiliated, I am cast into jail and forced to pay a fine for violating the Virginia laws. Every hour in the day Jim Crow cars filled with colored people, many of whom are intelligent and well to do, enter and leave the national capital . . .

Unless I am willing to engage in a few menial occupations, in which the pay for my services would be very poor, there is no way for me to earn an honest living, if I am not a trained nurse or a dressmaker or can secure a position as teacher in the public schools, which is exceedingly difficult to do. It matters not what my intellectual attainments may be or how great is the need of the services of a competent person, if I try to enter many of the numerous vocations in which my white sisters are allowed to engage, the door is shut in my face . . .

Some time ago a young woman who had already attracted some attention in the literary world by her volume of short stories answered an advertisement which appeared in a Washington newspaper, which called for the services of a skilled stenographer and expert typewriter. It is unnecessary to state the reasons why a young woman whose literary ability was so great as that possessed by the one referred to should decide to earn money in this way. The applicants were requested to send specimens of their work and answer certain questions concerning their experience and their speed before they called in person. In reply to her application the young colored woman, who, by the way, is very fair and attractive indeed, received a letter from the firm stating that her references and experience were the most satisfactory that had been sent and requesting her to call. When she presented herself there was some doubt in the mind of the man to whom she was directed concerning her [race], so he asked her point-blank whether she was colored or white. When she confessed the truth the merchant expressed great sorrow and deep regret that he could not avail himself of the services of so competent a person, but frankly admitted that employing a colored woman in his establishment in any except a menial position was simply out of the question . . .

And so I might go on citing instance after instance to show the variety of ways in which our people are sacrificed on the altar of prejudice in the Capital of the United States and how almost insurmountable are the obstacles which block his path to success. Early in life many a colored youth is so appalled by the helplessness and the hopelessness of his situation in this country that in a sort of stoical despair he resigns himself to his fate. "What is the good of our trying to acquire an education? We can't all be preachers, teachers, doctors, and lawyers. Besides those professions there is almost nothing for colored people to do but engage in the most menial occupations, and we do not need an education for that." More than once such remarks, uttered by young men and women in our public schools who possess brilliant intellects, have wrung my heart.

Mary Church Terrell, "What It Means to Be Colored in the Capital of the United States," *The Independent*, LXII (Jan. 24, 1907), pp. 181-182, 185.

EMMA GOLDMAN FIGHTS THE EVILS OF INDUSTRIALIZATION

Emma Goldman emigrated to the United States in 1885 from her native Russia. Gradually she came to believe in anarchism and violence as a means of achieving social change. A popular and able speaker, she lectured throughout the nation on anarchism and on the role of women. Here Goldman expresses her commitment to radical change.

. . . The industrial crisis. . . had thrown thousands out of employment, and their condition now reached an appalling state. Worst of all was the situation in New York. Jobless workers were being evicted; suffering was growing and suicides multiplying. Nothing was being done to [relieve] their misery.

[She returns to New York to help these people, but the man she loved objected to her working for the unemployed.]

It was bliss to know that someone cared so much for me, but I felt it at the same time a handicap. . . Did he consider me his property, a dependent or a cripple who had to be taken care of by a man? I had thought he believed in freedom, in my right to do as I wished. It was anxiety about me, fear for my health, he assured me, that prompted his words. But if I was determined to resume my efforts, he would help. He was no speaker, but he could be useful in other ways.

Committee sessions, public meetings, collection of food-stuffs, supervising the feeding of the homeless and their numerous children, and, finally, the organization of a mass meeting on Union Square entirely filled my time.

The meeting at Union Square was preceded by a demonstration, the marching columns counted many thousands. The girls and women were in front, I at their head carrying a red banner. Its crimson waved proudly in the air and could be seen for blocks. My soul, too, vibrated with the intensity of the moment.

I had prepared my speech in writing and it seemed to me inspiring, but when I reached Union Square and saw the huge mass of humanity, my notes appeared cold and meaningless.

The atmosphere in the ranks had become very tense, owing to the events of that week. Labor politicians had appealed to the New York Legislature for relief of the great distress, but their pleas met with evasions. Meanwhile the unemployed went on starving. The people were outraged by this callous indifference to the suffering of men, women, and children. As a result the air at Union Square was charged with bitterness and indignation, its spirit quickly communicating itself to me. I was scheduled as the last speaker and I could barely endure the long wait. Finally the [speeches were] over and my turn came. I heard my name shouted from a thousand throats as I stepped forward. I saw a dense mass before me, their pale, pinched faces upturned to me. My heart beat, my temples throbbed, and my knees shook.

"Men and women," I began amidst sudden silence, "do you not realize that the State is the worst enemy you have? It is a machine that crushes you in order to sustain the ruling class, your masters. Like naive children you put your trust in your political leaders. You make it possible for them to creep into your confidence, only to have them betray you to the first bidder. But even where there is no direct betrayal, the labor politicians make common cause with your enemies to keep you in leash, to prevent your direct action. The State is the pillar of capitalism, and it is ridiculous to expect any [help] from it. Do you not see the stupidity of asking relief from Albany with immense wealth within a stone's throw from here? Fifth Avenue is laid in gold, every mansion is a [place] of money and power. Yet there you stand, a giant, starved and [in chains], shorn of his strength. . . . You . . . will have to learn that you have a right to share your neighbor's bread. Your neighbors—they have not only stolen your bread, but they are sapping your blood. They will go on robbing you, your children, and your children's children, unless you wake up, unless you become daring enough to demand your rights. Well, then, demonstrate before the palaces of the rich; demand work. If they do not give you work, demand bread. If they deny you both, take bread. It is your sacred right!"

Uproarious applause, wild and deafening, broke from the stillness like a sudden storm. The sea of hands eagerly stretching out towards me seemed like the wings of white birds fluttering. [She is arrested the next day.]

Emma Goldman, *Living My Life* (New York: Alfred Knopf, Inc., 1931), Vol. I, pp. 121-123. Reprinted with the permission of Alfred A. Knopf, Inc.

MOTHER JONES LEADS THE WORKERS

The following passages are excerpts from the autobiography of "Mother (Mary) Jones" who spent the last fifty years of her life supporting and organizing American laborers. She was over 100 years old when she died and had earned the respect even of her enemies.

From 1880 on, I became wholly engrossed in the labor movement. In all the great industrial centers the working class was in rebellion. The enormous immigration from Europe crowded the slums, forced down wages and threatened to destroy the standard of living fought for by American working men. Throughout the country there was business depression and much unemployment. In the cities there was hunger and rags and despair.

Foreign agitators who had suffered under European despots preached various schemes of economic salvation to the workers. The workers asked only for bread and a shortening of the long hours of toil. The agitators gave them visions. The police gave them clubs . . .

Victory at Arnot

[Mother Jones goes to Pennsylvania in 1899 to lead the miners in a strike.]

. . . Then the company tried to bring in scabs. I told the men to stay home with the children for a change and let the women attend to the scabs. I organized an army of women housekeepers. On a given day they were to bring their mops and brooms and "the army" would charge the scabs up at the mines. The general manager, the sheriff and the corporation hirelings heard of our plans and were on hand. The day came and the women came with the mops and brooms and pails of water.

I decided not to go up to the Drip Mouth myself, for I knew they would arrest me and that might rout the army. I selected as leader an Irish woman who had a most picturesque appearance. She had slept late and her husband had told her to hurry up and get into the army. She had grabbed a red petticoat and slipped it over a thick cotton night gown. She wore a black stocking and white one. She had tied a little red fringed shawl over her wild red hair. Her face was red and her eyes were mad. I looked at her and felt she could raise a rumpus.

I said, "You lead the army up to the Drip Mouth. Take that tin dishpan you have with you and your hammer, and when the scabs and mules come up, begin to hammer and howl. Then all of you hammer and howl and be ready to chase the scabs with your mops and brooms. Don't be afraid of anyone. . ."

Up the mountain side, yelling and hollering, she led the women, and when the mules came up with the scabs and the coal, she began beating on the dishpan and hollering and all the army joined in with her. The sheriff tapped her on the shoulder.

"My dear lady," said he, "remember the mules. Don't frighten them."

She took the old tin pan and she hit him with it and she hollered, "To hell with you and the mules!"

He fell over and dropped into the creek. Then the mules began to rebel against scabbing. They bucked and kicked the scab drivers and started off for the barn. The scabs started running down hill, followed by the army of women with their mops and pails and brooms . . .

From that day on the women kept continual watch of the mines to see that the company did not bring in scabs. Every day women with brooms or mops in one hand and babies in the other arm wrapped in little blankets, went to the mines and watched that no one went in. And all night long they kept watch. They were heroic women. In the long years to come the nation will pay them high tribute for they were fighting for the advancement of a great country . . .

You Don't Need a Vote to Raise Hell

. . . Five hundred women got up a dinner and asked me to speak. Most of the women were crazy about women suffrage. They thought that the Kingdom-come would follow the enfranchisement of women.

"You must stand for free speech in the streets," I told them.

"How can we," piped a woman, "when we haven't a vote?"

"I have never had a vote," said I, "and I have raised hell all over this country! You don't need a vote to raise hell! You need convictions and a voice!"

Someone meowed, "You're an anti [suffragist]!"

"I am not an anti to anything which will bring freedom to my class," said I. "But I am going to be honest with you sincere women who are working for votes for women. The women of Colorado have had the vote for two generations and the working men and women are in slavery. The state is in slavery, vassal to the Colorado Iron and Fuel Company and its subsidiary interests. A man who was present at a meeting of mine owners told me that when the trouble started in the mines, one operator proposed that women be disfranchised [lose the vote] because here and there some woman had raised her voice in behalf of the miners. Another operator jumped to his feet and shouted, 'For God's sake! What are you talking about? If it had not been for the women's vote the miners would have beaten us long ago!'"

Some of the women gasped with horror. One or two left the room. I told the women I did not believe in women's rights nor in men's rights but in human rights. "No matter what your fight," I said, "don't be ladylike! God Almighty made women and the Rockefeller gang of thieves made the ladies. I have just fought through sixteen months of bitter warfare in Colorado. I have been up against armed mercenaries but this old woman, without a vote, and with nothing but a hatpin has scared them . . ."

Mary Harris Jones, *Autobiography of Mother Jones* (Chicago: Charles H. Kerr & Co., 1925), pp. 17, 34-35, 36, 203-204.

CHARLOTTE PERKINS GILMAN THINKS FAMILY LIFE SHOULD CHANGE

In her 1899 book *Women and Economics*, Charlotte Perkins Gilman encouraged a "revolution" in American family life. She felt that this, more than anything else, would change women's roles and create equality between females and males.

Is our present way of organizing home life, based on the economic dependence of women on men, the best way to maintain the individual in health and happiness? Will it develop higher abilities? The individual is not maintained in health and happiness,—that is visible to all; and how little the individual is developed in social relation is shown in the wastefulness of our economic system.

If women are to become economically independent there will have to be a change in the home and family relation. But, if that change is for the advantage of individual and race, we need not fear it. It does not involve a change in the marriage relationship except in taking away the economic dependence of women on men. It will not involve a change in the relation of mother to child except to improve it. But it does involve . . . women in social service and business rather than only in household service. This will of course require the introduction of some other form of living other than that which now exists. It will make impossible the present method of feeding the world by millions of private servants, and bringing up children in the same way . . .

If there should be built and opened in any of our large cities today a comfortable and roomy and well served apartment house for professional women with families, it would be filled at once. The apartments would be without kitchens; but there would be a kitchen belonging to the house from which meals could be served to the families in their rooms or in a common dining room, as preferred. It would be a home where the cleaning was done by efficient workers, not hired separately by the families, but hired by the manager of the establishment; and a roof garden, day nursery, and kindergarten, under well-trained professional nurses and teachers, would insure proper care of the children. The demand for such a way of life is increasing daily, and must soon be met, . . . by a permanent provision for the needs of women and children, of family privacy with advantage for everyone . . .

This division of housekeeping would require the service of fewer women for fewer hours a day. Where now twenty women in twenty homes work all the time and do not accomplish their varied duties, the same work in the hands of specialists could be done in less time by fewer people; and the others would be left free to do other work for which they were better suited, thus increasing the productive power of the world . . .

Charlotte Perkins Gilman, *Women and Economics* (Boston: Small, Maynard, and Co., 1899), pp. 210-211, 242, 245, adapted.

NELLIE BLY TRAVELS AROUND THE WORLD IN 72 DAYS

Elizabeth Cochrane, better known as Nellie Bly to her readers, was one of the most famous reporters of the late nineteenth century. Once she commited herself to an insane asylum to gain a "scoop" and in her most famous adventure she raced around the world in seventy-two days to beat the record of Jules Verne's fictional character in *Around the World in Eighty Days*. Here she describes how that trip came to be.

What gave me the idea?

It is sometimes difficult to tell exactly what gives birth to an idea. Ideas are the chief stock in trade of newspaper writers and generally they are the scarcest stock in market, but they do come occasionally.

This idea came to me one Sunday. I had spent a greater part of the day and half the night vainly trying to fasten on some idea for a newspaper article. It was my custom to think up ideas on Sunday and lay them before my editor for his approval or disapproval on Monday. But ideas did not come that day and three o'clock in the morning found me weary and with an aching head tossing about in my bed. At last tired and provoked at my slowness in finding a subject, something for the week's work, I thought fretfully: "I wish I was at the other end of the earth!"

"And why not?" the thought came: "I need a vacation; why not take a trip around the world?"

It is easy to see how one thought followed another. The idea of a trip around the world pleased me and I added: "If I could do it as quickly as Phileas Fogg [in Verne's book] did, I should go."

Then I wondered if it were possible to do the trip in eighty days and afterwards I went easily off to sleep with the determination to know before I saw my bed again if Phileas Fogg's record could be broken.

I went to a steamship company's office that day and made a selection of time tables. Anxiously I sat down and went over them and if I had found the elixir of life I should not have felt better than I did when I conceived a hope that a tour of the world might be made in even less than eighty days.

I approached my editor rather timidly on the subject. I was afraid that he would think the idea too wild and visionary.

"Have you any ideas?" he asked, as I sat down by his desk.

"One," I answered quietly.

He sat toying with his pens, waiting for me to continue, so I blurted out:

"I want to go around the world!"

"Well?" he said, inquiringly looking up with a faint smile in his kind eyes.

"I want to go around in eighty days or less. I think I can beat Phileas Fogg's record. May I try it?"

To my dismay he told me that in the office they had thought of this same idea before, and the intention was to send a man. However he offered me the consolation that he would favor my going, and then we went to talk with the business manager about it.

"It is impossible for you to do it," was the terrible verdict. "In the first place, you are a woman and would need a protector, and even if it were possible for you to travel alone you would need to carry so much baggage that it would detain you in making rapid changes. Besides you speak nothing but English, so there is no use talking about it; no one but a man can do this."

"Very well," I said angrily, "Start the man and I'll start the same day for some other newspaper and beat him."

"I believe you would," he said slowly. I would not say that this had any influence on their decision, but I do know that before we parted I was made happy by the promise that if any one was commissioned to make the trip, I should be that one.

After I had made my arrangements to go, other important projects for gathering news came up, and this rather visionary idea was put aside for a while.

One cold, wet evening, a year after this discussion, I received a little note asking me to come to the office at once. A summons, late in the afternoon, was such an unusual thing to me that I was to be excused if I spent all my time on the way to the office wondering what I was to be scolded for.

I went in and sat down beside the editor waiting for him to speak. He looked up from the paper on which he was writing and asked quietly: "Can you start around the world day after to-morrow?"

"I can start this minute," I answered, quickly trying to stop the rapid beating of my heart.

Elizabeth Cochrane, *Nellie Bly's Book, Around the World in 72 Days* (New York: Pictorial Weeklies, 1890), pp. 3-6.

EARNING A LIVING—THE LIFE OF A WINNEBAGO INDIAN

Mountain Wolf Woman began her life as a simple food gatherer in Wisconsin. Eighty years later she had seen great changes in the lives of her people as well as her own. She herself rode on trains, and lived in a modern home. In the following excerpt from her autobiography, Mountain Wolf Woman recalls her life as a young girl in the 1890's. Her experiences illustrate another one of the wide variety of lifestyles of American women in the late 1800's.

In March we usually travelled to the Mississippi River . . . and then we returned again in the last part of May. We used to live at a place on the edge of the Mississippi called Caved In Breast's Grave. My father, brother-in-law and brothers used to trap there for muskrats. When they killed the muskrats my mother used to save the bodies and hang them up there in great numbers. When there were a lot of muskrats then they used to roast them on a rack . . . When these were cooked, the women put them aside and placed some more on the rack. They cooked a great amount of muskrats. When they were cooled, the women packed them together and stored them for summer use.

In the spring when my father went trapping on the Mississippi and the weather became very pleasant my sister once said, "It is here that they dig yellow water lily roots." So, we all went out, my mother and sisters and everybody. When we got to a slough where the water lilies were very dense, they took off their shoes, put on old dresses and went wading into the water. They used their feet to hunt for the roots. They dug them out with their feet and then the roots floated up to the surface. Eventually, my second oldest sister happened upon one. My sister took one of the floating roots, wrapped it about with the edge of her blouse and tucked it into her belt. I thought she did this because it was the usual thing to do. I saw her doing this and when I happened upon a root I took it and did the same thing. I put it in my belt too. And then everybody laughed at me! . . . My sister had done that because she was pregnant . . .

After cranberry time they went on the fall migration to hunt deer . . . At that time my father did not have to buy any deer license. They never used to pay for such things. When they went deer hunting the white people did not spy on them. That is how it used to be at that time. They killed as many deer as they deemed necessary . . . They wrapped the deer in autumn leaves and carried the deer on their backs. As they were approaching you could see the red leaves moving along here and there, as they came home with the freshly killed deer . . .

Four or five households of Indians migrated to this area where they built long wigwams . . . Our family was large enough to require a two-fireplace wigwam. We lived in a rush wigwam. My grandmother and my mother made our house of cattail matting . . .

One time when we had been living there only a short time, as I recall, this old man, Daylight, died. When he was about to die he was very sick. He was really very sick but he said that he wanted to see the daylight, he wanted to go outside. He said this as he lay there. Upon hearing this my mother came home. She had evidently gone to visit him. She said, "My sons, he is to be pitied that he is saying this. Go and carry him. Take him outside. Let him see the daylight." So, my older brothers did as they were told to do . . . That is the way old people were; the old people were supposed to be respected. "Respect those old people," mother and father used to say to us. That is what we used to do. We respected the old people, but today they do not respect the old people. . .

Nancy Lurie, editor, *Mountain Wolf Woman, The Autobiography of a Winnebago Indian* (Ann Arbor, Michigan: University of Michigan Press, 1961), pp. 8-9, 15-16. © 1961 by the University of Michigan Press. Reprinted with permission.

8

Suffrage at Last

Thousands upon thousands of women gave years of their lives to getting the vote for American women. Carrie Chapman Catt, a leader of the struggle, described what it took to achieve suffrage in 1920:

> To get the word male in effect out of the constitution cost the women of the country 52 years of pauseless campaign . . .; 56 campaigns of referenda to male voters; 480 campaigns to urge Legislatures to submit suffrage amendments to voters; 47 campaigns to induce state constitutional conventions to write woman suffrage into State constitutions; 277 [state party convention campaigns]; 30 campaigns to urge presidential party conventions to adopt woman suffrage planks in party platforms; and 19 campaigns with 19 successive Congresses . . .

Why was American society so reluctant to give women suffrage, even after the black man had been granted that right? The complex and exciting lives of the major leaders of the suffrage movement tell the story of the conflicts involved in this struggle.

Leaders of the Suffrage Movement

Susan B. Anthony and Elizabeth Cady Stanton, the giants of the suffrage campaign, formed one of the unique partnerships in history.

Elizabeth Cady Stanton (seated) and Susan B. Anthony.

"No power in heaven, hell or earth can separate us," wrote Stanton to her friend, "for our hearts are eternally wedded together." Susan B. Anthony grew up in a home where girls were allowed to be self-sufficient. Her parents and sister became involved early in the woman's rights movement as well as in temperance and abolition. This progressive environment shaped her later life. She was an excellent organizer, an eloquent speaker, and a very determined woman. She remained unmarried her entire life and was able to devote her considerable energy to the suffrage cause.

From the first, when Anthony met Stanton in 1851, their abilities harmonized. They began to work together.

> We were at once fast friends, in thought and sympathy [wrote Stanton]. We were one, and in the division of labor, we exactly complemented each other. In writing we did better work together than either could do alone . . . I am the better writer, she the better critic. She supplied the facts and statistics, I the philosophy and rhetoric, and together we have made arguments that have stood unshaken by the storms of 30 long years.

Included in the group who worked with Anthony and Stanton were Lucy Stone and Julia Ward Howe. They had both participated in the fight for abolition and were respectable and respected. Carrie

Chapman Catt, another suffragist, became the leader of the movement after Stanton and Anthony stepped down, because she possessed organizational and political skills. Also important were Harriot Blatch, the daughter of Elizabeth Stanton, a woman determined to put life back into the movement in the early 1900's; and Alice Paul and Lucy Burns, who used more radical techniques, such as staging protests outside the White House, for which they went to prison.

From 1870 to 1920, these women plus thousands of others fought the established political system. They were finally rewarded for their efforts by the passage of the Nineteenth Amendment. Following the activities of some of these significant women gives an understanding of the excitement and the grueling hard work of picketing, parading, and petitioning to achieve political change.

Early Demands for Suffrage

As a result of the Civil War, the Fifteenth Amendment was passed. Its purpose was to give the vote to freed black males, but not to females, black or white. Although Anthony had held a convention in Washington to dramatize the need for woman suffrage, Congress took no apparent notice. The women of America, who had devoted all their efforts to preserving the Union during the war, became painfully aware that they were not to be rewarded for their hard work or their good will.

Stanton and Anthony, with the help of a few Congressmen, initiated an amendment that would have provided universal suffrage. For the next 50 years, the amendment would be known as the Susan B. Anthony amendment. It read: "The right of citizens of the United States to vote shall not be denied or abridged by the United States or by any state on account of sex." This amendment was introduced into Congress in early 1878, but it failed to pass. The amendment would be introduced almost every year for half a century until it was adopted in 1920.

In 1872 Susan B. Anthony decided to test the prohibition on women voting. After spending the required 30 days' residency in Rochester, New York, she walked into the polling place and cast her ballot for president. Elated, she wrote to her friend Stanton:

> Well I have gone and done it!!—positively voted the Republican ticket—straight this A.M. at 7 o'clock—and sworn my vote in at that.

On November 18, 1872, she was arrested for voting illegally. If convicted, she would have received a fine of up to $500 or even three years' imprisonment.

At her trial Susan B. Anthony spoke eloquently regarding the denial of her rights as one of the governed, of her denial of representation as one of the taxed, of her denial to a trial by a jury of her peers (women could not serve on juries) The final verdict was a $100 fine, arrived at by the judge who did not poll the jury. Some of the members of the jury, when able to speak out, confirmed that they could not have found her guilty. Anthony wanted to be sentenced to prison so that she could take the case to the Supreme Court. She refused to pay the fine hoping the judge would imprison her. However, he did not. Although Anthony did not get what she wanted, her principled action brought much publicity to the suffrage cause.

In 1874 Virginia and Francis Minor brought the same question to the Supreme Court. The Minors argued that women should have the right to vote because they were citizens of the United States. The Court, however, ruled that the states, having withheld suffrage from certain men, were within their rights to withhold it from women.

Suffrage Associations

It was evident in the 1870's that suffrage would be difficult to achieve. There were two associations that used different methods for achieving this goal. One, the National Woman Suffrage Association, worked at the national level for a constitutional amendment to grant suffrage to women. Anthony and Stanton were the leaders of this organization, which had been formed in 1869. The other group, the American Woman Suffrage Association, believed the vote could be won only by convincing the states to change their voting laws. Lucy Stone, Julia Ward Howe, and Henry Blackwell provided leadership for this group. The success of both the American and National Associations was minimal in the two decades after the Civil War. By 1887 it became evident that the two suffrage organizations had to work together, and a merger was completed in 1890. The association that emerged was called the National American Woman Suffrage Association (NAWSA).

By the beginning of the twentieth century the founders of the suffrage movement were gone. Lucy Stone died in 1893, Stanton in 1902, and Anthony in 1906. Their deaths created a vacuum, and the movement lost momentum. At this time, America was concerned with trustbusting, muckraking, the "Rough Riders," and territories overseas. These interests, by comparison, seemed to dull the importance of suffrage, but a new generation of women was ready to take over and bring new life to the movement.

New Leadership

Two women seemed fit to assume leadership of the suffrage struggle. Carrie Chapman Catt, who had become chairwoman of the organizational committee of the NAWSA in 1895, exhibited remarkable qualities as an organizer. She had immediately seen the need for a definite plan of action—for a state headquarters and a manual of organization. She instituted a consistent membership plan and encouraged the members to take political science and economics courses in order to become more effective. Catt was Anthony's choice to be her successor. She served as president of NAWSA from 1900 to 1904.

When Catt retired from national leadership, multitalented Anna Howard Shaw became the new president. Shaw had been a pioneer, a minister, and in 1885 received her M.D. degree. Her work in the slums brought her close to poor working women. But Shaw proved less effective than the previous leaders and during her presidency, NAWSA accomplished very little. As a result the state organizations became more powerful.

Harriot Stanton Blatch returned from England inspired by the methods that English women were employing to gain the vote. Blatch expressed her impatience with American methods:

> The suffrage movement was completely in a rut in New York State at the opening of the twentieth century. It bored its adherents and repelled its opponents ... Nothing better described the situation than the title of an address given by one of its leaders, "Enmeshed." The only method suggested for furthering the cause was the slow process of education. We were told to organize, organize, organize, to the end of educating, educating, educating public opinion.

With the help of trade union women as well as professional and business women, Blatch founded the Equality League of Self-Supporting Women in 1907. Later it was to be renamed the Women's Political Union. It had two purposes: (1) the introduction of new methods of propaganda, and (2) the entrance of suffrage into politics. The tactics of the league included distribution of leaflets near the polls on election day, making personal visits to labor unions, and speaking before politicians. People began to hear about woman's rights. The press, politics, and propaganda served the Equality League well. The league became political because its members believed theirs was a political cause.

Harriot Stanton Blatch was convinced that since emotion pushes people to action, a dramatic suffrage parade would be a good political tactic. The first one was set for New York City on May 21, 1910, to protest legislative indifference to the needs and demands of women. The league wanted the support of all suffrage groups, but was told by the conservative NAWSA members that their struggle would be set back by 50 years by an undignified parade. They were wrong. The *Evening Telegram* summed it up aptly; "Flying Their Banners and Wearing Yellow Votes-For-Women Sashes, the greatest suffrage parade and demonstration ever seen in New York moved on Union Square thousands strong this afternoon."

Parades became an annual event, and the Women's Political Union insisted that, from then on, all women would have to walk (many had ridden in carriages the first time) and would have to stay in the procession from the start to the finish. In May 1911, after the second annual parade, The New York *World* said:

> The ladies are campaigning. Early and late, afoot and in the horseless [automobiles], from the curbstone and the top of the tables, on street corners and door steps, not to mention canvassing the elusive voter in the seclusion of his home, they are demanding the vote and the scalps of the enemy . . .

Even *The New York Times*, which did not believe in suffrage, conceded that "the marchers, instead of injuring their cause by conduct that . . . was distinctly unfeminine and therefore obnoxious and ridiculous really accomplished something . . . and did not lose but gained respect."

Carrie Chapman Catt was also working in New York to get New York State to grant women the vote. Beginning in 1910, her Woman Suffrage Party organized sophisticated campaigns. Trained political workers visited every voter in a district to secure support. In 1915 the party finally was able to organize a referendum on the suffrage question, although there was tremendous opposition. Thousands of meetings to gather support were held, huge parades were planned, and millions of leaflets were distributed. However, the referendum was approved by only 42 percent of the vote. Undaunted, the suffragists started again and were finally successful in 1917.

At this time almost no work was being done on the constitutional amendment. The Susan B. Anthony amendment was introduced into Congress every year, but it was considered routine and unimportant by most congressmen. It had not been reported out of committee onto the floor of the Senate since 1887 and had never reached the floor of the House.

In order to publicize their cause suffragists often protested in front of the White House.

Alice Paul, who had been involved in the British suffrage movement, must be credited with giving the national movement new life. She became chairwoman of the congressional committee of the board of the National American Woman Suffrage Association. Along with Lucy Burns and many others, Paul organized a parade of 5,000 women to be held the day before Woodrow Wilson's inauguration. Lacking sufficient police protection, one newspaper reported, "the women had to fight their way from the start and took more than one hour in making the first ten blocks . . . The parade itself, in spite of the delays, was a great success. Passing through two walls of antagonistic humanity, the marchers, for the most part, kept their tempers."

The national movement was once again in the news. NAWSA, while welcoming the renewed interest in the woman's movement, feared that it would not be able to control the growing militancy. Paul formed the Congressional Union, or Woman's Party. Its belief in confrontation, which often led to violence, frightened the more conservative NAWSA.

By 1915 the National Association was out of money, leaders, and initiative, and the Congressional Union had become stronger. Their uncompromising approach to suffrage began to bring results. On March 19, 1914, the suffrage question finally reached the floor of the Senate, where it was defeated by only one vote. It was also defeated in the House at that time.

Opponents of woman suffrage were well organized.

Antisuffrage Ideas

Many organizations fought to defeat suffrage in the United States. In the South traditional attitudes about the proper role of women were still strong. Men feared the destruction of the family if women became involved in politics. Most Southern women felt that politics was men's work and that "every Southern woman has a protector and champion in every Southern man." The Southern woman wanted to keep the security she had. Southerners were aware that woman suffrage would increase the voting power of blacks, as black women as well as white women would be able to vote.

Liquor interests also complicated the suffrage struggle. Since temperance had been a woman's struggle, liquor interests were worried that, with the vote, women would act to prohibit the sale of liquor. According to Catt, had there been no temperance movement, women would have won the vote two generations earlier. One distiller remarked in 1914:

> In regard to the matter of woman suffrage, we are trying to keep from having any connection with it whatever. We are, however, in a position to establish channels of communication with the leaders of

the anti-suffrage movement for our friends in any state where suffrage is an issue.

Distillers spent thousands of dollars fighting for the defeat of suffrage.

Political organizations also opposed suffrage. "Machine" politicians such as the Tammany group in New York City feared that they would not be able to control the female vote. They worried that women who wanted labor reform, abolition of child labor, and improved schools would not be influenced by traditional backroom political deals. For similar reasons, business groups also were against woman suffrage. They felt that these new voters would support Progressive reforms that would threaten their established interests.

Finally, Americans who supported states' rights fought against a federal amendment granting suffrage. States' righters believed that each state should decide this controversial issue for itself.

The Final Effort

In spite of the strong opposition to their cause, suffragists pressed on with their work. World War I, which the United States entered in

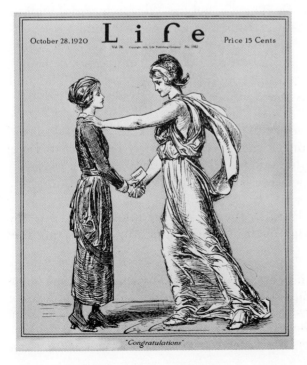

This Life *magazine cover celebrated the passage of the 19th Amendment in 1920.*

1917, gave suffrage the final push it needed. This war, like the Civil War, brought women out of their homes and into industry and public service. Women worked in oil refineries, steel mills, war goods manufacture, textiles, and all other important industries. Women also were appointed to government positions that dealt with such issues as how many hours a woman could work, whether or not working conditions were safe, and with the war effort in general.

The war also furnished the suffragists with moral arguments. World War I was fought to "make the world safe for democracy," stated President Wilson. If women could do their fair share during this period of national crisis, then surely they were capable of assuming political and social responsibility during peacetime as well. But during the war, women were once again urged to put aside their own concerns. This time, however, many were not willing to do so.

Alice Paul and Lucy Burns would not wait until peace came. On January 10, 1917, pickets sponsored by the Woman's Party stood outside the White House. On June 22 the arrests began. Alice Paul was arrested on October 20 for carrying a banner saying "The Time Has Come to Conquer or Submit." She was sentenced to seven months in prison. She and others were brutally treated and were force-fed when they went on starvation campaigns.

The tactics of the Woman's Party forced Congress to deal with the suffrage question. A vote was scheduled in the House of Representatives for January 10, 1918. The day before, Wilson declared himself in favor of suffrage. As the House session began, members of suffrage groups filled the galleries. Suspense increased as the voting began. Every vote was so important that one congressman, Henry Barnhart of Indiana, was carried in to vote on a stretcher. The final vote—274 yea, 136 nay—was just past the necessary two-thirds vote majority.

The struggle, however, was not over. It took all of 1918, half of 1919, and the election of a new Congress to get the suffrage amendment through the Senate. Militant demonstrations were resumed, and political persuasion and education were continued by NAWSA leaders.

On September 30, 1918, President Wilson appeared before the Senate to ask for passage of the Anthony amendment. He told the Senators:

> We have made partners of the women in this war; shall we admit them only to a partnership of suffering and sacrifice and toil and not to a partnership of privilege and right? This war could not have been fought, either by the other nations engaged or by America, if it had not been for the services of the women—services rendered in every

sphere—not merely in the fields of effort in which we have been accustomed to see them work, but wherever men have worked, and upon the very skirts and edges of the battle itself . . . .

In spite of this eloquent appeal, the amendment was voted down, two votes short of passage. The response of suffragists was a concentrated political campaign to defeat antisuffrage Senators. They were successful in defeating two Senators and although the women lost another Senate vote in February 1919, on May 20, 1919, Congress finally passed the Anthony amendment.

Thirty-six states had to approve the amendment to make it law. By January 1920, only one more state was needed. National attention turned to the Tennessee legislature, where a vote was to be held on August 26, 1920. The amendment seemed to be short the necessary votes. But Harry Burn, a 24-year-old Tennessee representative, had received a message from his mother which said:

> Hurrah! And vote for suffrage and don't keep them in doubt . . . Don't forget to be a good boy and help Mrs. Catt put "Rat" in Ratification.

Burn cast the deciding "yes" vote on August 26, 1920. Twenty-six million American women had finally won the right to vote.

THE PEOPLE VS. SUSAN B. ANTHONY

In 1872 Susan B. Anthony voted illegally in Rochester, New York. She was brought to trial for this crime and used the occasion to speak eloquently for the rights of woman.

The Court: The prisoner will stand up. Has the prisoner anything to say why sentence shall not be pronounced?

Miss Anthony: Yes, your honor, I have many things to say; for in your ordered verdict of guilty, you have trampled underfoot every vital principle of our government. My natural rights, my civil right, my political rights, are all alike ignored. Robbed of the fundamental privilege of citizenship, I am degraded from the status of a citizen to that of a subject; and not only myself individually, but all of my sex, are, by your honor's verdict, doomed to political subjection under this so-called Republican government.

Judge Hunt: The Court can not listen to a rehearsal of arguments the prisoner's counsel has already consumed three hours in presenting.

Miss Anthony: May it please your honor, I am not arguing the question, but simply stating the reasons why sentence can not, in justice, be pronounced against me. Your denial of my citizen's right to vote is the denial of my right of consent as one of the governed, the denial of my right of representation as one of the taxed, the denial of my right to a trial by jury of my peers as an offender against law, therefore, the denial of my sacred rights to life, liberty, property, and—

Judge Hunt: The Court can not allow the prisoner to go on.

Miss Anthony: But your honor will not deny me this one and only poor privilege of protest against this high-handed outrage upon my citizen's rights. May it please the Court to remember that since the day of my arrest last November, this is the first time that either myself or any person of my disfranchised class has been allowed a word of defense before judge or jury— . . .

Judge Hunt: The Court must insist—the prisoner has been tried according to established forms of law.

Miss Anthony: Yes, your honor, but by forms of law all made by men, interpreted by men, administered by men, in favor of men, and against women; and hence, your honor's ordered verdict of guilty, against a United States citizen for the exercise of "that citizen's right to vote," simply because that citizen was a woman and not a man. But, yesterday, the same man-made forms of law declared it a crime punishable with $1,000 fine and six months' imprisonment, for you, or me, or any of us, to give a cup of cold water, a crust of bread, or a night's shelter to a panting fugitive as he was tracking his way to Canada. And every man or woman in whose veins coursed a drop of sympathy violated that wicked law, reckless of consequences, and was justified in so doing. As then the slaves who got their freedom must take it over, or under, or through the unjust forms of law, precisely so now must women, to get their right to a voice in this Government, take it; and I have taken mine, and mean to take it at every possible opportunity.

Judge Hunt: The Court orders the prisoner to sit down. It will not allow another word.

Miss Anthony: When I was brought before your honor for trial, I hoped for a broad and liberal interpretation of the Constitution and its recent amendments, that should declare all United States citizens under its ⌐protection], that should declare equality of rights the national guarantee to all persons born or naturalized in the United States. But failing to get this justice—failing, even, to get a trial by a jury *not* of my peers—I ask not leniency at your hands—but rather the full rigors of the law.

Judge Hunt: The Court must insist—[Here the prisoner sat down.]

Judge Hunt: The prisoner will stand up. [Here Miss Anthony arose again.] The sentence of the Court is that you pay a fine of one hundred dollars and the costs of the prosecution.

Miss Anthony: May it please your honor, I shall never pay a dollar of your unjust penalty. All the stock in trade I possess is a $10,000 debt, incurred by publishing my paper—*The Revolution*—four years ago, the sole object of which was to educate all women to do precisely as I have done, rebel against your man-made, unjust, unconstitutional forms of law, that tax, fine, imprison, and hang women, while they deny them the right of representation in the Government; and I shall work on with might and main to pay every dollar of that honest debt, but not a penny shall go to this unjust claim. And I shall earnestly and persistently continue to urge all women to the practical recognition of the old revolutionary maxim, that "Resistance to tyranny is obedience to God."

Judge Hunt: Madam, the Court will not order you committed until the fine is paid.

E.C. Stanton, S.B. Anthony, M.J. Gage, editors, *The History of Woman Suffrage* (New York: Fowler and Wells, 1881), Vol. II, pp. 687-689.

"COMMON SENSE" APPLIED TO WOMAN SUFFRAGE

In 1894 Mary Putnam-Jacobi, the foremost female doctor of the late nineteenth century, wrote the reasons she felt justified the demand for woman suffrage. She was aware that the vote would not change the social order but believed that it would be the means by which women could achieve status as human beings, with the same potential as men.

No matter how well born, how intelligent, how highly educated, how virtuous, how rich, how refined, the women of today constitute a political class below that of every man, no matter how base born, how stupid, how ignorant, how vicious, how poverty-stricken, how brutal. The pauper in the almshouse may vote; the lady who devotes her philanthropic thought to making the almshouse habitable may not. The tramp who begs cold [food] in the kitchen may vote; the heiress who feeds him and endows universities may not. The half-civilized hordes pouring into our country through the open gates of our seaport towns, the Indian on [his own land], the negro on the cotton plantation,—all now, or in a few years, have a vote. But the white woman of purest blood, and who, in her own person, or that of her mother or grandmother has helped to sustain the courage of the Revolutionary war, to fight the heroic battle of abolition, and to dress the wound of the Rebellion,—this woman must keep silence. . . . The women—who embrace half the education, half the virtue, and but a fraction of the illiteracy or crime of the community—remain excluded from the franchise, buried behind this dense cloud of often [stupid] ignorance.

. . . After all, the most important effect of the suffrage is psychological. The permanent consciousness of power for effective action, the knowledge that their own thoughts have an equal chance with those of any other person, in being carried out by one's own will; this is what has always rendered the men of a free state so energetic, so acutely intelligent, so powerful. The influence of environment is only beginning to-day to be philosophically appreciated. It is just beginning to be suspected that the widely [spread] ignorance of women is not a necessary organic peculiarity, but explicable by the fact that until recently they were forbidden to learn anything. Similarly we may inquire whether much of the observed practical feebleness of women, even in carrying out the thoughts they may have justly conceived, is not due to the social customs which, in multiple directions, forbid their will to have any effect. The brain is not only the origin of activities, it is a result of them.

... The ignorance of the ignorant women differs in no wise from that of ignorant men ...

Mary Putnam-Jacobi, *"Common Sense" Applied to Woman Suffrage* (New York: G.P. Putnam's Sons, 1894), pp. 74-75, 180-181.

MARY DUFFY SPEAKS BEFORE THE LEGISLATURE

Mary Duffy, a member of the Overall Worker's Union, was among the first working women who became active members of suffrage groups. She worked for suffrage in the Equality League of Self-Supporting Women and spoke out for her rights as a citizen. "Gentlemen," she said, "we don't want charity, we want justice." Her participation in the movement served to motivate other working women to organize. Here, she testifies before a legislative committee in Albany, New York, in 1907 and pleads her cause.

Trade unionism is not very popular with some of you; but, gentlemen, it is the only protector we working women have.

... We are ruled out in the State, and why shouldn't our trade union get all our feeling of patriotism?

Miss Schneiderman,* who wanted to come here today, but could not leave the city, sent you a message by me. Rose Schneiderman is a cap-maker. She is a Russian, but has been a long time in America. She told me to tell you how we women who were born in America, or have lived here a long time and have learned to understand the laws in this country, feel when we see some man from Europe who knows nothing of free government and is too old to learn, just put right over our heads. And, gentlemen, this shows in our working life. That man learns his lesson quickly, and thinks himself superior to every woman. He won't take his place in any organization according to his ability, but wants to push in and lead, when he is not up to it.

Some one asked me the other night at the League of Self-Supporting Women if my union aimed to make women's wages equal to men's. Why, I told them, the whole effort was to keep men's up to ours. In some of the clothing trades almost all the workers a little time ago were women. They were self-respecting women, and skilled in their trade. Then came foreign men. They knew nothing about the country or the conditions here, but the State told them they knew everything better than any woman. Well, in such unions we women have a tough job bringing the men up to our standard. The State has much to answer for in filling those men full of conceit.

*Rose Schneiderman—a well-known labor leader

Gentlemen, that training school of mine, the trade union, has taught me that men and women must stand as equals. The big, strong man doesn't want any advantage over us, and the small man ought not to have any advantage in citizenship, for it only makes him cocky. Two million of the big, strong men, the men in the National Federation of Labor, have declared that they want us working women to be their equals in the State. And I bring you a resolution from the Central Federated Union in New York, asking you to help us get the vote.

Harriot Stanton Blatch and Alma Lutz, *Challenging Years* (New York: G.P. Putnam's Sons, 1940), pp. 95-96.

CARRIE CHAPMAN CATT ADDRESSES CONGRESS

Carrie Chapman Catt, recognized for her organizing ability, brought order to a haphazard National American Woman Suffrage Association. She made a contract with her husband which provided that she could work four months a year for suffrage. In the following excerpts from a speech she gave before Congress, she presents her fundamental arguments for suffrage.

Woman suffrage is inevitable. Suffragists knew it before November 6, 1917; opponents afterward. Three distinct causes make it inevitable.

1. The history of our country. Ours is a nation born of revolution; of rebellion against a system of government so securely entrenched in the customs and tradition of human society that in 1776 it seemed [strong enough to resist attack.] From the beginning of things nations had been ruled by kings and for kings, while the people served and paid the cost. The American revolutionists boldly proclaimed the heresies.

"Taxation without representation is tyranny."
"Governments derive their just powers from the consent
of the governed."

Our Theories Make Woman Suffrage Inevitable.

The colonists won and the nation which was established as a result of their victory had held unfailingly that these two fundamental principles of democratic government are not only the spiritual source of our national existence but have been our chief historical pride and at all times the sheet anchor of our liberty.

Eighty years after the Revolution, Abraham Lincoln welded those two maxims into a new one.

"Ours is a government of the people, by the people
and for the people."

Fifty years more passed and the President of the United States,
Woodrow Wilson, in a mighty crisis of the nation, proclaimed to the
world: "We are fighting for the things which we have always carried
nearest our hearts—for democracy, for the right of those who
submit to authority to have a voice in their own government." . . .

Woman suffrage became an assured fact when the Declaration of
Independence was written. It matters not at all whether Thomas
Jefferson and his compatriots thought of women when they wrote
the immortal document. They conceived and voiced a principle
greater than any man. . . .

Our Practice Makes Woman Suffrage Inevitable

2. The suffrage for women already established in the United
States makes woman suffrage for the nation inevitable.

When Elihu Root as President of the American Society of International Law, at the 11th annual meeting in Washington, April 26,
1917 said "the world cannot be half democratic and half autocratic.
It must be all democratic or all Prussian. There can be no com-
promise," he voiced a general truth. Precisely the same intuition has
already taught the blindest and most hostile foe of woman suffrage
that our nation cannot long continue a condition under which government in half its territory rests upon the consent of half the
people and in the other half upon the consent of all the people; a
condition which grants representation to the taxed in half its territory and denies it in the other half; a condition which permits women
in some states to share in the election of the President, Senators and
Representatives and denies them the privilege in others.

Our Leadership Makes Woman Suffrage Inevitable

3. The leadership of the United States in world democracy compels the enfranchisement of its own women. The maxims of the Declaration were once called "fundamental principles of government."
They are now called "American principles" or even "Americanisms."
They have become the slogans of every movement toward political
liberty the world around; of every effort to widen the suffrage for
men and women in any land. Not a people, race or class striving for
freedom is there, anywhere in the world, that has not made our
axioms the chief weapon of the struggle.

These are new times and, as an earnest [sign] of its sincerity in the
battle for democracy the government of Great Britain has not only

pledged votes to its disenfranchised men and to its women, but the measure passed the House of Commons in June 1917 by a vote of 7 to 1 and will be sent to the House of Lords in December with the assurance of Premier Lloyd George that it will shortly become a national law.

. . . Canada, too, has enfranchised the women of all its provinces stretching from the Pacific Coast to northern New York, and the Premier has predicted votes for all Canadian women before the next election.

Russia, whose opposing forces have made a sad farce of the new liberty, is nevertheless pledged to a democracy which shall include women . . . "Without the partnership of women, suffrage is not universal," [slogan of women of new Russia].

France has pledged votes to its women as certainly as a Republic can. Italian men have declared woman suffrage an imperative issue when the war is over . . . . Even autocratic Germany has debated the question in the Imperial Reichstag.

The Logic of the Situation Calls for Immediate Action

Is it not clear that American history makes woman suffrage inevitable? That full suffrage in twelve states makes its coming in all 48 states inevitable? That the spread of democracy over the world, including votes for the women of many countries, in each case based upon the principles our Republic gave to the world, compels action by our nation. Is it not clear that the world expects such action and fails to understand its delay?

In the face of these facts we ask you Senators and members of the House of Representatives of the United States, is not the immediate enfranchisement of the women of our nation the duty of the hour? . . .

. . . . Gentlemen, we hereby petition you, our only designated representatives, to redress our grievances by the immediate passage of the Federal Suffrage Amendment and to use your influence to secure its ratification in your own state, in order that the women of our nation may be endowed with political freedom before the next presidential election, and our nation may resume its world leadership in democracy.

Woman suffrage is coming—you know it. Will you, Honorable Senators and Members of the House of Representatives, help or hinder it?

Carrie Chapman Catt, "An Address to the Congress of the United States," (New York: National Woman's Suffrage Publishing Co. Inc, 1921), adapted.

THE WOMAN'S PARTY FIGHTS FOR CHANGE

The following poems capture the spirit of the radical Woman's Party of which Alice Paul was the inspired leader. Paul and her followers did much to gain attention for the suffrage issue.

On the Picket Line

The avenue is misty gray,
And here beside the guarded gate
We hold our golden blowing flags
And wait.

The people pass in friendly wise;
They smile their greeting where we stand
And turn aside to recognize
The just demand.

Often the gates are swung aside:
The man whose power could free us now
Looks from his car to read our plea—
And bow.

Sometimes the little children laugh;
The careless folk toss careless words,
And scoff and turn away, and yet
The people pass the whole long day
Those golden flags against the gray
And can't forget.

Beulah Amidon, "On The Picket Line," *The Suffragist*, March 3, 1917, p. 6.

Alice Paul

I watched a river of women,
Rippling purple, white, and golden,
Stream toward the National Capitol.

Along its border,
Like a purple flower floating,
Moved a young woman, worn, wraithlike,
With eyes alight, keenly observing the marchers.
Out there on the curb, she looked so little, so lonely;
Few appeared even to see her;
No one saluted her.

Yet commander was she of the column, its leader;
She was the spring whence arose that irresistible river of women
Streaming steadily towards the National Capitol.

Katherine Rolston Fisher, "Alice Paul," *The Suffragist,* January 19, 1918, p. 9.

NOTES FROM OCCOQUAN

On October 20, 1917, Alice Paul carried the following banner in front of the White House: "The Time has come to Conquer or Submit. For Us There Can Be But One Choice. We Have Made It." She was arrested and sentenced to seven months in prison. She and suffragist Rose Winslow went on a hunger strike which lasted three weeks and a day. During the last two weeks they were fed forcibly and became so weak that they had to be hospitalized. Many other protestors were also imprisoned at the Occoquan Workhouse in Virginia.

[Mrs. Gilson Gardner wrote on July 28, 1917] The short journey on the train was pleasant and uneventful. From the station at Occoquan the women sent to the Workhouse were put into three [buses]; two were filled with white women and a third with colored women. In the office of the Workhouse we stood in a line and one at a time were registered and given a number. The matron called us by number and first name to the desk. Money and jewelry were accounted for and put in the safe. We were then sent to the dining-room. The meal of soup, rye bread, and water was not palatable . . . .

From the dining room we were taken to the dormitory. At one end of the long room, a white woman and two colored women were waiting for us. Before these women we were obliged, one by one, to remove all our clothing, and after taking a shower bath, put on the Workhouse clothes. These clothes consisted of heavy unbleached muslin chemises and drawers, a petticoat made of ticking, and a heavy, dark gray cotton mother hubbard dress. The last touch was a full, heavy, dark blue apron which tied around the waist. The stockings were thick and clumsy. There were not enough stockings, and those of us who did not have stockings during our [stay] there were probably rather fortunate. We were told to wear our own shoes for the time being, as they did not have enough in stock. The one small rough towel that was given to us we were told must be folded and tucked into our aprons. The prisoners were permitted to have only what they could carry.

. . . The great nervous strain came at meal time. All the woman ate in one big room. The white women sat on one side. The meal lasted thirty and sometimes forty minutes. The food to us was not palatable, but we all tried to be sensible and eat enough to keep up our strength. The real problem, however, was not the food; it was the enforced silence. We were not allowed to speak in the dining-room, and after a conscientious effort to eat, the silent waiting was curiously unpleasant . . .

The use of the pencil is forbidden at all times. Each inmate is permitted to write but two letters a month, one to her family and one business letter. All mail received and sent is opened and read by one of the officials . . . .

[Many of the women went on hunger strikes. At one time, the Superintendent was afraid that Mrs. Lawrence Lewis and Lucy Burns might die. He had them taken to the hospital of the District Jail. They had been forcibly fed at Occoquan, and the feeding was continued at the jail.]

Mrs. Lewis writes:

I was seized and laid on my back, where five people held me, a young colored woman leaping upon my knees, which seemed to break under the weight. Dr. Gannon then forced the tube through my lips and down my throat, I gasping and suffocating with the agony of it. I didn't know where to breathe from, and everything turned black when the fluid began pouring in. I was moaning and making the most awful sounds quite against my will, for I did not wish to disturb my friends in the next room. Finally the tube was withdrawn. I lay motionless. After awhile I was dressed and carried in a chair to a waiting automobile, laid on the back seat, and driven into Washington to the jail hospital. Previous to the feeding I had been forcibly examined by Dr. Gannon, I struggling and protesting that I wished a woman physician.

Lucy Burns was fed through the nose. Her note, smuggled out of jail, is as follows:

Wednesday 12 m. Yesterday afternoon at about four or five, Mrs. Lewis and I were asked to go to the operating room. Went there and found our clothes. Told we were to go to Washington. No reason, as usual. When we were dressed Dr. Gannon appeared, said he wished to examine us. Both refused. Were dragged through halls by force, our clothing partly removed by force, and we were examined, heart tested, blood pressure and pulse taken. Of course such data was of no value after such a struggle. Dr. Gannon told me that I must be fed. Was stretched on bed, two doctors, matron, four colored prisoners present, Whittaker [superintendent] in hall. I was held down by five people at legs, arms, and head. I refused to open mouth, Gannon pushed the tube up left nostril. I turned and twisted my head all I could, but he managed to push it up. It hurts nose and throat very much and makes nose bleed freely. Tube drawn out covered with blood. Operation leaves one very sick. Food dumped directly into stomach feels like a ball of lead. Left nostril, throat, and muscles of neck very sore all night. After this I was brought into the hospital in an ambulance. . . .

This morning Dr. Ladd appeared with his tube. Mrs. Lewis and I said we would not be forcibly fed. Said he would call in men guards and force us to submit. Went away and we not fed at all this morning. We hear them outside now cracking eggs.

[Paula Jakobi accounted]

We were summoned two days later to appear at Alexandria jail next day, Friday of that week—that would make nine days spent in the Workhouse.

A writ of habeas corpus had been issued for our unjust imprisonment at Occoquan when we had been sentenced to Washington jail. This day I fainted. It was now seven and a half days since I had started hunger-striking. Three young doctors came in to have a look at the hunger-strikers. They did not take our pulse; they just gazed and departed. Later in the day, I was told that I could not go to court next day if I did not eat, as they would not take responsibility for my trip. They prepared to forcibly feed me. I concluded to eat voluntarily, since I had to break my fast, so that evening I had a baked potato and a baked apple . . .

Inez Haynes Irwin, *The Story of the Woman's Party* (New York: Harcourt, Brace and Co., 1921), pp. 265-266, 280-281.

PROLIQUOR ADVOCATES JOIN WITH ANTISUFFRAGISTS

During the years immediately preceding the suffrage victory, the women "antis" and the liquor men worked for a common aim —the defeat of the woman suffrage amendment. Often the newspapers, which were against prohibition, included in their issues material designed to convince readers not to support enfranchisement for women. Street cars in Stark County, Ohio, 1914 carried advertisements for the liquor amendment and at the same time urged readers to see the advertisement "opposite," which asked for votes against the suffrage amendment.

The Macomb County Michigan Retail Liquor Dealers' Association addressed the following letter to newspapers—one of which turned the copy over to suffrage headquarters:

Macomb County Retail Liquor Dealers' Association,
Office of the Secretary,
Mt. Clemens, Michigan

March 31st, 1913

To the Publisher:
I enclose herewith copy for an advertisement which I wish you would insert in this week's issue of your paper . . . .

I will thank you to see that this is done, and mail statement of charges and also marked copy to me and we will remit for the same. . . .

Joseph Matthews
Secretary

Enclosure.
The enclosure for the publication of which the Macomb County Retail Liquor Dealers' Association guaranteed payment, read:

AN APPEAL TO MEN!

You should vote against woman suffrage for ten thousand reasons.
We mention but six.
As women, we do not want the strife, bitterness, falsification and publicity which accompany political campaigns.
We women are not suffering at the hands of our fathers, husbands and brothers because they protect us in our homes.
We have women's greatest right—to be free from political medley.
We do not want to lose this freedom.
We have refrained from protest heretofore, depending upon men to protect women from the ballot. We now ask the men of Michigan to defend us and vote NO on suffrage.

Keep mother, wife and sister in the protected home. Do not force us into partisan politics. Put a cross before the word 'NO' on April 7th, and win our gratitude.

Carrie Chapman Catt and Nettie Rogers Shuler, *Woman Suffrage and Politics* (New York: Charles Scribner's Sons, 1923), p. 275.

ANTISUFFRAGISTS LOBBY TO KEEP THE SUFFRAGE BILL FROM REACHING THE FLOOR OF CONGRESS

The following speech was made at a hearing of the House of Representatives on whether or not to report the suffrage bill out of committee. Mrs. Arthur Dodge of the National Association Opposed to Woman Suffrage spoke on behalf of her group. Her argument was based on two ideas: that suffrage was a question for the states to decide individually, and that women should be represented by men.

Mr. Dyer [Congressman from Missouri]. What is the position of your organization with reference to the question of whether or not women should have the right to vote at all? Are you in favor of women voting?

Mrs. Dodge. We are in opposition to woman suffrage generally. We have never opposed women voting in school matters; we think that is a perfectly legitimate line for them to vote upon. The only trouble is they do not vote upon those questions where authorized; only two percent of them do so.

Mr. Dyer. That is as far as you want them to go?

Mrs. Dodge. Yes; that is a perfectly legitimate line for them, we have always taken that position from the first, but that does not mean that women are to be drawn into politics and government and we only draw the line at their taking part in politics and government.

Mr. Dyer. I understand your position is that you favor submitting this question to the States directly.

Mrs. Dodge. Yes. We have always rather inclined to the idea that it should be submitted to the women themselves . . .

Mr. Taggart [Representative from Kansas]. Would you say that it was just to require a woman to pay the income tax demanded by the government and then deny her the right to any voice as to who should be the Representative that voted that tax on her?

Mrs. Dodge. I certainly should. I have paid taxes in five states myself. I feel that I am entirely protected—that is what the tax is for. I think that taxpaying men are just as capable of taking care of my rights as of their own and I feel that I am justified in saying that the men can quite as well look after that which ought to be and is their business as I can.

E.C. Stanton and S.B. Anthony, *The History of Woman Suffrage* (New York: NAWSA, 1921), Vol. V, pp. 476-477.

SUFFRAGE WINS IN THE HOUSE

The following editorial, which appeared in *The Suffragist* on January 12, 1916, demonstrated how politically alert the woman's movement had become. It was a long way back to the beginning, when supporters talked mainly to one another rather than debating with the public and representatives of government. Here they pressured President Wilson to get members of his party on the side of the suffrage bill coming before the Senate.

The Federal suffrage amendment passed the House on January 10 with an exact two-thirds majority.

Women are earnestly rejoicing over the victory. And they are keenly alive to the narrow margin by which that victory was obtained.

274 Congressmen voted for the amendment, 163 voted against. . . A change of one vote, save for the help of the Speaker, would have defeated the amendment.

The closeness of this margin has caused grave concern—and not to women only. If this great enfranchising act had gone down to defeat, it would not have been difficult for the women of this nation to fix the responsibility for the injustice done them.

Of the Republicans who voted on the measure, 83% voted in favor of it; of the Democrats only 50%. The Democratic vote, taken alone would have defeated the amendment; the Republican saved it; they gave it more than enough votes, over and above a two-thirds majority, to compensate for the Democrats' deficiency.

It is quite evident that Democratic leaders saw the danger to their party in this opposition to a fundamental democratic reform.

Representative Cantrill, of Kentucky, a veteran Democrat standing high in the party's councils and regular beyond party reproach, issued, four days before the vote was taken, a public appeal to his fellow Democrats from the South to support the federal suffrage amendment if they would avoid "political suicide."

That this plea, frankly official as it was, was not enough to turn southern Democratic sentiment to the support of national woman suffrage was plain, when on the evening of January 9 President Wilson first allowed himself to be publicly quoted in favor of national woman suffrage.

This was clear; it turned votes, and as events proved it turned enough votes, and just enough, to pass the Susan B. Anthony Amendment.

That is well, Mr. President, the women's bill is safe; they are satisfied. But you, diplomat as you are, cannot be satisfied to see your party, now playing a bold part in the government of the world, come so close to political suicide. You can do better than that. We have seen you in effective action during five years of national party leadership. When you have wanted other measures passed, you have gone to the Capitol and demanded their passage. We look to you to do as much for us, and to give the suffrage amendment in the United States Senate all the help it needs.

The Suffragist, January 12, 1916, p. 10.

9

World War I
and the Twenties

The woman machinist and the different sort of work she is capable of doing have created not a little interest and curiosity. At first it would seem, I admit, that women are fitted neither by training nor physical makeup for the machinist trade. And yet during the war women entered the machine industry quite extensively. And they were not at all backward, I may add, in tackling a real man's job.

The president of the Machinists' Ladies Auxiliary was proud of the part women were playing in winning World War I. For the machinist described above and other women, the war expanded opportunities.

Before the United States entered World War I in 1917, leading American women had been active in trying to obtain peace among the warring powers. In January 1915 the Woman's Peace Party was organized. Its goals were to stop the war that was raging in Europe and to establish a system of cooperation among nations. Prominent women, including Jane Addams and Carrie Chapman Catt, provided leadership in this pacifist movement. Many women agreed that the war was "an exhibition of masculinity run amuck."

Other women, however, supported the war and encouraged United States involvement. Some feminist leaders hoped that women would

During World War I job opportunities for women expanded. This welder worked on the boiler of a tug boat.

benefit both economically and politically if the United States was drawn into war.

Women Join the War Effort

As in all wars, women played a large and supportive role in World War I. The Council of National Defense established a Committee of Women's Defense to coordinate the war activities of American women. It was put under the direction of 70-year old Dr. Anna Howard Shaw, who was later to receive a Distinguished Service Medal for her war services. Her committee registered women throughout the nation in an attempt to gather information and to place women in suitable jobs. Shaw encouraged women to conserve food and fuel, plant gardens, sell Liberty Bonds, and to involve themselves in the economy.

More than a million women moved into industry to replace men who had gone off to war. Women worked in nearly every type of job and were the objects of much attention and admiration. Yet the Women in Industry Service of the Labor Department, later to become the Women's Bureau, noted at the end of the war that women in war work made less than men to start. Women were promoted much more slowly, were not organized, and were almost all discharged at the war's end.

Black women were the least well off of the wartime work force. They were hired for the worst jobs and were fired first. Mary

Church Terrell, a suffragist and spokeswoman for black women, worked in government service during the war. She found that most government agencies usually would not hire black women, and if they did, segregated them. The wages of black female workers were much lower than those of white employees.

Women, black and white, sailed abroad to work for the Red Cross canteen service. Addie Hunton was one of three black women who organized cultural, athletic, and religious activities for nearly 200,000 black soldiers. She encountered much prejudice, as did Adah Thoms, who fought for and won the right for black nurses to serve in the United States Army Nurse Corps. Thousands of women volunteered to serve in the United States Naval Reserve force as clerks, stenographers, typists, translators, and telephone operators, releasing men for service in combat. Belle Dunn and Helen O'Shaughnessy became the first women to serve aboard a navy ship, and in May 1917, Mrs. Marion Taylor enrolled as the first woman telegrapher. She received secret reports of ship movements in the U-boat-infested waters of the Atlantic.

Both women and men believed that World War I was the "war to end all wars," the "war to make the world safe for democracy." By the war's end, as they began to realize that trench warfare was horrible, gas warfare was barbaric and our allies were often undemocratic societies, Americans began to lose their ideals.

On November 11, 1918, Woodrow Wilson addressed the American people about the coming of peace. He said:

> My fellow countrymen, the armistice was signed this morning. Everything for which America fought has been accomplished. It will now be our fortunate duty to assist by example, by sober, friendly counsel, and by material aid in the establishment of democracy throughout the world.

Wilson's vision was not to become a reality, however. Americans preferred to withdraw from world affairs rather than to remain leaders.

Political and Economic Issues of the Twenties

Women were granted suffrage in 1920. Many feminists had believed that the female vote would mean the releasing of a great moral force that would make American life better. But Anna Howard Shaw felt that younger women would have great difficulties to face that the vote would not solve. Shortly before her death she said:

You younger women will have a harder task than ours. You will want equality in business and it will be even harder to get than the vote, for you will have to fight for it as individuals and that will not get you far. Women will not unite, since they will be in competition with each other.

She was proved to be correct. After the vote was gained, unity among women disappeared. This was partly due to a conservative reaction at the end of the war. Many women's organizations were linked with Communist activity by those opposed to their work. These problems led to many divisions among women. An example of this can be seen in the difficulties in achieving child-labor legislation. Prewar child-labor legislation was declared unconstitutional in 1918 and 1922. The attempt to pass a child-labor amendment, led by Florence Kelley of the National Consumers League, was unsuccessful. It was labeled a Communist plot. With this defeat the Consumers League declined in importance, as did many other of the progressive women's groups.

Suffrage did lead to the formation of one new group. In 1921 the League of Women Voters was organized. It was designed to educate newly enfranchised women and to promote good government.

Women discovered that suffrage gave them even less political power than they had had earlier because there was no bloc vote of women after suffrage was granted. They gained few high offices. In 1925 there were two women governors, Nellie Ross of Wyoming and Miriam (Ma) Ferguson of Texas, both following their husbands into the position. (Ferguson's husband had been impeached and convicted, and her slogan was "Two Governors for the Price of One.") Jeannette Rankin had become the first female Representative in 1916; Alice Robertson was elected to the House in 1920, and in 1922 Winnifred Huck succeeded her dead father. "Widow's succession" was to become the most common means for women to achieve political office. Some women were successful, but generally feminists were greatly disappointed by their failure to gain political power.

The most controversial political involvement for women in the 1920's was the struggle for the passage of an equal rights amendment to the Constitution. The proposed amendment read, "Men and women shall have equal rights throughout the United States and every place subject to its jurisdiction." The Woman's Party believed that such an amendment was necessary to end widespread discrimination in marriage, divorce, and property laws as well as in employment. Those opposed, including most labor and women's groups, favored protective legislation providing pensions for

widowed mothers, minimum wages for women, working-hours regulation, and the limitation of nightime and dangerous work. These
groups were fearful that such benefits would be lost if an equal
rights amendment were passed. The amendment and the Communist scare proved destructive to women's unity during the decade
after World War I.

The issues of protective legislation and job equality were real to
many of the millions of women who worked in the 1920's. By 1920
women made up 21.2 percent of the total American labor force, and
by 1925 over 8½ million women worked outside the home (a growth
of nearly 6 million from 1880). The 1920 census listed women as
lumber workers, woodchoppers, blacksmiths' apprentices, stonecut-
ters, boarding-house keepers, marshals, typists, clerks, and in hundreds of other jobs. The percentage of women workers in professional occupations was growing. Also growing were differences
between male and female salaries.

Congress recognized the significance of women workers when in
June 1920 it established the Women's Bureau as part of the Department of Labor. The bureau's purpose was to "formulate standards
and policies that shall promote the welfare of wage-earning wom-
en. . . ." Mary Anderson, a veteran of the Trade Union League,
served as its head.

Social Issues of the Twenties

The decade following the world war became important in the story
of women in America for reasons other than political or economic.
The twenties was labeled with names reflecting the importance of
private life—"Roaring Twenties," "The Jazz Age," "Return to Nor-
malcy." It was an era shaped by peace, Prohibition, gangsters, the
growth of the automobile industry, a virtual end to immigration, in-
tolerance, and tremendous creativity in the arts. For many women,
the twenties also brought a "loosening" of strict moral teachings.

Writers spent much time trying to define the "new woman" of the
decade. She was labeled the "flapper," "lovely, expensive, and about
nineteen." Old-line feminists were distressed with the new morality
of the young, but they had helped to create the "new woman." They
had emphasized independence and a fighting spirit in women by
working to break down political and social barriers. This changed
women's private lives too.

The flapper reflected the dress reform that had started before
World War I. In July 1920 a fashion reporter for *The New York Times*
wrote that "the American woman . . . has lifted her skirts far beyond

The flapper look reflected the changing attitude of many women toward their lives. One fashion editor called the dress revolution "a release of women from clothing."

any modest limitation . . ." The hem was nine inches off the ground and most people were betting it would go down. But it continued to rise. By 1927 women wore knee-length dresses, short-sleeved or sleeveless, with rolled-down, flesh-colored stockings, which showed a bit of knee. A slim, boyish figure was popular. Girls stopped wearing corsets—those who wore them had to risk being called "Old Ironsides" by young men!

The flapper cut her hair and used cosmetics more and more. By 1929 American women were using an average of one pound of face powder a year, and the *Ladies' Home Journal* carried lipstick ads for the first time.

Drinking liquor and smoking cigarettes were included in the behavior of these young girls, as well as dancing cheek to cheek and "necking" and "petting." Parents began to wonder about the changes the war years had brought to their daughters. How many times had their girls been kissed, they asked themselves?

The new sexual morality was encouraged by the popularity of psychology during the decade. By the early 1920's the ideas of Sigmund Freud had been introduced in America. Americans spoke of the "id, ego, and repressions" and used other Freudian terms. Freud had emphasized the harmful effects that repression of feelings, especially sexual feelings, could have on personality. This idea was twisted by the generation of the twenties to mean that the repression of all natural impulses was dangerous and wrong. Therefore, sexual freedom was approved. Women openly challenged the "double standard" of morality that said one way of behavior was acceptable for men but not for women.

People who believed in the traditional values of the country tried to prevent the new sexual freedom from growing further. Many groups attacked the young generation for its behavior. In Philadelphia, for example, a Dress Reform Committee of leading citizens sent a questionnaire about proper dress to 1,000 clergymen. The results led to the design of a "moral gown," the main characteristics of which were that it was loose-fitting, had sleeves below the elbow, and a hem seven and one-half inches off the floor. In 1921 in Utah a bill was introduced to fine or imprison those whose skirts were three inches above the ankle. In Ohio two inches was to be the limit.

Birth Control

The conflicts over the new morality appeared in the controversy over birth control. Most American women were forced to worry about unwanted pregnancies because of the lack of contraceptives and contraceptive information.

Birth control was at best an upper-class luxury. In 1873 Anthony Comstock, a fighter against liquor and pornography, had led the Congress to pass the "Comstock Law." This bill banned the distribution of "obscene, lewd, lascivious, filthy, and indecent" materials. An addition to the bill prohibited the distribution of any information about contraception. Comstock became a Post Office inspector whose job it was to find this material and prosecute offenders. Comstock obtained many convictions, including one of a doctor who had answered two letters from women requesting contraceptive advice. The doctor was sentenced to six years at the Leavenworth prison.

At this time, Margaret Sanger was nursing her sick mother. When her mother died, Sanger decided to become a doctor, realized she could not afford to attend medical school, and went to nursing school instead. She specialized in obstetric cases. In her work she discovered great differences in the conditions of rich and poor children and wanted and unwanted children. She was often asked about contraception but had little useful information herself. "Finally," she wrote, in *My Fight For Birth Control*, "the thing began to shape it-

Margaret Sanger (left) with her sister in court after their arrest in 1916.

self . . . during the three weeks I spent in the home of a desperately sick woman" in New York City. Mrs. Sacks was 28 and had three children under five. She became pregnant again, attempted to abort herself, and became very ill. Sanger nursed her for three weeks and when the doctor arrived, Mrs. Sacks asked him, "What can I do to prevent getting [pregnant] again?" The doctor advised her to tell her husband to sleep on the roof. Sanger was horrified, but also had no information to give the woman. Several months later, Mrs. Sacks died from a cheap abortion.

This incident spurred Sanger to begin her fight to develop and make contraceptive information available in America. She traveled to Europe in 1913, and in the following year she founded *The Woman Rebel,* a newspaper, and the National Birth Control League. Late that year she was indicted for violating the Comstock Law. She had published articles in her paper that advocated that women should be able to control their own bodies. In 1916, acting on her belief that all women were entitled to contraceptive information, she opened the first American birth control clinic in New York City. She was arrested soon after and jailed. Sanger was imprisoned eight times, but each struggle helped to liberalize laws relating to contraception.

Other women also worked to change these laws. Mary Coffin Dennett organized supporters for birth control. Her goal was the repeal of all contraceptive laws. She disagreed with Sanger, who wanted to leave doctors in control of the distribution of contraception. However, both wanted women to have more control over their reproductive lives. By 1930 many major groups in the United States, including Protestant and Jewish organizations and the General Federation of Women's Clubs, had endorsed the movement for birth control.

Technology and the Arts

That the twenties was a decade of shifting values, of conflict and confusion, was clearly shown by the literature of the period. Ernest Hemingway, F. Scott Fitzgerald, and others wrote about a "lost" or confused generation of men and women. Women poets and novelists also reflected changing ideas and morality. Willa Cather wrote many novels recording life in frontier America. Her writing generally reflected the more traditional American beliefs that were being challenged during the twenties. In 1922 her novel *One of Ours,* which described the decline of pioneer values, received the Pulitzer Prize.

Popular too throughout the decade was the poetry of Edna St. Vincent Millay. Millay graduated from Vassar in 1917 and went to live in New York's Greenwich Village, a popular place among artists and intellectuals of the time. Redheaded and petite, Millay was described by a friend as "very much a revolutionary in all her sympathies, and a whole-hearted Feminist." Her poems often expressed strong feelings about the need for women to be free. She won the Pulitzer Prize in 1923 for her book of poems *Ballad of the Harp-Weaver.*

Changes in the world of dance also reflected the new freedom of the decade. Isadora Duncan exhibited in her life and in her revolutionary approach to dancing the new woman of the twenties. She danced barefoot, expressing her feelings through free movement of her body. This approach led to enormous changes that are still influencing the world of dance today. Duncan lost her life in 1927 in a bizarre accident. Her long scarf became entangled in the wheel of the car in which she was riding and strangled her. Duncan's death became a symbol of the romantic attitude of the 1920's.

The growing entertainment industry provided women with new ways to express themselves. Records became popular as more and more people bought phonographs. Bessie Smith, a black singer, had traveled throughout the South in the decade before the twenties as a blues singer. Between 1923 and 1930 she made over 160 recordings and was recognized as the "Empress of Blues."

In these same years the movie industry was developing rapidly and growing in its influence. Millions of Americans went to the movies every week and saw such female stars as Clara Bow (the "It" girl), Janet Gaynor, Mary Pickford (America's Sweetheart), and the Gish sisters. These women became models for the dress and behavior of thousands who saw them.

The conflicts and liberation created by the changes in the twenties were speeded up and encouraged by a developing technology that affected women's roles. Canned foods and other prepared foodstuffs became more common and acceptable. Thousands of women added electric washing machines, refrigerators, irons, and vacuum cleaners to their homes. The automobile brought America into a motor age—and encouraged the changing sexual morality. Each invention expanded the horizons and thus created even more conflicts in women's lives.

Mary Pickford was an idol for millions of women and girls who attended the increasingly popular movie theaters. Movies created a national female model and young girls copied their heroines in an attempt to achieve this ideal.

Housewives learned about a variety of new, timesaving appliances from advertisements in magazines and newspapers. The vacuum cleaner and the electric cooking range seemed like miracles to women who had previously swept with a broom and cooked on a wood-and-coal burning stove.

Just at the time that conflicting roles were becoming a difficult problem for many women, art and technology combined to produce an "image-maker" that encouraged dreams and shaped people's life styles. Advertising grew in prominence and women were used in ads to encourage buying and spending. They were often used as "the promise"—that is, if you bought the car, you'd get the girl too. Advertisers began to publicize, and even create, an ideal American woman.

Summary

The decade of the twenties changed many American women. They had been actively involved in winning World War I. Suffrage had been granted in 1920. Women had accepted new attitudes toward sexuality, dress, work, and leisure. Some women had become leaders in the arts. Traditional ways of acting no longer served as a guide to acceptable behavior. But before the new social attitudes became widespread, economic and political crises changed these social attitudes again.

AMERICAN WOMEN AND WORLD WAR I

On May 5, 1917, Secretary Houston of the Department of Agriculture appealed to women to share in war work while maintaining their homes. He urged women to conserve resources, to make sacrifices, and to be proud of this kind of participation in the war.

To the Women of the United States:

Every woman can render important service to the Nation in its present emergency. She need not leave her home or abandon her home duties to help the armed forces. She can help to feed and clothe our armies and help to supply food to those beyond the seas by practicing effective thrift in her own household.

Every ounce of food the housewife saves from being wasted in her home—all food which she or her children produce in the garden and can or preserve—every garment which care and skilled repair make it unnecessary to replace—all lessen that household's draft on the already insufficient world supplies.

To save food the housewife must learn to plan economical and properly balanced meals, which, while nourishing each member of the family properly, do not encourage overeating or offer excessive and wasteful variety. It is her duty to use all effective methods to protect food from spoilage by heat, dirt, mice or insects . . .

Clothing is largely an agricultural product and represents the results of labor on the sheep ranges, in cotton fields and in mills and factories. Whenever a useful garment is needlessly discarded, material needed to keep some one warm or dry may be consumed merely to gratify a passing fancy. Women would do well to look upon clothing at this time more particularly from the utilitarian point of view . . .

. . . While all honor is due to the women who leave their homes to nurse and care for those wounded in battle, no woman should feel that because she does not wear a nurse's uniform she is absolved from patriotic service. The home women of the country, if they will give their minds fully to this vital subject of food conservation and train themselves in household thrift, can make of the housewife's apron a uniform of national significance.

Demonstrate thrift in your homes and encourage thrift among your neighbors.

Make saving rather than spending your social standard.

Make economy fashionable lest it become obligatory. . .

Ida Clyde Clarke, *American Women and the World War* (New York: D. Appleton and Co., 1918), pp. 63-64.

WOMAN POWER AT WORK

As men left their factory jobs to enter the war, women replaced them in the plants and on the railroads. Their ability to master the skills necessary to do the work effectively surprised both themselves and the men in charge. Harriot Stanton Blatch visited women on the job and described with pride what she saw.

. . . . the American woman is going over the top. Four hundred and more are busy on aeroplanes at the Curtiss works. The manager of a munition shop where to-day but fifty women are employed, is putting up a dormitory to accommodate five hundred. An index of expectation! Five thousand are employed by the Remington Arms Company at Bridgeport. At the International Arms and Fuse Company at Bloomfield, New Jersey, two thousand, eight hundred are employed. The day I [Harriot Blatch] visited the place, in one of the largest shops women had only just been put on the work, but it was expected that in less than a month they would be found handling all of the twelve hundred machines under that one roof alone.

The skill of the women staggers one. After a week or two they master the operations on the "turret," gauging and routing machines. The best worker on the "facing" machine is a woman. She is a piece worker, as many of the women are, and is paid at the same rate as men. This woman earned, the day I saw her, five dollars and forty cents. She tossed about the fuse parts, and played with that machine, as I would with a baby. Perhaps it was in somewhat the same spirit—she seemed to love her toy.

. . . Nor are the railways neglecting to fill up gaps in their working force with women. The Pennsylvania road, it is said, has recruited some seven hundred of them. In the Erie Railroad women are not only engaged as "work classifiers" in the locomotive clerical department, but hardy Polish women are employed in the car repair shops. They move great wheels as if possessed of the strength of Hercules. And in the locomotive shops I found women working on drill-press machines with ease and skill. Just as I came up to one operator, she lifted an engine truck-box to the table and started drilling out the studs. She had been at the work only a month, and explained her skill by the information that she was Swedish, and had always worked with her husband in their auto-repair shop. All the other drill-press hands and the "shapers," too, were Americans whose husbands, old employees, were now "over there." Not one seemed to have any sense of the unusual; even the little blond check-clerk seated in her booth at the gates of the works with her brass discs about her head in a few months' time changed a revolution into an established custom. She and the discs seemed old friends. Women are adaptable.

Harriot Stanton Blatch, *Mobilizing Woman-Power* (New York: The Woman's Press, 1918), pp. 94-96.

WOMEN WORK WITH THE AMERICAN FORCES OVERSEAS

Addie Hunton was a black woman who was active in YWCA work before World War I. When the United States entered the war, she volunteered for YMCA service and was sent to France in June 1918. There she was one of three black women who worked among 200,000 black troops.

It was our privilege to go overseas as welfare workers under the auspices of the YMCA, and from the time we entered active duty until we finished our work at Camp Pontanezen, we can conscientiously say we had the greatest opportunity for service that we have ever known; service that was constructive and prolific, with wonderful and satisfying results . . .

But to help mar the beauty and joy of this service was the ever-present war with its awful toll of death and suffering; and then the service of the colored welfare workers was more or less clouded at all times with that biting and stinging thing which is ever shadowing us in our own country. . .

Upon our arrival in Paris we met Mr. Matthew Bullock and his staff of four secretaries, including the first colored woman, who had been ordered home as *persona non grata* [unacceptable person] to the army; this was done on recommendation of army officials in Bordeaux, who had brought from our southland their full measure of sectional prejudice.

This incident resulted in the detention of many secretaries, both men and women, from sailing for quite a period of time, and no more women came for nearly ten months, thus leaving three colored women to spread their influence as best they could among 150,000 men. . .

[She tells the background of her adventure.]

Press and pulpit, organizations and individuals were beseeching and demanding in 1918 that the Red Cross add some of our well-trained and experienced nurses to their "overseas" contingent, but no favorable response could be obtained. Meantime, the Paris Headquarters of the Young Men's Christian Association cabled as follows! "Send six fine colored women at once!". . . .

Six women! A small number to be sure, but the requirements for eligibility were not so easy to meet and one must not have a close relative in the army. Many questions were asked. "Was there a real need for women over there?" "Could they stand the test?" "Would they not be subjected to real danger?" "Were not gruesome stories being told relative to terrible outrages perpetrated on women who had gone?" To these questions and others there seemed to be just one reply. It was that if hundreds of other women had answered the call to serve in the armies of the Allies, surely among the thousands of colored troops already in France and other thousands who would soon follow there would be some place of service for six colored women. . . [Mrs. Curtis, Mrs. Hunton and Miss Johnson left.]

For all the period of the war and the dreary winter that followed it, there were just these three colored women with the American Expeditionary Forces in France. . . Two hundred thousand colored soldiers and three colored women in France!
[She describes canteen services.]

Over the canteen in France, the woman became a trusted guardian of that home back in America. To her were revealed its joys and sorrows. Because of that same loneliness—that loss of background—the soldier poured out to the canteen worker his deepest and dearest memories and dreams . . .

Over the canteen in France meant not simply the eat and drink of it when rightly interpreted. It meant that we must not rely alone on the "Movies" and entertainments sent from Headquarters to the soldiers—but we must supply games, entertainments of our own and even parties. . . [It] meant much letter writing and the wrapping and sending home little presents that had been approved by the company commanders . . . [It] included not only a cozy reading room and the selection of books for the men to read, but it meant also, reading to them or with them in leisure moments. . .

Addie Hunton and Kathryn Johnson, *Two Colored Women with the American Expeditionary Forces* (New York: Brooklyn Eagle Press, 1920), pp. 22, 23-24, 135-136, 142-143, 146, 148.

DISCRIMINATION IN GOVERNMENT SERVICE DURING THE WAR

Some black women were able to break into the federal civil service during World War I, in spite of obstacles placed in their way. Mary Church Terrell, a club woman, suffragist, and outstanding black leader did government work. She describes her experiences and the discrimination she encountered.

During the World War almost everybody in Washington who knew how to write and spell was taking an examination of some kind, so as to get a job in one of the Government departments. . . Accordingly, I decided to take an examination as typist and presented myself with my machine at the building designated for that date.

I knew I had passed, but I took it for granted that it would be a long time before I would be called if, indeed, I ever received an appointment. So I thought very little about it. Ten days after I took the examination our doorbell jangled one morning between two and three o'clock and a telegram addressed to me was handed to me. "Come immediately to the Aetna Building, Room 305," it read. . .

About nine o'clock, therefore, I presented myself at Room 305 and handed the telegram to General Crozier's secretary. The young man soon ushered me into his presence, and I found him reading a paper. It was my questionnaire at which he was looking, for everybody who took an examination for Government service was required to answer certain questions showing what his preparation and record were.

When General Crozier first saw me, he merely glanced at me but greeted me very cordially, nevertheless. His eyes were fastened upon my questionnaire, which showed that I had received the A.B. and A.M. degrees from Oberlin College, that I had traveled abroad, that I could speak, read and write both German and French and that I had once spoken Italian quite well. Perhaps I should state here that, in replying to the question concerning race, I simply wrote "American," without specifying what particular kind of American I am.

After the General had carefully read my record, he laid it on the table and looked at me squarely for the first time. "You have had very fine training indeed," he said. "We need the services of those who understand German and French." Then he studied me intently for a second and a shadow passed over his countenance. He began to appear puzzled and then displeased, as he looked at me. The longer he looked, the more puzzled and displeased he became. A light of some kind seemed to be dawning on him. . . [She did not get the job, supposedly because she had no office experience.]

By those in a position to know I have been informed that at that time college graduates were being eagerly sought, especially those who could speak and translate both German and French. Had I been a white woman there is no doubt I would have secured a responsible and lucrative position in the Government service at that time.

Shortly after that I was summoned to the War Risk Insurance Bureau and appointed to a clerkship. The man before whom I then appeared did not consume enough time in giving me the "once over" to note any peculiarity in my complexion which would suggest to him that I was "different from the rest." That little oversight on his part undoubtedly accounts for the fact that I was placed in the room with white women. After I had been appointed and assigned to this room, I learned that the women who were known to be colored had been placed in a section to themselves.

[After about two months she was suspended from duty for acting contrary to rules and regulations.]

There was not a [bit] of truth in any of these charges. It was a case of "framing" a colored woman, so as to remove her from a room in which she had been placed by mistake where they did not want one of her race to work. If I had really "taken action contrary to the rules and regulations of the Bureau and of the chief medical advisor," those responsible for the proper conduct of the office would have called me to account the very first time they learned I was guilty of the infraction of the rules. If they allowed me to persist in such a disobedient, inefficient course, they themselves were derelict in their duty, and deserved to be punished as well as the offending clerk. . .

Nobody who understands conditions in the National Capital would believe that a colored woman working in one of the Government departments in a room with white women "would cause considerable disturbance" when mistakes were called to her attention if she were sane and wished to retain her job. Colored women know all too well if they make themselves conspicuous or objectionable, either to their fellow clerks or to their superior officers, they are courting disaster and ruin. . .

The truth of the matter is that when some of the superior officers of the Bureau saw that a colored woman was working in that particular room, they decided to remove her at all hazards. The easiest way to do this was to prefer charges against the colored woman, and they decided to resort to this method to get rid of me. . .

Mary Church Terrell, *A Colored Woman in a White World* (Washington, D.C.: Ransdell Inc., 1940), pp. 250-253, 255.

THE STATUS OF WOMEN WORKERS

In 1925 the Women's Bureau conducted a survey of the family status of breadwinning women in four representative American cities. The conclusions drawn from the study seemed to indicate that governmental action would be needed.

Outline of salient truths of broad social significance revealed by this study.

1. Because of present economic organization of society many women are forced by stress of circumstances to become breadwinners.

2. A larger proportion of foreign-born and negro women than native-born are driven into breadwinning activities by economic stress.

3. Marriage does not necessarily spell a release for women from breadwinning activities, but frequently means greater economic responsibilities.

4. Many women are compelled to enact the double role of breadwinner and homemaker.

5. The coupling of economic responsibilities and domestic duties for women tends to menace the health of women and the happiness of the home.

6. Single women breadwinners as well as married ones often must carry heavy domestic and financial responsibilities for the family.

7. The need for mothers to engage in breadwinning activites outside the home frequently means inadequate and casual care of children.

8. The performance by mothers of breadwinning activites within the home tends to upset the normal relations, since any diversion of a home to such purposes impinges upon its efficiency as a place of relaxation and of nurture of family life.

9. The failure of men to secure a living wage for the family necessitates the entrance of wives and mothers into breadwinning activities outside or within the home.

10. Better wages for men would frequently mean withdrawal of a large group of wives and mothers from breadwinning activities.

11. Better and more extensive mothers' pension laws would mean the withdrawal of many more mothers from breadwinning activities.

12. Women compelled by unavoidable circumstances to support dependents should receive a wage sufficient to cover the cost of living of such dependents.

13. The foregoing statements are applicable to practically every average civic community in the country.

14. The disastrous effects resulting from our neglect of the urgent problems related to breadwinning women undermine each community where harmful conditions are allowed to exist and in the final analysis weaken the strength and prosperity of the Nation.

U.S. Women's Bureau Survey of Family Status of Breadwinning Women in Four Selected Cities, Bulletin #41, 1925, p. 20.

THE FLAPPER

The flapper became the symbol of the twenties; a young, thin, boyishly built, stylishly dressed girl who loved to flirt and dance. Although flappers comprised only a small percent of the young women of America, they captured the imagination of American society.

. . . The other day I found myself walking a few [yards] behind a girl who must have been approaching sweet sixteen. She held to the middle of the broad sidewalk. It was just after four, and she was apparently on her way home from high school. We were on a long block that passed a college campus, where the students were foregathering for afternoon sports. She was not chewing gum, but was occasionally bringing some tidbit from her pocket to her mouth, taking in everything in sight, and her gait was swagger and superior. 'Howdy, Billy,' she called to a youth whom I fancied a classmate; and 'Hello, boys,' was her greeting to three more a little later.

Soon she turned on her heel and wandered back, so that I had to meet her. A glance at her comely, happy, innocent, and vividly tinted face, as I swerved to one side that she might keep the middle of the walk, almost made me feel that it would not surprise her overmuch if I stepped to the very edge of the gutter, and removed my hat, as if apologizing for trespassing on preserves that belonged to her. Had I done so, however, it might have made no difference; for I suspect that she would have remained unconscious of my very existence, although just then we were almost the only ones on the block. . . .

I now felt at liberty to look at her a little more carefully. She wore a knitted hat, with hardly any brim, of a flame or bonfire hue; a henna scarf; two strings of Betty beads, of different colors, twisted together; an open short coat, with ample pockets; a skirt with vertical stripes so pleated that, at the waist, it seemed very dark, but the alternate stripes of white showed progressively downward, so that, as she walked, it gave something of what physiological psychologists call a flicker effect. On her right wrist were several bangles; on her left, of course, a wrist watch. Her shoes were oxfords, with a low broad heel. Her stockings were woolen and of brilliant hue. But most noticeable of all were her high overshoes, or galoshes. One seemed to be turned down at the top and entirely unbuckled, while the other was fastened below and flapped about her trim ankle in a way that compelled attention. This was in January, 1922, as should be particularly noted because, by the time this [essay] meets the reader's eye, flapperdom, to be really *chic* and up-to-date, will be quite different in some of these details. . .

A good dance is as near heaven as the flapper can get and live. She dances at noon and at recess in the school gymnasium; and, if not in the school, at the restaurants between courses, or in the recreation and rest-rooms in factories and stores. She knows all the latest variations of the perennial fox-trot, the ungainly contortions of the camel walk; yields with abandon to the fascination of the tango; and if the floor is crowded, there is always room for the languorous and infantile toddle; and the cheek-to-cheek close formation—which one writer ascribes to the high cost of rent nowadays, which necessitates the maximum of motion in the minimum of space—has a lure of its own, for partners must sometimes cling together in order to move at all. Verticality of motion and, at least, the vibrations of the 'shimmy' are always possible.

G. Stanley Hall, "Flapper Americana Novissima," *Atlantic Monthly*, Vol. 129 (June, 1922), pp. 772-773. Reprinted by permission.

THE "NEW WOMAN" IN LITERATURE

The following excerpt is taken from *This Side of Paradise*, a novel by F. Scott Fitzgerald. The main character, Amory, is attending a party at a friend's house. Rosalind, with whom he falls in love, has been described as "one of those girls who need never make the slightest effort to have men fall in love with them." She characterized the ideal of the "new woman" of the twenties.

The corner of a den down-stairs, filled by a very comfortable leather lounge. A small light is on each side above, and in the middle, over the couch hangs a painting of a very old, very dignified gentleman, period 1860. Outside the music is heard in a fox-trot.

Rosalind is seated on the lounge and on her left is Howard Gillespie, a [lifeless] youth of about twenty-four. He is obviously very unhappy, and she is quite bored.

Gillespie: (Feebly) What do you mean I've changed. I feel the same toward you.

Rosalind: But you don't look the same to me.

Gillespie: Three weeks ago you used to say that you liked me because I was so blasé, so indifferent—I still am.

Rosalind: But not about me. I used to like you because you had brown eyes and thin legs.

Gillespie: (Helplessly) They're still thin and brown. You're a vampire, that's all.

Rosalind: The only thing I know about vamping is what's on the piano score. What confuses men is that I'm perfectly natural. I used to think you were never jealous. Now you follow me with your eyes wherever I go.

Gillespie: I love you.

Rosalind: (Coldly) I know it.

Gillespie: And you haven't kissed me for two weeks. I had an idea that after a girl was kissed she was—was—won.

Rosalind: Those days are over. I have to be won all over again every time you see me.

Gillespie: Are you serious?

Rosalind: About as usual. There used to be two kinds of kisses: First when girls were kissed and deserted; second, when they were engaged. Now there's a third kind, where the man is kissed and deserted. If Mr. Jones of the nineties bragged he'd kissed a girl, every one knew he was through with her. If Mr. Jones of 1919 brags the same every one knows it's because he can't kiss her any more. Given a decent start any girl can beat a man nowadays.

Gillespie: Then why do you play with men?

Rosalind: (Leaning forward confidentially) For that first moment, when he's interested. There is a moment—Oh, just before the first kiss, a whispered word—something that makes it worthwhile.

Gillespie: And then?

Rosalind: Then after that you make him talk about himself. Pretty soon he thinks of nothing but being alone with you—he sulks, he won't fight, he doesn't want to play—Victory!

F. Scott Fitzgerald, *This Side of Paradise* (New York: Charles Scribner's Sons, 1920), pp. 193-194. Reprinted by permission of Charles Scribner's Sons. Copyright 1920 Charles Scribner's Sons.

"THE SERIOUS-MINDED YOUNG—IF ANY"

The feminists who had worked to get the vote for women were often surprised and distressed at the reaction of young women to their new rights. According to this article, the "mothers and daughters" differed in the things they considered to be important.

Mary telephoned from the laboratories that she would not be home for dinner. Her mother protested; she had counted on Mary, who was tall and strawberrily blonde and lazy-voiced and swift-witted, to help entertain the unknown out-of-towners whom Father was wishing upon her that night. But Mary refused to see that she had a duty to her mother's dinner table, her father's business, or to society in general as constituted.

"Nothing doing, darling," she said to her mother [lazily] but very firmly. "Kate and I have had a rotten hard day and we're going to eat at the Club where we won't have to say a word, and then we're going to see "The Lass From Labrador," where we won't have to think a thought. . . Father'd do a lot better to take his Rotarian couple there than to dump them on you. . . Now, Mother angel, don't be [old-fashioned]. . ."

The Rotarian couple proved unexpectedly congenial, and by and by Mother found herself telling all about Mary.

"She's working immediately under Dr. Grinnelle himself, at the Metchnikoff Laboratories," she boasted. "She specialized in biology in college. Yes, she is serious-minded. In science, that is," she added honestly. "Outside science she's totally indifferent to serious things. I couldn't drive her around the corner last fall to register for the elections, and yet I couldn't induce her to take any holiday all the summer because of some culture she was watching develop at the Laboratories. She goes by choice to musical comedies instead of Moscow Players, and she reads detective stories instead of Dreiser and those. She says that detective stories don't pretend to be concerned with life or philosophy, and that what she can't stand is the allegedly realistic artists who seem to her about as realistic as the Blue Fairy Book. She's a contradictory sort of person."

"They all seem to be like that nowadays, girls," said the visiting Rotarian's wife comfortably. "Apparently they don't think they must spread their solemnities thinly over all human affairs, as we did in our generation. If they're serious about their own businesses or professions, they seem to believe that is enough. Like men," she concluded. "Men have generally used up all their earnestness in their own work, haven't they?"

"Men have generally been selfish," said Mother with sudden grimness. "And I hate to think that women are growing like them. I don't know what is to become of the world if they do. Who is going to purify politics? Who is going to give a standard to social life? Who is going to keep the outside activities of the churches going—the applied religion? Who will run the settlements and fill the community chests? What is going to become of good works in general?"

The Rotarian's wife showed an unexpected lack of alarm. "Do you really think that our way had been such an unqualified success that we need despair because our daughters are seeing things differently?" she said. "If they are. . ."

They are. There isn't any doubt about that. The new generation wears its seriousness with a difference, when it wears it at all.

External [signs] of character have changed and are changing. . . When the young of today are serious, it is about something quite other than those things about which the late Nineties and the early Nineteen Hundreds were serious.

If you don't believe it, ask yourself what new blood has come into your organization this year? What are the ages of the youngest women in the thousands of clubs organized a score or twoscore years ago for one form or another of civic or personal improvement?. . . Where are the young women? Where are the girls? Where are the daughters of the serious-minded mothers of the generation that might be pardoned if it were now taking to easy chairs and knitting needles and pottering among the rose bushes?

An inquiring reporter, I have been out sleuthing among these mothers and their daughters. . . Here are some of the instances, typical, I think, which I have run against. . .

Luella major [the mother], aged now about fifty, is the full and admirable fruit of the [charitable] spirit that flowered in the late nineties. She is chairman of this hospital board; she is a trustee of that fund for encouraging worthy endeavor; she fought gallantly for suffrage and she avails herself to the full of the privileges and duties which enfranchisement landed upon her; she is on the state committee of her political party; she makes speeches, she nominates mayors, and sometimes she elects them. She organizes drives and collects tens of thousands of dollars for community centers and health posts.

And what is Luella minor [the daughter], now about twenty-five, doing? Luella minor is studying stage dancing with ardor and the brightest jewel in her crown to this date is that she was taken on as an extra elf when a certain internationally acclaimed foreign pageant gave a two-night performance in her city. Luella minor regards house-to-house visitations in the meaner portions of the town. . . as a dreary and unimportant waste of time. She declines to have any part or lot in it. She won't even bother to cast a vote for Alderman Jones; and she shrugs her shoulders, in effect, over the housing situation. . .

Luella major indignantly points out that it is this spirit of detachment from the common concerns of society which causes them to be so mismanaged. Luella minor smiles speculatively.

"And yet your generation, dearest, put in its time and energy in getting into the very middle of the muddle—and here's the muddle, as bad as ever! Come on and learn to dance with me. . ."

Anne O'Hagan, "The Serious-Minded Young—If Any", *Woman's Journal* (April, 1928), Volume 13, pp. 5-6.

FEMINIST–NEW STYLE

Much writing was done in the 1920's in an attempt to define the "new woman" of that period. Compare the attitude of this writer to O'Hagan's in the previous article.

. . . Since men must have things pointed out to them in black and white, we beg leave to enunciate the tenets [principles] of the modern woman's credo. Let us call her "Feminist—New Style."

First Tenet. Our modern young woman freely admits that American women have so far achieved but little in the arts, sciences, and the professions as compared with men. . .

. . . So far as the arts are concerned, it cannot be stated categorically that women lack creative power, in view of their original work in fiction, poetry, and the plastic arts. As for their status in the professions, it might fairly be claimed that they have scarcely had time to get a running start. . .

Second Tenet. Why, then, does the modern woman care about a career or a job if she doubts the quality and scope of women's achievements to date? There are three good reasons why she cares immensely: first, she may be of that rare and fortunate breed of persons who find a certain art, science, or profession as inevitable a part of their lives as breathing; second, she may feel the need of a satisfying outlet for her energy whether or not she possesses creative ability; third, she may have no other means of securing her economic independence. . .

In brief, Feminist—New Style reasons that if she is economically independent, and if she has, to boot, a vital interest in some work of her own she will have given as few hostages to Fate as it is humanly possible to give. Love may die, and children may grow up, but one's work goes on forever.

Third Tenet. She will not, however, live for her job alone, for she considers that a woman who talks and thinks only shop has just as narrow a horizon as the housewife who talks and thinks only husband and children. . .

Fourth Tenet. Nor has she become hostile to the other sex in the course of her struggle to orient herself. On the contrary, she frankly likes men and is grateful to more than a few for the encouragement and help they have given her. . .

Fifth Tenet. . . . Feminist—New Style professes no loyalty to women *en masse*, although she staunchly believes in individual women. Surveying her sex as a whole, she finds their actions petty, their range of interests narrow, their talk trivial and repetitious. . .

Sixth Tenet. [New Woman dresses and speaks to set off feminine charms.]

Seventh Tenet. Empty slogans seem to Feminist—New Style just as bad taste as masculine dress and manners. They serve only to prolong the war between the sexes and to prevent women from learning to think straight. Take these, for instance, "Keep your maiden name," "Come out of the kitchen," "Never darn a sock." After all, what's in a name or in a sock?. . .

Eighth Tenet. As for "free love," she thinks that it is impractical rather than immoral. With society organized as it is, the average man and woman cannot carry on a free union with any degree of tranquility. . .

Ninth Tenet. She readily concedes that a husband and children are necessary to the average woman's fullest development, although she knows well enough that women are endowed with varying degrees of passion and of maternal instinct. . .

But no matter how much she may desire the sanction of marriage for the sake of having children, she will not take [just] any man who offers. . .

Tenth Tenet. But even while she admits that a home and children may be necessary to her complete happiness, she will insist upon *more freedom and honesty within the marriage relation . . .*

Finally, Feminist—New Style proclaims that men and children shall no longer circumscribe her world, although they may constitute a large part of it. . . She is acutely conscious that she is being carried along in the current of. . . sweeping forces, that she and her sex are in the vanguard of change. She knows that it is her American, her twentieth-century birthright to emerge from a creature of instinct into a full-fledged individual who is capable of molding her own life, and in this respect she holds that she is becoming man's equal. . .

Dorothy Dunbar Bromley, "Feminist—New Style", *Harper's Magazine* (October, 1927) Vol. CLV, pp. 553-560. Copyright 1927 by Harper's Magazine. Reprinted by special permission.

MARGARET SANGER OPENS THE FIRST BIRTH CONTROL CLINIC IN THE UNITED STATES

In the early years of the twentieth century, Margaret Sanger started her fight to make birth control information generally available. In 1916 she opened the first American birth control clinic in New York City. Sanger was arrested and her clinic was closed, but the incident was publicized throughout the nation. It was to be repeated in the 1920's as Sanger continued her difficult struggle.

To Fania Mindell, Ethel Byrne—the nurse, and myself [the three women who started the clinic]. . . women told the constantly reiterated but ever-varying story of low wages and high rent, or irregular employment and steadily rising prices. They told us of a so-called home having only two rooms and one window, with two beds for a family of seven; of another in which three cots and a soap box had to suffice for eight children. Fine, hopeful men came to us with stories of wives broken in health and husbands broken in spirit, of sons sent to prison and daughters to prostitution. And always there were the helpless tales of children that were not wanted but came in neverending numbers. . .

. . . A gaunt skeleton of a woman suddenly stood up one day and made an impassioned speech to the women who were present: "They come with their charity when we have more children than we can feed, and when we get sick with more children for trying not to have them they just give us more charity talk! I tell you that some day they will erect a monument to Margaret Sanger on the spot where she came to help women like us!" She had been married fifteen years, was the mother of seven living children and four dead ones, and had undergone twenty-eight self-induced abortions.

. . . It was on October 16, 1916, that the three of us. . . opened the doors of the first birth control clinic in America. I believed then and do today, that the opening of those doors to the mothers of Brownsville was an event of social significance in the lives of American womanhood.

News of our work spread like wildfire. Within a few days there was not a darkened tenement, hovel or flat but was brightened by the knowledge that motherhood could be voluntary; that children need not be born into the world unless they are wanted and have a place provided for them. For the first time, women talked openly of this terror of unwanted pregnancy which had haunted their lives since time immemorial. . . .

. . . It was whispered about that the police were to raid the place for abortions. We had no fear of that accusation. We were trying to spare mothers the necessity of that ordeal by giving them proper contraceptive information. It was well that so many of the women in the neighborhood knew the truth of our doings. Hundreds of them who had witnessed the facts came to the courtroom afterward, eager to testify in our behalf.

One day a woman by the name of Margaret Whitehurst came to us. She said that she was the mother of two children and that she had not money to support more. Her story was a pitiful one—all lies, of course, but the government acts that way. She asked for our literature and preventives, and received both. Then she triumphantly went to the District Attorney's office and secured a warrant for the arrest of my sister, Mrs. Ethel Byrne, our interpreter, Miss Fania Mindell, and myself.

The crusade was actually under way! It is no exaggeration to call this period in the birth control movement the most stirring period up to that time, perhaps the most stirring of all times, for it was the only period during which we had experienced jail terms, hunger strikes, and intervention by the Chief Executive of the state. It was the first time that there was any number of widespread, popular demonstrations in our behalf. . .

. . . The arrest and raid on the Brooklyn clinic was spectacular. There was no need of a large force of plain clothes men to drag off a trio of decent, serious women who were testing out a law on a fundamental principle. . . We were not surprised at being arrested, but the shock and horror of it was that a *woman*, with a squad of five plain clothes men, conducted the raid and made the arrest. A woman—the irony of it!. . . .

. . . When the policewoman entered the clinic with her squad of plain clothes men and announced the arrest of Miss Mindell and myself (Mrs. Byrne was not present at the time and her arrest followed later), the room was crowded to suffocation with women waiting in the outer room. The police began bullying these mothers, asking them questions, writing down their names in order to subpoena them to testify against us at the trial. . . .

Crowds began to gather outside. A long line of women with baby carriages and children had been waiting to get into the clinic. Now the streets were filled, and police had to see that traffic was not blocked. The patrol wagon came rattling through the streets to our door, and at length Miss Mindell and I took our seats within and were taken to the police station. . .

As I sat in the rear of the car and looked out on that seething mob of humans, I wondered, and asked myself *what* had gone out of the race. Something had gone from them which silenced them, made them impotent to defend their rights. . . But as I sat in this mood, the car started to go. I looked out at the mass and I heard a scream. It came from a woman wheeling a baby carriage, who had just come around the corner preparing to visit the clinic. She saw the patrol wagon, realized what had happened, left the baby carriage on the walk, rushed through the crowd to the wagon and cried to me: "Come back! Come back and save me!" The woman looked wild. She ran after the car for a dozen yards or so, when some friends caught her weeping form in their arms and led her back to the sidewalk. That was the last thing I saw as the Black Maria [patrol wagon] dashed off to the station.

Margaret Sanger, *My Fight for Birth Control* (New York: Farrar & Rinehart, 1931), pp. 156-160. Reprinted by permission.

THE PROBLEM OF BIRTH CONTROL

The following letters were published in a pamphlet by Margaret Sanger in 1921 as part of an appeal to change the laws which made it a crime to distribute contraceptive information.

Minnesota, May 20, 1921

Dear Mrs. Sanger:

Your book of "Women and the New Race" received. But did not get what I most needed in it. . . Now I would like to ask you to help me as soon as you can. I am a mother of 11 children, 10 living. Green, that is what I am, only 34 years old and am 3 months in a family way again. I have a man that thinks it's my fault because we have children. I do confess it is. I am out here on the farm, no money or way to get to the doctors. I would not care how I would get [through]. I would now take almost poison, for I do hate life again. Our children are all very strong and healthy, but I am the one has to suffer. Can you not tell me or help me in some way. . . I have a daughter 17 and 15. I want them to know and be better than I, for this is sure hell; that is what this is. Well, will close now and remain waiting for an answer soon.

Mrs. S.J.

Wisconsin May 5, 1921

Dear Madam:

Have read your book "Women and the New Race," and am more than interested in its contents. I think it's just wonderful. It expresses everything that many women have felt, but never dared breathe. I have been married seventeen years and have had mostly all the troubles the majority of married women have, have four living children, had one miscarriage and eight abortions. No doubt you will think it almost unbelievable, but nevertheless it's true, and true only because I'm ignorant in these things as most women are, so I come to you for advice. Please tell me what a contraceptive is, and where to get such. It will be a blessing to me, and I will bless you to the end of my days.

Sincerely yours
Mrs. R.S.

Margaret Sanger, *Appeals From American Mothers*(New York: Woman's Publishing Co. Inc, 1921), pp. 4-5.

10
The Depression and World War II

On October 24, 1929, or "Black Thursday" as it came to be called, 13 million shares of stock changed hands on the New York Stock Exchange. By October 29, the Exchange had lost between $8 and $9 billion. There had been unmistakable signs of economic trouble earlier, but people had been too eager to "get rich" to see them. Experts had ignored the overexpansion of credit, the excessive volume of stock being traded, and the problems of the American farmer.

At first most Americans optimistically assumed that this economic panic would be short-lived. However, it was not long before the effects of economic depression could be seen and felt everywhere. Consumer buying declined sharply. In panic, people tried to take their savings out of the banks, which caused many banks to fail. By 1932, 12 million persons, or 25 percent of America's normally employed workers, were out of work. How did this severe economic crisis affect the American woman?

Effects of the Depression

At first it appeared that the average woman was affected less than the man—that her world of cooking, sewing, keeping house, and childraising could go on, at least as long as there was food to cook, clothes to mend, and a house to keep. To supplement their family needs, women often returned to traditional crafts such as soap making, fruit drying, pickling, bread baking, and sewing. In 1931 the sale of glass jars zoomed while the sale of canned goods declined sharply. Domestic activities kept many women active and optimistic, while men, faced with no work, often felt useless and depressed.

In 1930, one out of every five women, a total of 11 million, were employed outside the home. They were usually paid less than men, even though many of them were responsible for the support of their families. As the depression worsened, women were often the first to lose their jobs. It was believed that at worst they would be inconvenienced, while unemployment among men would cause "anguish on account of responsibilities which cannot be met. . ." In ten studies conducted by the Women's Bureau, it was found that over 43,000, or 13 percent, of the 370,000 women studied were the sole support of families of two or more persons. Firing these people because they were women resulted in the same "anguish" as unemployed men would feel.

Working married women were discriminated against in many jobs. For example, in 1932 the Women's Bureau reported that most major cities had banned the employment of married women in their schools. This created a situation in which women either did not marry or did not live with their husbands. A surprisingly large number of persons felt that the crisis could be lessened if married women returned to homemaking, and the federal government restricted a family to one job and one paycheck. A law was passed to that effect, but was repealed when it was realized that it did not improve conditions.

Black women faced additional hardships. At best these women were the last hired and first fired. In 1930, one-fifth of all white women worked outside the home, while two-fifths of black women were employed, although at lower wages. In the cigar industry, for example, black women earned an average of $10.10 a week as compared to $16.30 earned by white women. In one survey of over 100 working black women, 63 were domestics or in personal service, which were very low-paying jobs. By 1931, 42 percent of black female workers were unemployed as compared with 18 percent of American-born white women. Often black women were discharged and whites were given their jobs.

To those who watched the breadlines, it might have appeared that women were eating better than their male counterparts because "you never see a woman on a breadline." An article written in December 1932 for the paper *Labor* contradicted this assumption. It

The face of this Ozark mountain woman reflects the hopelessness many women felt as a result of the depression.

was entitled "Forgotten Women, Reluctant to Beg, Starve in Cold Garrets."

> All but neglected for three years, one of the most tragic phases of the depression—the plight of unemployed and homeless women—was brought to the foreground this week . . . . Miss Mary Anderson, Director of the Women's Bureau, has been working without success for many months to get the condition of these unfortunate women before the government and the public. . . . Practically no provision has been made for their care. Because they hesitate to beg on the streets or resort to breadlines, many of the homeless women are literally starving to death in cold garrets and other out-of-the-way places.

According to the Family Aid Society, there were actually "thousands of forgotten women" who were "clinging desperately to life" and who needed immediate care.

Attempts to Deal with the Crisis

The Women's Bureau, which had been established in 1920, was deeply concerned with the problem of women workers during the depression. The bureau tried to help

> the woman who makes candlewick bedspreads in her Southern mountain home for a pittance, the maid who toils for long hours in someone else's kitchen, the waitress who serves food to the public. . . the

woman whose health is endangered by unsanitary working conditions or a hazardous occupation, the married woman responsible for the support of her children who is denied a job because of prejudice, the qualified Negro woman who is barred from this or that kind of employment because of her race. . . .

The Women's Bureau sought to increase wages, shorten hours, improve working conditions, and increase the efficiency of working women. In 1934 the Women's Bureau presented specific demands to various government agencies. These included jobs through the Civil Works Administration (CWA) for all unemployed women without regard to race, nationality, or marital status; adequate relief, no discrimination against blacks in wages, equal pay for equal work, free nursery schools, and free medical and maternity care. These demands called attention to the economic problems of women.

In 1933 Congress passed the National Industrial Recovery Act (NIRA). It was a major part of President Franklin D. Roosevelt's plan to improve the economic health of the United States. The NIRA also aided women workers. Title I of the act provided for labor codes to govern all industry. These codes regulated hours, working conditions, and encouraged the process of collective bargaining. Although NIRA was declared unconstitutional in 1935, women did gain higher wages, which reduced the gap between salaries paid to men and women.

Many of the codes unfortunately set minimum wages for women below those for men. This meant that it was legal to pay a woman less than a man for the same job. For example, in the boot and shoe industry, the minimum wage was 35 cents an hour for men and 30 cents an hour for women. Since the codes were confined to industries involved in interstate commerce, nearly one-half of all employed women were not covered; professional, agricultural, and domestic workers were left unprotected.

The Works Progress Administration (WPA) aided women by putting them to work. In 1933, 450,000 women were involved; mostly widows, single women, and married women whose husbands were unable to secure jobs. Attempts were made to suit the woman to the job. There were over 250 occupational classifications, including sewing, providing hot lunches for school children, nursing and public health, library work, and positions in adult education and recreation.

The right of collective bargaining was assured when the Supreme Court upheld the constitutionality of the National Labor Relations Act of 1935. Unions began to grow rapidly during this period. By

The WPA attempted to provide work for the jobless. These women are making clothing for distribution to unemployed families.

1938 women made up a large part of the International Ladies Garment Workers Union (ILGWU) and the Amalgamated Clothing Workers of America (ACWA). Dorothy Jacobs Bellanca, an immigrant from Latvia, became an active union organizer for the ACWA. Her index finger had become misshapen on her ten-hour-a-day job as a hand-buttonhole sewer in a men's overcoat factory. She contributed much to the growth of the Amalgamated Clothing Workers during the 1920's and 1930's. In spite of these real gains, however, agricultural and household employees remained outside union protection.

Minimum wage legislation became one of the controversial issues of the 1930's. During the Progressive era many states, in order to protect women workers, had passed minimum wage laws that applied only to women. But some feminists, such as the National Women's Party, began to argue that one could not be protected by special legislation and still expect equal pay for equal work. "Special treatment" and "equality," they felt, were contradictory. In contrast, the Women's Bureau argued that women would at least be assured of fair wages by minimum wage legislation. In 1936 New York State's minimum wage law for women was declared unconstitutional.

Women in Government

During the 1930's women became active in government. Frances Perkins was appointed Secretary of Labor by President Roosevelt, the first woman to achieve Cabinet rank. Impressed with her hard-headedness, the Baltimore *Sun* wrote:

> The lady is better than you are . . . and what's more, she is not afraid of you. And that makes an awful combination. A woman smarter than a man is something to get on guard about. But a woman smarter than a man and also not afraid of a man, well, good-night.

As Secretary of Labor Perkins worked hard for a five-day week, a minimum wage for all, and the abolition of child labor.

Nellie Taylor Ross, once Governor of Wyoming, became the Treasurer of the United States. To represent the United States, Ruth Bryan Owen, the daughter of William Jennings Bryan, was sent to Denmark as a foreign minister.

Mary McLeod Bethune, the first freeborn child in a family of 17 children, educated herself and started a school for black girls in 1904. She founded Bethune Cookman College in Daytona Beach, Florida and was president from 1932 to 1942. President Roosevelt recognized Bethune's unique abilities and appointed her director of the Division of Negro Affairs of the National Youth Administration. Her function was to supervise the training of 600,000 black children, a job she accepted eagerly. She wrote, "I am my mother's daughter, and the drums of Africa still beat in my heart. They will not let me rest while there is a single Negro boy or girl without a chance to prove his worth."

Eleanor Roosevelt was the most active first lady in America's history. In spite of an unhappy and difficult childhood, she matured to command the respect of the entire world in her humanitarian ef-

In the early years of her husband's Presidency Eleanor Roosevelt performed the traditional, ceremonial duties expected of a President's wife. Dissatisfied with this limited role, she developed into one of Franklin Roosevelt's most influential advisers.

forts. During the political life of Franklin D. Roosevelt, she helped him fulfill his goals and programs through her writing and speechmaking. In 1945, after his death, she became the United States delegate to the General Assembly of the United Nations. She was elected Chairman of the United Nations Human Rights Commission and helped to draft the Universal Declaration of Human Rights.

In 1931 there were nine women in Congress, five of whom had inherited their husbands' positions. Hattie Caraway of Arkansas was appointed to the Senate upon the death of her husband in 1931 and in 1932 was elected on her own. A writer remarked in the *Woman's Journal* in 1931 that a feminist must be loyal to men to get reelected; therefore, she could not act freely to improve the status of women.

By June 1939 almost 173,000 (or one-fifth) of all workers in the federal service were women. In their favor was the United States Civil Service Commission's ruling that opened all exams and positions to women at the same wages as men.

Social Values in the 1930's

Changes in American social values in the 1930's did not become apparent until the beginning of the New Deal in 1933. Economic problems and fears during the depression forced people to think more conservatively than they had done in the 1920's.

In the early 1930's understanding and affection within marriage were emphasized as the 1920's encouragement of experimentation and fun came to be considered less important. One young man remarked, "I keep away from girls for fear I'll fall in love and make matters worse," for it was difficult to think about marriage when neither the boy nor the girl had a job. The marriage rate fell from 10.14 per 1,000 in 1929 to 7.87 in 1932, and the birth rate fell from 18.9 per 1,000 in 1929 to 17.4 in 1932 and 16.5 in 1933. The sale of contraceptives increased sharply. Contraceptives were sold not only in drugstores but also in filling stations and tobacco shops.

Fashions were another indicator of social change. Boyish figures, long-waisted short dresses, and bobbed hair gave way to more conservative-length dresses with waistlines, figures that showed the curves of the body, and hair styles that were softer and curlier.

A "typical" middle-class family of 1937, not on relief, accurately reflected life for the average American. This family probably consisted of two adults and 1.6 children living in a rented 6.4-room house or a 4.5-room apartment. The gross annual income was $1,348. Life in the 1930's had become home-centered.

Film star Jean Harlow.

The family's main source of entertainment was the radio. By 1931, 28 million families, or 85 percent of the population, owned their own sets. Housewives tuned in melodrama or "feminine interest" programs featuring fashions or childcare during the day. They listened to children's programs during the early evening and top-rated shows at night. Professional baseball was also eagerly followed on the radio.

If the family went out, it probably went to the movies. The movies continued to grow in popularity—the "talkies" replacing the "silents." Heroines of the period included Greta Garbo, Carole Lombard, Mae West, and Marlene Dietrich. Actress Jean Harlow made "platinum blond" hair the sex symbol of the decade. Movies were attended by most Americans as a major source of entertainment outside the home.

The arts of the 1930's began to emphasize social realism, picturing life as it was rather than as it might be. Women had become successful in the arts and many works by females were well known. Photographers Margaret Bourke-White and Dorothea Lange reflected the stark realities of the depression in their well-known photographs. But not all creative work dealt with social realism. A popular novel in the romantic tradition was Margaret Mitchell's *Gone With the Wind,* which sold over 12 million copies and won the Pulitzer Prize for literature in 1937. Other women who successfully competed in the literary field were novelists Pearl Buck and Edna Ferber; short story writers Dorothy Parker and Katherine Anne Porter; playwright Lillian Hellman; and journalist Dorothy Thompson.

Traditional male-dominated fields such as aviation, sports, and the sciences were opened to women in the 1930's. Amelia Earhart became the first female passenger on a transatlantic flight in 1928. In 1932 she flew alone across the Atlantic; in 1937, while attempting to fly around the world, she was lost in the Pacific. Another heroine of the 1930's was Mildred "Babe" Didrikson, winner of two gold medals and one silver in track and field events at the 1932 Olympics. She was described as "lean with big arms and leg muscles, large hands and a rather angular jaw." She could sew and cook, as well as compete athletically, which was carefully pointed out to her fans.

Two internationally known women worked in the field of anthropology. Ruth Benedict received recognition for her classic work *Patterns of Culture*, and her student, Margaret Mead, became one of the world's foremost anthropologists.

Florence Rhena Sabin, a graduate of Smith College and an M.D. from Johns Hopkins, became the first female professor at the Rockefeller Institute of Medicine in New York. She taught and did research from 1925 to 1948. Sabin specialized in diseases of the lymph glands and the blood.

Amelia Earhart in the cockpit of her plane.

The United States Enters World War II

The outbreak of war in Europe in 1939 affected the lives of all Americans. The United States began to produce armaments, which resulted in an increase in employment. World War II thus provided the means to new economic prosperity.

Americans turned their attention to the rise of fascism in Europe. Leading American feminists were concerned that the fascist notion of women's place would hamper their efforts in America. The Nazi slogan "Kinder, Kirche, und Kuche" (children, church, and kitchen) demanded that married women remain in their traditional roles in the home. After the Japanese attack on Pearl Harbor on December 7, 1941, America was fully at war, and women were to play an increasingly important role both on the domestic front and on the fighting field.

As more and more men were drafted to serve in the armed forces, women took over in the factories that provided the support for the army. A Women's Bureau study in 1942 predicted that by the end of that year there would be a half-million increase in the number of women working in essential nonwar activities. By 1945 over 4 million additional women would be employed in the economy. New York employers, for example, expected to hire women to operate drilling machines, lathes, power sewing machines and as filers and riveters; also as grinders, drill-press operators, solderers, cementers, and welders.

Black women also benefited from these economic developments. In 1942 the Brooklyn Navy Yard began to employ women, and a black woman received the highest rating out of 600 women who took the Civil Service Exam for those jobs. At that time, of the 125 women hired, 12 were black. Black women were increasingly hired to fill war-related vacancies.

The Women's Bureau established guidelines for hiring women. It fought for improved working conditions and higher salaries for women, who received 60 percent less than men for similar jobs. But little was gained in the fight for equal pay for equal work during this time.

Full-time employment created many new problems for women: adequate housing, especially for single girls, transportation, recreation, and time for shopping.

"There ought to be a law," said Mrs. Tom Clark, wife of a marine, mother of four, as she pushed her way onto an already overflowing bus. Mrs. Clark, a welder in the big aircraft company 12 miles from

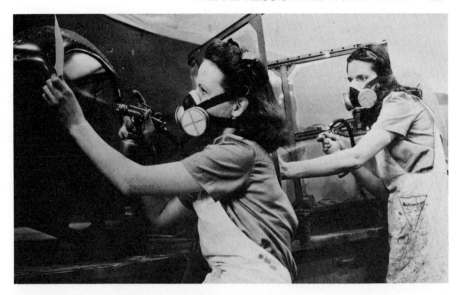

An airplane assembly line during World War II.

town, had arrived at the grocery store just three minutes too late. The store was closed . . . For a week Mrs. Clark hadn't been able to get to the store before it closed. The Clarks that night would dine on the one remaining can of peas—a nourishing meal for a woman welder and four growing children.

In many war plants women's divisions in personnel and industrial relations were established to solve these problems.

As a result of the father's leaving to fight the war and the mother's working outside the home, family life changed considerably. The need for day care centers increased, and some factories provided day care for their employees' children. However, at the end of the war, these reforms were eliminated.

Women also directly participated in the war. A total of 216,000 women served as nurses, Navy WAVES, Army WACS, Coast Guard SPARS, and female marines. Colonel Oveta Culp Hobby was appointed Director of the Women's Army Corps, created by Congress on May 14, 1942. Its task was to provide women for noncombatant service in order to release men for combat. The requirements for membership in the corps included: age between 20 and 49; United States citizenship; married or single, but no children under 14; excellent character and good health; and at least two years of high school or similar educational experience. These requirements were much stricter than those for male soldiers. These women recruits became accountants, bakers, bookkeepers, cashiers, chauffeurs, radio operators, and typists. In the Army Air Force, women trained student pilots in instrument flying. The Navy Nurse Corps was given sea duty to train hospital corpsmen.

There were 3½ million women volunteers in the American Red Cross in 1943. They worked in canteens, hospitals, recreation centers, and motor corps, and they aided in the recruitment of the United States Army Nurse Corps.

Toward the end of the war, there was concern about the future of the woman civilian worker. Returning servicemen who had previously been permanently employed were to be given their old jobs, or the equivalent. As a result many women would lose the jobs they had held while the men were away. Married women were especially affected, for the view was still held that they did not need to work.

Summary

During the depression, economic problems dominated American life. No longer could Americans allow themselves the luxury of thinking about the concerns of the "roaring twenties"—fashion, sexual freedom, and acquiring new gadgets. American social attitudes became more conservative in the 1930's. As the number of jobs decreased, working women were regarded with mounting disapproval.

When the United States entered World War II, attitudes toward acceptable behavior for women changed again. Work outside the home for women had been considered un-American in the 1930's, but conditions in the 1940's made work patriotic.

According to a survey made at the end of the war, most women and men believed that the scars of the preceding years could best be healed by accepting traditional patterns again.

> The average thinking American woman has a fairly modest, though as yet utopian, dream of the good life. It would be something like this: She would live in a comfortable, though not pretentious home, probably with a backyard grill, equipped by science to relieve her from drudgery and give her time for the subtler phases of homemaking.
> Her husband would have a secure and stable job in an economy that had a minimum of unemployment. He would probably work six hours a day, thus having time to help make the home a center of education and enjoyment.

This conservative reaction created conflicts in the decade that followed.

SHOULD WOMEN WORK?

Alice Stone Blackwell, daughter of Lucy Stone and Henry Blackwell, worked for many causes including suffrage, temperance, peace, and rights for blacks. In the following 1931 editorial she asks an important question: if women were to be denied work because they had male support, shouldn't rich men be denied work in favor of the jobless and poor. Rules, she feels, should apply equally to all.

The hard times have brought out a fresh crop of protests against the earning of money by women, especially married women, unless they are compelled to do it. We are told over and over that every salaried woman who could live without her job ought to give it up in favor of the jobless.

An argument can be made for this, from the standpoint of the Golden Rule. But, if it is sound, it does not apply to women only. No one suggests that every man who could live without his job ought to retire in favor of the jobless. On the contrary, if a rich man's son, sure of inheriting enough for himself and his family, goes to work for a salary, he is universally praised. But if that young man's sister, married or single, does the same, she is blamed.

School Boards are even urged to dismiss all married women from the teaching force; but it is never suggested that all male teachers ought to be dismissed who could live without their pay.

A young scoffer once told a distinguished clergyman that the religion he preached might be very good for old women, but would not do for men. The clergyman answered, "Sir, either the religion that I preach is true or it is not true. If it is true, it is good for everybody. If it is not true, it is neither good for old women nor for anybody else."

All believers in human rights should set themselves against these attempts to impose upon women a rule which would be [rejected] in the case of men. Either it applies to both sexes, or it does not apply at all.

Alice Stone Blackwell, "May Women Earn?" *The Woman's Journal* (January, 1931) Vol. XVI, pp. 26-27.

"WOMEN AVAILABLE"–EDUCATED WOMEN AND THE DEPRESSION

The following story provides a good example of the experiences of thousands of well-educated young women in all parts of the country whose lives were affected by the Depression. The charges made by Americans that women's unemployment was not as important or serious a problem as men's unemployment are contradicted by Vera's situation.

Vera has never had a job. Almost every day of her first year in New York was spent in the discouraging routine all too familiar to the inexperienced college graduate looking for work. Employment agencies and prospective employers were equally indifferent to her plight when they discovered her lack of experience. And the money she spent on stamps for answering want ads was wasted; her letters never elicited replies.

For a time she lived on a small inheritance. But by the summer of 1934 it was gone and she seemed as far as ever from any hope of getting a job. Despite the intense heat and the growing nausea and weakness of slow starvation she continued to look for work for a month after her funds gave out. During this period she did not pay any rent for her furnished room and for food she depended almost entirely on occasional dinner invitations from her friends. There were not many of these invitations because she did not tell anyone how desperate her situation really was. Sometimes, though, she would borrow a dollar which usually went for carfare when she got so tired she couldn't walk further or, contrary to her better judgment, for food.

After four weeks of assuring her landlady that she would soon get a job and pay her rent she came home one night to find that all her clothing and personal belongings had disappeared during her absence. Frantic, she appealed to the landlady who told her that everything would be returned when she paid her rent . . .

In a daze, she went to the park and sat on a bench and cried until a policeman threatened to arrest her on a charge of vagrancy if she stayed any longer. That night she slept, or tried to sleep, in the waiting room of the Grand Central. Once a guard told her to leave, but when he discovered she was so weak and sick that she couldn't stand he relented. Later she discovered that homeless women often sleep in the big stations, pretending to be waiting for a morning train. She also found women lying behind the heating and ventilating shafts in subway toilets . . .

Vera herself slept in all the Y.W.C.A.'s in town in rotation: homeless girls can spend one night in each . . . [She finally borrows a little money from a friend and finds a tenement room which she shares with another homeless girl.]

Vera is now in the third year of her unemployment. If she is completely discouraged, she does not say so. In fact, she told me that she had recovered sufficiently from [an accident] to start looking for work again. "Only I'll have to have something to wear first," she said. "No one will hire me looking this way." Her one dress has been cleaned and mended until there is nothing left of it; she has no hat and there are large holes in her shoes.

Lately she applied for relief, but so far nothing has come of it . . .

Ruth L. Porterfield, "Women Available," *The American Mercury* (April, 1935) Vo. xxxiv, pp. 473-475. Reprinted by permission of *Mercury*, P.O. Box 1306, Torrance, Calif. 90505.

BLACK WOMEN AND THE DEPRESSION

Although all groups of women encountered hardship during the years of the Depression, black women were in especially difficult circumstances. Hired for the lowest-paying jobs and fired first, they then met discrimination in government relief projects. Even those who continued to work suffered.

. . . Along with lowered wages have come increased responsibilities for many Negro as well as white women who still hold jobs. Case after case found by the Women's Bureau agents in their home visits [to the homes of employed women] testifies to the desperate economic struggle of working people, to the burden of support that is being thrown upon employed women as pay is cut and as other wage earners in the family lose jobs, and to the methods undertaken for reducing expenses, often to the point of doing without the bare necessities of life.

For example, cases may be cited of several Negro women who worked in laundries in a city in the South and who were visited late in 1932 or early in 1933. The essential problems they show could be duplicated in almost any city.

In a family of five the mother was the sole support except that the husband had been provided with some "made work." She had earned $5 a week in 1931 but received only $4 in 1932. The rent had not been lowered, and was always behind. The three children were all under 16. The oldest had to be taken from school as she was nearly blind. She had had some free treatment, but the family had never been able to get the glasses prescribed for her.

Another family had been increased to four when a brother-in-law had brought his wife to live with her mother and sister. Except that the brother-in-law was given some "made work", the sister was the only wage-earner and her pay had been cut in the 2 years preceding the date of the study. She said, "We are just living here till they put us out." She was walking to work to save car fare. They had discontinued taking a newspaper and had to make over their clothing. They were eating only two meals a day. . .

In another case, a woman of 37 was supporting a family of three including her mother and a niece. She claimed to have worked in the same laundry since the age of 9. Her regular time had been 9 hours a day, and her normal wage had been only $9 but this had been twice cut toward the end of 1932. She stated that the employer had tried to spread work to avoid dismissal, though another worker in the same laundry spoke as follows: "They laid off everybody they could think of, then worked the devil out of us who were left." This family had not asked for public aid. Their rent had been somewhat reduced, and they had cut down on clothing and ate sparingly. . .

U. S. Women's Bureau, *The Employment and Unemployment of Negro Women* (July 1934), p. 8.

ELEANOR ROOSEVELT WORKS TO END THE DEPRESSION

When Franklin Roosevelt was President, his wife Eleanor was well respected for her own work. In addition, she often served as her husband's representative and adviser. Her role in the New Deal is illustrated in the following description of her work.

People do not realize how much pressure is brought to bear on a president, and how the various pressures sometimes loom so important that the real desires of the man himself must be subordinated. War hysteria, for example, had an effect not only on some of the campaign speeches but on administration policies.

Often people came to me to enlist his support for an idea. Although I might present a situation to him, I never urged on him a specific course of action, no matter how strongly I felt, because I realized he knew of factors in the picture as a whole of which I might be ignorant. I would do all I could for the people who came to me, short of stating what my husband might think or feel, and he never asked me to refrain from speaking my own mind. . .

One of the ideas I agreed to present to Franklin was that of setting up a national youth administration. Harry Hopkins, then head of the WPA, and Aubrey Williams, his deputy administrator and later head of the National Youth Administration, knew how deeply troubled I had been from the beginning about the plight of the country's young people, for I had talked to them about it a number of times. One day they said: "We have come to you about this because we do not feel we should talk to the president about it as yet." They went on: "There may be many people against the establishment of such an agency in the government and there may be bad political repercussions. We do not know that the country will accept it. We do not even like to ask the president, because we do not think he should be put in a position where he has to say officially 'yes' or 'no' now."

I agreed to try to find out what Franklin's feelings were and to put before him their opinions and fears. I waited until my usual time for discussing questions with him and went into his room just before he went to sleep. I described the whole idea, which he already knew something of, and then told him of the fears that Harry Hopkins and Aubrey Williams had about such an agency. . . [The President accepts the idea.]

I went back to Harry Hopkins and Aubrey Williams the next day with Franklin's message. Shortly after, the NYA came into being and undoubtedly benefited a great many young people. . .

It was one of the occasions on which I was very proud that the right thing was done regardless of political considerations. As a matter of fact, however, it turned out to be politically popular and strengthened the administration greatly.

As time went by, I found that people no longer considered me a mouthpiece for my husband but realized that I had a point of view of my own with which he might not at all agree. Then I felt freer to state my views. However, I always used some care, and sometimes, for example, I would send Franklin one of my [newspaper] columns about which I was doubtful. The only change he would ever suggest was occasionally in the use of a word, and that was simply a matter of style. Of course, this hands-off policy had its advantages for him, too; for it meant that my column could sometimes serve as a trial balloon. If some idea I expressed strongly—and with which he might agree—caused a violent reaction, he could honestly say that he had no responsibility in the matter and that the thoughts were my own. . .

Eleanor Roosevelt, *This I Remember* (New York: Harper and Row, 1949), pp. 162-164. Abridged and reprinted by permission of Harper & Row, Publishers, Inc.

AMELIA EARHART FLIES THE ATLANTIC

Amelia Earhart was the first woman to fly alone across the Atlantic Ocean. In this magazine article, written after her flight in 1932, she has some advice for women and men; do what you think is right for you.

I flew the Atlantic because I wanted to. If that be what they call "a woman's reason," make the most of it. It isn't, I think, a reason to be apologized for by man or woman. It is the most honest motive for the majority of mankind's achievements. To want in one's heart to do a thing, for its own sake; to enjoy doing it; to concentrate all one's energies upon it—that is not only the surest guarantee of its success. It is also being true to oneself.

Whether you are flying the Atlantic, or selling sausages, or building a skyscraper, or driving a truck, or painting a picture, or skiing down an unknown hill, or nursing shell shock patients in a hospital, or running a grocery store in Atchison, Kansas, your greatest power comes from the fact that you want tremendously to do that very thing, and do it well.

If you worry about the money you will make from it, or what people will say about you, or whether you will stub your toe or bark your shins, then you are frittering away that power—that inner concentration on the goal itself. "To thine own self be true. . . thou canst not then be false to any man." Thus Mr. Shakespeare gave the answer more than 300 years ago.

Some of my friends have suggested that I made very little preparation for my recent Atlantic flight. I took with me only what I wore—jodphurs, silk shirt, windbreaker, and a leather flying suit—no dresses for the other side. I sent ahead no agents to greet and attend to my affairs on my arrival in Europe. I made no advance announcements to the newspapers. I carried with me only $20.00 in bills. My supply of food included only a thermos bottle of soup and a can of tomato juice.

The extras, as a matter of fact, were of as little value to me as a monocle to a man going over Niagara in a barrel. If I succeeded they would take care of themselves; if I failed, they were irrelevant. A pilot whose land plane falls into the Atlantic is not consoled by three-decker caviar sandwiches, and bank notes are not legal tender in Davy Jones's locker.

My concern was simply to fly alone to Europe. Extra clothes and extra food would have been extra weight and extra worry. They would have distracted my attention from the main object. . . I wanted to fly because I *wanted* to. . .

Amelia Earhart, "Flying the Atlantic," *American Magazine* (August, 1932) Vol. 114, pp. 15.

LEARNING SEX ROLES

Anthropologist Margaret Mead has made major contributions in the study of sex roles in various societies. In the following analysis she discusses how society assigns sex roles and why people follow them so closely.

Sex Membership

The human child, born into a world which regards sex as the most important difference between human beings, wants very much to belong to its own sex, for only so can he or she attain full membership in the human race. A person without full sex membership is worse off than a man without a country.

Nor do human societies believe that mere possession of the appropriate anatomy is enough to ensure membership in the right sex. If this were so, we would not find so much anxiety, so many rituals—cutting the girl's umbilical cord on her yam masher, cutting the boy's cord on a war club, or sealing the boy's cord up in a pot to ensure him a harsh, deep voice. There is always the chance that the girl may not take to her feminine role, that the boy may not show the hardy, virile character which will proclaim him a man. And the fear of each generation of parents, expressed in ritual, in costume, in admonitions, infects the child with fear: "If I play with dolls, I won't be a man." "If I want to shoot with a gun I won't be a woman." Fear of being disenfranchised stands at the elbow of every growing boy and girl.

As the boy grows older, he learns that it is not so much playing with dolls which he must avoid as playing baseball and football which he must cultivate. No one will commend him and pronounce him a *real boy* for the things which he abstains from doing. They watch anxiously for signs of positive achievement in the fields of decreed masculine activity. He can neglect the avoidances which were necessary when he was smaller and still longed to play with dolls and hide behind his mother's skirts just in proportion to the skill and enthusiasm with which he wields a baseball bat.

In most historical discussions of sex differences it has been assumed that the little girl learned the same kind of lesson, that she learned that, if she directed enough attention toward dolls, toward daintiness, toward feminine shrinking and fluttering, she too would be safe.

But this is only half the story, and it is the other half which is the more significant. For the boy, as he grows older, the emphasis upon avoiding feminine occupations grows less, until, as the proud captain of the winning eleven he can even hold a baby in his arms and so proclaim his masculinity. For the girl the exact opposite occurs. Her main task is not to achieve in the feminine field but to *avoid achieving* in the masculine. While the boy is merely required to document his masculinity, the girl is required to prove both that she *is* feminine and that she is *not* masculine, that she will not try to achieve success in any masculine field.

A typical example is the Eskimo woman, forced in her husband's absence to build a snowhouse to shelter her family from a sudden storm. She can build a snowhouse, but it is unwomanly to do so. Afraid that her skill will be held against her, she chatters disarmingly as she works and, when her husband returns and asks who has built the house, she answers: "Just an attempt of a simple woman to put a few blocks together." With such cautious phrases has her formal, many-thousand-years' old culture equipped her to protect her femininity in the moment of achievement.

So the boy is taught to achieve, the girl to prove that she doesn't achieve, will never achieve. The same threat hangs over the unachieving boy and the achieving girl, the threat that he or she will never be chosen by a member of the opposite sex.

Margaret Mead, "Sex and Achievement," *Forum* (November, 1935) Vol. XCIV, No. 5, p. 302. Reprinted with permission.

WOMEN IN THE ARMED SERVICES

The following description is from a Women's Army Corps (WAC) publication.

What the Wacs do—

THEY ARE MAKING A GLORIOUS WAR RECORD —IN ALL THREE ARMY FORCES!

The Army in warfare today is a vast organization of "specialists" . . .

Pilots and bombardiers and engineers . . obviously, these are jobs for men.

Stenographers and typists and map makers and telephone operators . . .

Just as obviously, these are jobs for women as well as men.

So the Army takes both men and women specialists and places them where their own particular skills will do the most good.

Wacs serve with the Air Forces, the Ground Forces, and the Service Forces. Finely trained Wacs, at mobile switchboards, flash combat messages to front lines.

Clear-headed Wacs handle the high-pressure routine of an overseas headquarters as calmly as if they were in an office back home. Turn out an incredible volume of secret orders, reports, dispatches in record-breaking time, thereby keeping our infantry moving forward.

Wacs serve in Army hospitals, helping wounded men to overcome handicaps and battle shock. Wacs check troop sailing lists, handle V-Mail at the ports of embarkation. Wacs make strategy maps for invading enemy territory.

Wacs decode, file, tabulate, take blood counts, repair cameras and radios, issue supplies to men bound for overseas. Wacs do 239 Army jobs.

And above all, Wacs do every job—little or big—with a thrilling competence that awakens respect in the eyes of even the ablest G.I.

For wherever they serve—around the world and back—Wacs are doing a job. A gallant, soldier's job. Making a glorious war record!

A Book of Facts About the WAC (Washington, D.C.: Women's Army Corps, 1944), p. 3.

WITH LOVE, ISABEL

Many women joined the WACS, WAVES, SPARS, and Nurse Corps during World War II and were generally assigned as support for the men in combat. Captain Isabel Kane, a WAC, wrote to her father after her arrival in Normandy with her outfit. Her letter shows how she felt about her role in the war.

At Sea, 13 July 1944

I have just come down from the deck—watching the brilliant sunset fade to purple and finally the blackness of ships silhouetted against the sky. My thoughts were with you as I leaned against the ship's rail—drifting and dreaming—all was so peaceful—so relaxed—and yet the scene around me recalled the tenseness of D-Day and the silver barrage balloons attached to each craft were not part of the holiday scene . . . And tomorrow is Bastille Day. We have been learning the words and tune of the Marseillaise. Those words do make your blood tingle—"To arms—to arms ye brave . . . All hearts resolved to victory or death" . . . . .

I really shouldn't try to write. It all seems so unreal. I wonder if it is I—and that we are really the first Wacs to land in France. We started off into the great unknown and gradually the mystery is unfolding. The trip to the marshalling area—the time spent there—the trip to the docks and now the ship. Soon will come the beaches—the debarkation and a new home to make. It is so thrilling, and has so many angles that I can't write about. I'll continue tomorrow . . .

And this is tomorrow—almost time now. The harbor is a maze of ships and I want to close this so I can get it off on the first courier. We have been prepared to be rugged, but so far it has been very easy. This is the trip of trips and worth waiting two years for. I'll soon be celebrating my 2nd anniversary of joining the WAC . . . .

Alma Lutz, *With Love Jane* (New York: John Day Co., 1945), pp. 116-117. Reprinted with permission.

AFTER THE ARMY—WHAT?

What will happen to the women who served in the armed forces during World War II, asked Doria Higgins, a Washington reporter. She believed women would face a shrinking job market as the men came home from the war and received job priority.

A prediction that by mid-November more than 2,500,000 women will be looking for jobs has been made by Miss Frieda S. Miller, Chief, Women's Bureau, Labor Department. The dearth of postwar employment will be felt first by civilian workers, for the servicewomen will be discharged more gradually. The thought uppermost in the minds of the nearly 100,000 women already in the Women's Army Corps is—When do I get out of the Army and after that—what?

They all are eligible for benefits under the GI bill of rights, and if they wish can complete or further their education at the expense of the Government.

The time has come when the women who left their homes and donned uniforms to travel, who accepted the regimentation and discipline of Army life, the responsibilities of a large organization, will return to a life of personal decisions and responsibilities.

The impressions gained from interviews is that they are eager to resume "a regular, normal life," to return to their husbands, or to get married and start a home.

A recent First Air Force questionnaire on the postwar ambitions of the Wacs declares 73 percent want marriage and home-making. That finding is in accord with the opinion of a young infantry lieutenant. "Aw, lady," he drawled, "you know as well as I do a woman's place is in the home."

Although most of the Wacs joined for patriotic reasons, some said restlessness had been a secondary factor and that the restlessness was with them again. They want to travel. One group is planning to buy a car and leisurely tour the United States.

One definite note was struck in the words of a young corporal who said, "I don't feel prepared for the peace. I don't want to get out because I don't know what I want to do."

The question of a regular Wac army is still undecided. At a recent press conference Gen. Stephen C. Henry, assistant chief of staff in charge of personnel, said that it was a legislative matter, and so far Congress has made no moves.

At the other extreme an attractive sergeant, asked if she was glad to get out, cried, "Are you kidding? I bought my first dress in three years yesterday—black and slinky."

Regardless of what they do and any temporary bewilderment, they'll take with them not only new and valuable training in different trades, but a sense of independence and a greater tolerance toward people and ideas.

Doria Higgins, " 'After the Army-What'—Women in Uniform Ask?" *Washington News Digest* as cited in the Appendix to the *Congressional Record*, Volume 91, Part 13, 79th Congress, pp. A-5369.

11

Life in the Fifties

"I wanna be Bobby's girl," the singer in the 1950's song pleaded. "I wanna be Bobby's girl; that's the most important thing to me," she continued. And if one were to believe the magazines, songs, and many of the books that appeared during the decade, being someone's "girl" was indeed the most important thing to the American female. The depression and the war years had been uncertain and difficult. Part of the return to a normal way of life in the United States seemed to mean a restructuring of male and female roles, with women making the home the central concern of their lives.

The Feminine Mystique

The model of the ideal woman as housewife-mother could be seen very clearly in the women's magazines from the late 1940's to the early 1960's. Betty Friedan, in her important and controversial book *The Feminine Mystique*, published in 1963, called the magazines' image of women the "happy housewife heroine." Friedan explained that in the late 1930's the majority of heroines in the magazine stories were career women, adventurous and proud. They were attractive to men because they were interesting individuals. For example, one heroine gave up a date to continue her work at her office;

Betty Friedan.

another had been secretly learning to fly an airplane. Both "got" their men in addition to leading lives of their own choosing. Yet, Friedan found, during the 1950's there were almost no articles or stories about women involved outside their homes. Instead, "the happy housewife" had become the typical heroine. Stories urged women to love their roles as wives and mothers. The following excerpt from a 1960 *McCall's* magazine story illustrated the popular image of women. Radie Lester has been sent to charm camp by her parents. She recalls her parents saying:

> "Now, darling . . . it isn't that we think you aren't attractive, because you are. It's just that—oh, Reginald, tell her why we're giving her this wonderful vacation." And her father had looked up dourly from the *Wall Street Journal.* "It's simple," he had said. "We want you to learn how to throw a tennis match. You've beaten the last four boys you played with. . . . You're nineteen and by normal American standards I am now entitled to have you taken off my hands. . . ."

Almost all fiction conveyed the same message to readers—a man and a family were the only legitimate interests healthy women should have.

Feature articles also reflected society's emphasis on woman's role as housewife-mother. Typical of the tone of the articles was Dorothy Thompson's "Occupation-Housewife" in the March 1949 *Ladies' Home Journal.* Thompson, a well-known journalist, described the advice she gave a woman friend who was ashamed to write "housewife" on an official questionnaire because she felt she had never made anything out of her life. Thompson said, "You might write, business manager, cook, nurse, chauffeur, dressmaker, interior decorator, accountant, caterer, teacher, private secretary. . . ." Her friend complained that in becoming "housewife-mother" she had had to give up her music. Thompson reminded her that all her children were musical. "You are one of the most successful people I know," praised Thompson. Hundreds of articles said similar things.

During the 1950's millions of women tried to live the role of housewife-mother. But housewives who had every convenience imaginable and who followed the advice of hundreds of magazine articles were both more bored and busier than they should have been. Typical housewife Jane Smith, for example, lived in an urban center and had a dishwasher, washing machine, vacuum cleaner, freezer, and other conveniences. But she spent 80.57 hours a week on housework, a study showed. Something seemed to be wrong.

Friedan labeled the problem "the feminine mystique." This, she wrote, was the belief that the highest value and the only commitment for women was to fit into the housewife-mother ideal. These jobs, according to the mystique, were the only suitable work for females. Those who created the mystique said that the cause of women's troubles in the past had been their envy of men and their attempt to be like men. The mystique taught that it was best for women to accept their nature. This nature was described as passive, accepting of male domination, and nurturing. The mystique taught the women of the 1950's to see themselves solely in terms of these qualities.

Throughout the 1950's this message was conveyed to the convinced and the unconvinced through radio, television, magazines, books by sociologists and psychologists, and advertising. All relied on psychoanalytic thought to support their message. Popular writers wrote and rewrote Freud. Novels, plays, short stories, and magazines "popularized the popularizers."

Chief among the popularizers of Freudian theories were Ferdinand Lundberg and Marynia Farnham, authors of *Modern Woman: The Lost Sex*. The book was published in 1947 but had its largest sale several years later. Its main idea was that large numbers of modern women were "psychologically disordered," and their problems were having terrible social and personal effects throughout society. Their problems came from their attempts over the past century to copy men. Lundberg and Farnham believed that women's dissatisfactions and therefore, many of society's problems, could be solved if women regained a feeling of worth from being in the home. Lundberg and

Illustrations of this kind suggested the roles that Americans of the 1950's were expected to play.

Farnham felt that women had to be convinced into organizing their lives around the home and their children—their proper and healthy destiny. (Lundberg and Farnham went so far as to say, for example, that spinsters should be forbidden from teaching because they were not good models of complete women, and children had to be "saved" from them.)

The influence of such theories was clear in magazine articles such as the feature article on American women in the Christmas 1956 issue of *Life* magazine. The psychologist-authors wrote that career women were maladjusted and not properly accepting of the feminine role. Women worked, they said, because they rejected the role of wife and mother. The family of a career woman suffered psychological damage, and the woman herself had to be unhappy.

So the American woman of the 1950's was told in a variety of ways that she could be normal only by centering her life around domestic concerns. These women were urged to express their creativity by buying products for their homes. This was a kind of conspiracy, Friedan believed, in which American industry collaborated. Because it was profitable, she felt, the feminine mystique was taught throughout the decade.

Changing Social Patterns

Statistics certainly proved that patterns of social life were changing in postwar America. By 1950 more girls between 15 and 19 years of age were marrying than women in any other age group. This was the lowest age in the nation's history. One-half of all women were married by the age of 20. In 1959, 14 million young women were engaged by the age of 17. After marriage, they were twice as likely to have more than three children than women had been 20 years earlier.

The percentage of women attending college in comparison with men dropped from 47 percent in 1920 to 35 percent in 1958. Sixty percent of women students dropped out of college to marry or to "avoid becoming overeducated" and spoiling their chances of marriage, such as Radie Lester in the story quoted above.

College professors and other educators voiced their concern over the patterns that were developing in both women's and coeducational colleges during the 1950's. Of the brightest 40 percent of American high school graduates, only one-half went on to college. Of those who stopped their education before college, two-thirds were female. By 1958, five women's colleges had closed and 21 had become coed. Fewer than one out of every ten doctorates granted went to women, as compared to one in six in 1920. Educators complained of the boredom and lack of interest of their female students, many of whom chose the less demanding secretarial and home economics courses of study.

Some educators explained these changes by pointing to cultural teachings that conditioned women not to become involved in subjects that required intense study. Others criticized the direction that education had taken, saying that education had "defemininized" American women. Lynn White, a prominent male educator and Mills College president, called for a curriculum for women that would emphasize the teaching of adjustment to home and family. Educating women as men were educated, he felt, produced frustration in later life. White believed education for women should teach them applied arts they would use as buyers, cooks, and mothers. Women were discouraged from the areas of pure science and fine arts and urged into home economics, psychology, and education.

The Women's Bureau studied 3,000 randomly selected female college graduates of the class of June 1955. The bureau found that 80 percent had jobs; nearly 1500 were teachers. The bureau also found that these women graduates viewed their college education as something other than preparation for future employment. By their own reports, only one-quarter of the group were interested in a career. Another one-quarter said they expected to work "only as necessary" but did not have a career in mind. About 50 percent of those graduates considered paid employment a temporary activity between school and marriage.

The World of Work

Not everyone accepted the belief that women belonged in the home. Some educators and community leaders were becoming aware of the growing role of work in women's lives. Educators also realized the increasing needs of postwar America for trained man- and woman-power. And, in actuality, the feminine mystique's understanding of the reality of women's lives was not accurate. Not only were many housewives unable to identify with the image of the perfect housewife-mother, but many of them were not even full-time housewives. Throughout the depression and war, and into the 1950's, there was a steady movement of wives and mothers from household activities into the world of paid employment.

It was a matter of extensive public concern during World War II as to how many women would stay in the labor force after the war. Many men recalled the high unemployment of the 1930's and believed that when defense production came to an end, jobs would be scarce again. Women in the labor force would make competition for jobs even keener. But a Women's Bureau survey in 1945 showed that 75 percent of the women workers intended to continue working.

Between June and September 1945, one out of every four employed women was fired or quit. By 1947 the female labor force had decreased by about 5 million. The trend started to reverse after this, however, especially for married women. In 1940, 17 percent of all married women worked for pay. By 1950 the percentage had grown to 24 percent and by 1962, 33 percent of all white married women were employed. Nearly 50 percent of all black and Puerto Rican wives worked. Contrary to the feminine mystique, working women were becoming the rule rather than the exception in the 1950's.

By 1959 the labor force included about 36 percent of all females over the age of 14. The American economy had become very dependent on the work of women. The schoolgirl of 1959 would never know from reading the *Ladies' Home Journal* that she was likely to spend one-half of her adult years in paid employment. And the income from her work would probably not be used to buy luxuries. Many women worked because their income was needed to maintain a comfortable standard of living for their families. Over one-half of these working women either supported themselves or were primarily responsible for the support of their families.

But the society of the 1950's had little sympathy for the 22 million working women. Most were in low-paying clerical or service jobs, and the median wage for women in 1956, $1,363, was more than $2,000 less than the $3,552 the average man earned. This was only partly explained by differences in pay caused by part-time and temporary work patterns. The least awareness and sympathy went to the over 2.5 million working mothers of children under six. Most psychologists and sociologists believed these women were doing terrible damage to their families and society. But famed anthropologist Margaret Mead disagreed. At present, she wrote, the child's

> need for care by human beings [is being] hopelessly confused in the growing insistence that child and biological mother . . . must never be separated. . . . This is a new and subtle form of anti-feminism in which men . . . are tying women more tightly to their children than has been thought necessary since the invention of bottle feeding and baby carriages. . . .

Mead criticized psychologists for their insistence on constant mother-child contact.

In spite of isolated objections, however, it was true that the society of the 1950's pressured all married women who worked to consider work secondary to their home responsibilities.

Women did work, in spite of the mystique, and they became successful and respected during the decade. Though few in number, women were a part of the government of the nation. Oveta Culp Hobby was appointed Secretary of Health, Education and Welfare by President Eisenhower and Ivy Baker Priest served as United States Treasurer. The United States Ambassador to Italy from 1953 to 1956 was Clare Booth Luce, a former congresswoman and a suc-

Elizabeth Eckford was followed by a jeering crowd after troops barred her from entering Little Rock's Central High School.

Marilyn Monroe.

cessful playwright. Another capable woman, Margaret Chase Smith, of Maine, won a prestigious Senate seat in 1948.

Women served as forceful leaders in the struggle for civil rights. This struggle led to violent confrontation between whites and blacks during the later years of the 1950's. Charlotte Bass, a journalist and publisher, broke with the Republican Party after World War II over civil rights and peace issues and became a founding member of the Progressive party. In 1950 this black woman took the unusual step of running for Congress, and in 1952 she was a candidate for Vice-President. Although unsuccessful, she remained a militant community leader.

When the civil rights movement erupted in violence in Little Rock, Arkansas, in 1957, the leader of the Arkansas NAACP was Daisy Lee Bates, a newspaper editor and publisher. She guided the nine black students who had been chosen to integrate Little Rock's all-white Central High School. Six of those students were girls, and many Americans watched as one of them, 15-year-old Elizabeth Eckford, tried to enter the school on September 4. She was turned away by the bayonets of National Guardsmen and faced a mob of white women and men screaming to lynch her. The struggles of these six girls brought into sharp focus the double discrimination faced by black women.

Women continued to participate in sports. Althea Gibson was recognized as one of the world's great tennis players throughout the decade. She became the first black to compete in tennis matches in Forest Hills, New York and Wimbledon, England, winning both titles in 1957 and 1958.

In literature, women continued their successes in educating and entertaining the public. In *Gift From the Sea,* Anne Morrow Lindbergh questioned the role American women were expected to play. Gwendolyn Brooks became the first black poet to win a Pulitzer Prize. An educated and thoughtful scientist, Rachel Carson, exposed the dangers Americans faced from pollutants in her influential study *Silent Spring.*

But, in spite of continuing involvement in government, literary, and scientific life, the idealized American woman was still quite different from Margaret Chase Smith or Althea Gibson. Many young girls chose as their ideal the major film star of the period, Marilyn Monroe. Blond, soft-spoken, innocent but enormously sexy, she starred in a variety of successful films. She was photographed nude for *Playboy* magazine, which rapidly became one of the most successful publications in the country. Monroe became the leading sex symbol of the 1950's. The stardom her talent and body brought her also drove her to kill herself in 1962 when she was only 36 years old.

Summary

The belief that women were healthiest when they were housewives and mothers remained strong throughout the decade of the 1950's, in spite of the conflicting realities. When she was 32 years old, the average American woman's last child was in school. With a life expectancy of 77 years, she had 45 "leftover" years to live. Sociologists urged society to change its role expectations of women who often felt lonely and useless. But attitudes changed very little, if at all, until 1963 when Betty Friedan published *The Feminine Mystique,* her study of the 1950's. Her work and those of others caused Americans to sharply question their views about male and female roles.

THE FEMININE MYSTIQUE

In 1963 Betty Friedan's book *The Feminine Mystique* was published. Her analysis of the role society encouraged women of the 1950's to play was widely publicized and became the center of much controversy.

The Problem That Has No Name

The problem lay buried, unspoken, for many years in the minds of American women. It was a strange stirring, a sense of dissatisfaction, a yearning that women suffered in the middle of the twentieth century in the United States. Each suburban wife struggled with it alone. As she made the beds, shopped for groceries, matched slipcover material, ate peanut butter sandwiches with her children, chauffeured Cub Scouts and Brownies, lay beside her husband at night—she was afraid to ask even of herself the silent question—"Is this all?"

For over fifteen years there was no word of this yearning in the millions of words written about women, for women, in all the columns, books and articles by experts telling women their role was to seek fulfillment as wives and mothers. Over and over women heard in voices of tradition and of Freudian sophistication that they could desire no greater destiny than to glory in their own femininity. Experts told them how to catch a man and keep him, how to breastfeed children and handle their toilet training, how to cope with sibling rivalry and adolescent rebellion; how to buy a dishwasher, bake bread, cook gourmet snails, and build a swimming pool with their own hands; how to dress, look, and act more feminine and make marriage more exciting; how to keep their husbands from dying young and their sons from growing into delinquents. They were taught to pity the neurotic, unfeminine, unhappy women who wanted to be poets or physicists or presidents. They learned that truly feminine women do not want careers, higher education, political rights—the independence and the opportunities that the old-fashioned feminists fought for. Some women, in their forties and fifties, still remembered painfully giving up those dreams, but most of the younger women no longer even thought about them. A thousand expert voices applauded their femininity, their adjustment, their new maturity. All they had to do was devote their lives from earliest girlhood to finding a husband and bearing children . . .

Just what was this problem that has no name? What were the words women used when they tried to express it? Sometimes a woman would say "I feel empty somehow . . . incomplete." Or she would say, "I feel as if I don't exist." Sometimes she blotted out the feeling with a tranquilizer. Sometimes she thought the problem was with her husband, or her children, or that what she really needed was to redecorate her house, or move to a better neighborhood, or have an affair, or another baby . . .

The Happy Housewife Heroine

The feminine mystique began to spread through the land, grafted onto old prejudices and comfortable conventions which so easily give the past a stranglehold on the future. Behind the new mystique were concepts and theories deceptive in their sophistication and their assumption of accepted truth. These theories were supposedly so complex that they were [known only to a few and therefore impossible to disprove.] It will be necessary to break through this wall of mystery and look more closely at these complex concepts, these accepted truths, to understand fully what has happened to American women.

The feminine mystique says that the highest value and the only commitment for women is the fulfillment of their own femininity. It says that the great mistake of Western culture, through most of its history, has been the undervaluation of this femininity. It says this femininity is so mysterious and intuitive and close to the creation and origin of life that man-made science may never be able to understand it. But however special and different, it is in no way inferior to the nature of man; it may even in certain respects be superior. The mistake, says the mystique, the root of women's troubles in the past is that women envied men, women tried to be like men, instead of accepting their own nature, which can find fulfillment only in sexual passivity, male domination, and nurturing maternal love.

But the new image this mystique gives to American women is the old image: "Occupation: housewife." The new mystique makes the housewife-mothers, who never had a chance to be anything else, the model for all women; it presupposes that history has reached a final and glorious end in the here and now, as far as women are concerned. Beneath the sophisticated trappings, it simply makes certain concrete, finite domestic aspects of feminine existence—as it was lived by women whose lives were confined, by necessity, to cooking, cleaning, washing, bearing children—into a religion, a pattern by which all women must now live or deny their femininity.

Fulfillment as a woman had only one definition for American women after 1949—the housewife-mother. As swiftly as in a dream, the image of the American woman as a changing, growing individual in a changing world was shattered. Her solo flight to find her own identity was forgotten in the rush for the security of togetherness. Her limitless world shrunk to the cozy walls of home.

Betty Friedan, *The Feminine Mystique* (New York: W. W. Norton and Co., 1963), pp. 15-16, 20, 43-44. By permission of W. W. Norton and Company, Inc.

THE "REAL" AMERICAN WOMAN

In 1956, *Life* magazine published a special Christmas issue on the American woman. The introduction, which set the tone of the issue, described most Americans' feelings about the role of the woman in the United States.

. . . In addition to her new responsibilities this present-day woman finds that she has certain strong urges and instinctive needs. If she is to be a truly happy person, those needs must be met. Ask any thoughtful, honest woman what the most satisfying moments of her life have been and she will never mention the day she got her first job or the day she outwitted her boss on his ground. But she will always speak of the night when, as a teen-ager, she wore her first formal and twirled in the arms of a not-so-bad date to tingly music. Or the night the man she loved took her in his arms, bringing a special look to her face. Then there was the moment when she held her first baby in her arms. It was not just releasing, it was completely fulfilling.

When women do *not* have the deep satisfaction of these experiences, their troubles begin . . .

Catherine Marshall, "The American Woman," *Life* (December 24, 1956), Vol. 41, #26, p. 2.

MARGARET MEAD ANALYZES FEMALE AND MALE ROLES IN AMERICA

In her 1949 book *Male and Female,* famed anthropologist Margaret Mead analyzed the very different roles that females and males play in other cultures and then discussed the different sexual patterns she found here in her native land. In the excerpt that follows she discussed the ways American family patterns were changing and offered some suggestions for the future.

Each Family in a Home of Its Own

Perhaps the most significant word in family relationships that has been invented for a very long time is the word "sitter"—the extra person who must come into the family and sit whenever the two parents go out of it together. The modern wife and mother lives alone, with a husband who comes home in the evening, and children, who as little children are on her hands twenty-four hours out of twenty-four, in a house that she is expected to run with the efficiency of a factory—for hasn't she a washing machine and a vacuum cleaner?—and from which a great number of the compensations that once went with being a home-maker have been removed. Except in rural areas, she no longer produces, in the sense of preserving and pickling and canning. She has no [bursts] of house-cleaning twice a year. She doesn't give the sort of party where she is admired because of the heaps of food that she has . . . prepared [to show off], but instead she is admired just in proportion to the way she "looks as if it had taken her no time at all." As our factories move towards the ideal of eliminating human labor, our home ideals have paralleled them; the successful homemaker today should always look as if she had neither done any work nor would have to do any; she should produce a finished effect effortlessly, even if she has to spend all day Saturday rehearsing the way in which she will serve an effortless Sunday-morning breakfast. The creativity that is expected of her is a creativity of management of an assembly-line, not of materials lovingly fashioned into food and clothes for children. She shops, she markets, she chooses, she transports, she integrates, she co-ordinates, she fits little bits of time together so as "to get through the week," and her proudest boast often has to be "It was a good week. Nothing went wrong."

To Both Their Own

. . . If we once accept the premise that we can build a better world by using the different gifts of each sex, we shall have two kinds of freedom, freedom to use untapped gifts of each sex, and freedom to admit freely and cultivate in each sex their special superiorities. We may well find that there are certain fields, such as the physical sciences, mathematics, and instrumental music, in which men by virtue of their sex, as well as by virtue of their qualities as specially gifted human beings, will always have that razor-edge of extra gift which makes all the difference, and that while women may easily follow where men lead, men will always make the new discoveries. We may equally well find that women, through the learning involved in maternity, which once experienced can be taught more easily to all women, even childless women, than to men, have a special superiority in those human sciences which involve that type of understanding which until it is analyzed is called intuition . . .

Once it is possible to say it is as important to take women's gifts and make them available to both men and women . . . as it was to take men's gifts and make the civilization built upon them available to both men and women, we shall have enriched our society . . .

Margaret Mead, *Male and Female* (New York: William Morrow and Co., 1949), pp. 332-333, 382. Reprinted by permission.

WORKINGMAN'S WIFE

In 1959 a book called *Workingman's Wife* was published. Its purpose was to explain the findings of a study of the lives of the "working class woman". The authors found that the daily concerns of these women centered on the tasks of home-making, child-rearing and being a good wife to their husbands. In the following selection, some of the women they interviewed speak for themselves about their daily lives.

. . . The first description was given by a 24-year old woman from Trenton, New Jersey. She lives in one of Levittown's modest new houses:

"Well, naturally, I get up first, make breakfast for my husband and put a load of clothes in my washer while breakfast cooks. Then I wake him up, give him his breakfast and he's off to work. Then I make breakfast for the children. After the children eat I dress them and they go out to play. Then I hang the clothes up and clean lightly through the house. In between times I do the dishes—that's understood, of course. Then I make lunch for the children and myself and I bring them in, clean them up, and they eat. I send them out to play when they're done and I do the dishes, bring the clothes in, and iron them. When I'm ironing it's usually time to make supper, or at least start preparing it. Sometimes I have time to watch a TV story for half an hour or so. Then my husband comes home and we have our meals. Then I do dishes again. Then he goes out to work again—he has a part-time job—at his uncle's beverage company. Well, he does that two or three nights a week. If he stays home he watches TV and in the meantime I get the kids ready for bed. He and I have a light snack, watch TV awhile and then go to bed . . . "

Here is a story of harassment told by a 23-year old Louisville [Kentucky] mother of two young children:

"Well, I fight with the children to eat for one thing. They don't want to eat. The little girl—she's 4—is hungry and then she won't eat. They usually go on outside after breakfast. I feed the baby and give him a bath and then I put him on the floor. Then I make the bed up, dust the floors and dust the furniture and by that time it's time for dinner. Then I fix dinner and do the dishes. In between time I have to feed him and give him a bath and put him to bed. Then it's time to fix supper and Daddy comes home. After supper we just sit here and watch TV or I visit one of the neighbors. We very seldom go out during the week because he works. My husband may wash the car or something like that. Other than that he just watches TV or goes to sleep. He putters around the yard or reads maybe. He is usually too tired after he comes home from work. The children just spend the whole day playing and getting messed up. Then they watch TV after supper with me. Then they get washed and go to bed about 9 o'clock."

Another wife describes her day and her feelings about it:

"Crowded, just crowded—that's what every day is like. They're all busy. They're just dull too. We just don't do much except work. They're dull compared to those you read about in the newspapers of people who run around all the time.

Oh, it's housework all day long. We really don't do very much—I would like to get out more if I weren't so isolated out here. My husband has the car all day long, so I'm sort of stuck here.

All I ever seem to do is mess around. I get up at 8—I make breakfast, so I do the dishes, have lunch, do some more dishes, and then some more work in the afternoons. Then it's supper dishes and I get to sit down for a few minutes before the children have to be sent to bed. That's it—that's all there is to my day.

My day's just like any other wife's. It's just routine. Humdrum. It's really just what every other housewife does.

We don't do much of anything special. I imagine my day is spent doing what any housewife does. Just cooking and cleaning, washing the dishes and mending clothes. Then the biggest part of the time I am chasing kids."

Lee Rainwater, Richard Coleman, and Gerald Handel, *Workingman's Wife* (New York: Oceana Publications, 1959), pp. 27-28, 32. Copyright 1959 by Social Research Inc. Reprinted by permission of the publisher.

THE YOUNG WOMEN OF LITTLE ROCK

In September 1957, as a result of a court order, nine black students were chosen by Little Rock, Arkansas school authorities to enter all-white Central High School. The attention of much of the world was focused on this city as it blocked integration attempts with violence and lawlessness. Among the nine students, six were young women who endured terrible experiences and became symbols for the nation. Daisy

Bates, the leader of the Arkansas NAACP, described their experiences in her memoir, *The Long Shadow of Little Rock*. Two of the stories follow.

Elizabeth Eckford [in her words]

That night I was so excited I couldn't sleep. The next morning I was about the first one up. While I was pressing my black and white dress—I had made it to wear on the first day of school—my little brother turned on the TV set. They started telling about a large crowd gathered at the school. The man on TV said he wondered if we were going to show up that morning . . .

Before I left home Mother called us into the living-room. She said we should have a word of prayer. Then I caught the bus and got off a block from the school. I saw a large crowd of people standing across the street from the soldiers guarding Central. As I walked on, the crowd suddenly got very quiet. Superintendent Blossom had told us to enter by the front door. I looked at all the people and thought, "Maybe I will be safer if I walk down the block to the front entrance behind the guards."

At the corner I tried to pass through the long line of guards around the school so as to enter the grounds behind them. One of the guards pointed across the street. So I pointed in the same direction and asked whether he meant for me to cross the street and walk down. He nodded "yes." So, I walked across the street conscious of the crowd that stood there, but they moved away from me.

For a moment all I could hear was the shuffling of their feet. Then someone shouted, "Here she comes, get ready!" I moved away from the crowd on the sidewalk and into the street. If the mob came at me I could then cross back over so the guards could protect me.

The crowd moved in closer and then began to follow me, calling me names. I still wasn't afraid. Just a little bit nervous. Then my knees started to shake all of a sudden and I wondered whether I could make it to the center entrance a block away. It was the longest block I ever walked in my whole life.

Even so, I still wasn't too scared because all the time I kept thinking that the guards would protect me.

When I got right in front of the school, I went up to a guard again. But this time he just looked straight ahead and didn't move to let me pass him. I didn't know what to do. Then I looked and saw that the path leading to the front entrance was a little further ahead. So I walked until I was right in front of the path to the front door.

I stood looking at the school—it looked so big! Just then the guards let some white students go through.

The crowd was quiet. I guess they were waiting to see what was going to happen. When I was able to steady my knees, I walked up to the guard who had let the white students in. He too didn't move. When I tried to squeeze past him, he raised his bayonet and then the other guards closed in and they raised their bayonets.

They glared at me with a mean look and I was very frightened and didn't know what to do. I turned around and the crowd came toward me.

They moved closer and closer. Somebody started yelling, "Lynch her! Lynch her!"

I tried to see a friendly face somewhere in the mob—someone who maybe would help. I looked into the face of an old woman and it seemed a kind face, but when I looked at her again, she spat on me.

They came closer, shouting, "No nigger bitch is going to get in our school. Get out of here!"

I turned back to the guards but their faces told me I wouldn't get help from them. Then I looked down the block and saw a bench at the bus stop. I thought, "If I can only get there I will be safe." I don't know why the bench seemed a safe place to me, but I started walking toward it. I tried to close my mind to what they were shouting, and kept saying to myself, "If I can only make it to the bench I will be safe."

When I finally got there, I don't think I could have gone another step. I sat down and the mob crowded up and began shouting all over again. Someone hollered, "Drag her over to this tree! Let's take care of the nigger." Just then a white man sat down beside me, put his arm around me and patted my shoulder. He raised my chin and said, "Don't let them see you cry."

Then a white lady—she was very nice—she came over to me on the bench. She spoke to me but I don't remember what she said. She put me on the bus and sat next to me. She asked my name and tried to talk to me but I don't think I answered. I can't remember much about the bus ride, but the next thing I remember I was standing in front of the School for the Blind, where Mother works.

Minnijean Brown

Minnijean Brown, sixteen years old and in the eleventh grade, was tall, attractive, and outgoing. Her manner was friendly and good-natured . . .

The first of these incidents took place on October 2, 1957. Minnijean and Melba Pattilo were roughed up by several unidentified boys and girls in the corridors as they left their second class for the day.

One girl deliberately ran into Minnijean, and a group of boys formed a line to block her entrance to her classroom. Then followed an incredible catalogue of violence:

Minnijean was kicked by a boy as she was going to her seat at "pep" assembly, prior to a football game.

She was threatened by a pupil who said, "I will chase you down the hall and kick all your teeth out the next time you do what you did yesterday afternoon." The boy alleged that she had made insulting gestures at him. Minnijean insisted she did not remember ever seeing him before. The boy was taken to the principal's office and reprimanded.

By the middle of December Minnijean had had enough. After repeated provocation by white pupils blocking her path as she attempted to reach a table in the cafeteria, she warned her persecutors that they might get something on their heads. On December 17, when chairs had been shoved in her way, she emptied her tray on the heads of the two boys. These boys excused her, saying that she had been annoyed so frequently they "didn't blame her for getting mad." The boys were sent home to change their clothing. But Minnijean was suspended for six days because of the incident.

Soon after she returned to her classes, a pupil emptied a bowl of hot soup on Minnijean. The reason he gave was that he remembered she had earlier spilled chili on two white boys. He was suspended for three days . . . [Minnijean was eventually expelled for the term and went to school in New York City.]

Daisy Bates, *The Long Shadow of Little Rock: A Memoir* (New York: David McKay Co. Inc., 1962), pp. 73-75, 116-118. Reprinted by permission.

EDUCATED WORKING WOMEN

In the middle of the 1960's a study was published which described the lives of some of the women who had attended Columbia University in the 1940's and 1950's and who had been judged to be outstanding. Ideas about her proper role were different for Florence Usher, a psychiatrist, than for many other American women of the time.

Florence Usher

. . . All of the women in my family worked. It was expected that I would. Both of my parents were professionals and this influenced my choice to take up a professional occupation, especially since the limitations of a non-professional life appeared substantial . . . [My father] shared the view that women should do whatever work they were equipped to do and gave me faith in myself, determination and moral support.

I was born in Philadelphia in 1919, the second of three children, and I grew up in Chicago. My older sister, who died a few years ago, was an architect, and my younger brother is an engineer. I entered Swarthmore College in 1936, and transferred the following year to Vassar, where I majored in psychology with the goal of becoming a psychologist. By the end of my undergraduate years, I had changed my goal to psychiatry. . . .

My husband, who had one year of college, was a statistical clerk and later an accountant in New York. For the few years after I graduated from college, I worked in that city, first in various clerical jobs and later as a biochemical technician, in order to acquire the money I needed. The latter position was the only one which provided not only a salary but also interesting work. By 1943 I was ready to enter medical school, but my applications to three New York City schools were rejected. Because of my husband's work, I was limited to institutions in New York. Fortunately, I was finally admitted to one of them, the College of Physicians and Surgeons, in 1944. These rejections of my applications to medical school are the only evidence of sex discrimination that I have encountered. It was probably World War II and the shortage of male applicants which finally secured my admission, for a woman, 25 years old, married, and out of college 4 years had a better chance than at other times. Being a Negro may have hindered my career in spots, but it had aided it in others . . .

I gave birth to my only child during the winter of my last year in medical school and received my M.D. the following spring . . . In 1952 I opened a private practice in addition to my part-time clinic consulting, and in 1954 I completed my training and received a certificate as a psychoanalyst.

Five years later I was appointed associate attending psychiatrist at a large hospital where I engaged in part-time hospital practice and clinic work, for which I was paid $6,800 a year. I continued in private practice until 1961, when I became director of the department of psychiatry at a public hospital, at a salary of $25,000 a year. This was an opportunity I had always wanted . . .

Of the women who went to college with me and had the capacity for graduate study, those who went on seem more satisfied than those who didn't. Their families do not appear to have suffered in major ways, though I am sure that there is a physical toll on a working mother which is very real. . . .

Eli Ginzberg and Alice M. Yohalem, *Educated American Women: Self-Portraits* (New York: Columbia University Press, 1966), pp. 30-34. Reprinted by permission of the publisher.

DEVELOPMENT OF WOMANPOWER— RECOMMENDATIONS IN EDUCATION

During the 1950's a number of Americans wrote about the potential power that women could exercise if their training were different and the expectations of society changed. In 1957 the National Manpower Council published an analysis of women in the labor force. Some of their recommendations follow.

In preparing young women not only for the obligation of citizenship and for a rich adult life, but also for work, our secondary schools play a critical part in manpower development. In 1956, girls accounted for just over half of almost 700,000 secondary school graduates, but for many decades they comprised an even larger proportion of the students completing high school. The high schools have long placed a strong emphasis upon vocational courses in which large numbers of girls have been enrolled. The secondary school experience of girls has in part been designed to prepare them not only for the functions of women in the home, but also for initial employment after they leave school.

The expectation that their lives as adults will be defined primarily by marriage and motherhood, and that their experience with paid employment will occur when they leave school and will be of short duration, leads many girls to pursue commercial and other vocational curricula. Existing patterns of employment strongly influence them to prepare for work chiefly in the small number of fields in which women are already heavily concentrated. Fewer girls than boys plan to go to college, and this is reflected in the fact that they are less well represented in high school curricula which prepare for college entrance . . . [However, traditional patterns are changing; especially, older women are returning to work after raising their families.]

With respect to expanding the opportunities for the effective development of womanpower, the National Manpower Council recommends that:

1. School and college officials, boards of education, and Federal, state and local governments expand and improve educational and vocational guidance, in order to help young women make sound decisions with respect to their self-development, the growing and changing employment opportunities open to them, and the probability that paid employment will occupy a significant place in their adult lives.

2. The Federal and state governments, employers, unions, and voluntary organizations cooperate to increase occupational guidance and placement services for mature women who want to work, in

order to help them make sound decisions in the light of their individual interests, capacities, and employment opportunities.

3. The Federal and state governments, employers, labor unions, voluntary groups, and individuals expand their support of scholarship and fellowship programs, in order to enable more young women of high ability to continue their formal education in college or in professional or graduate schools.

4. State governments, in cooperation with local communities, educational institutions, employers, and labor unions, initiate surveys to determine whether existing training facilities are adequate to meet the needs of mature women who want to work, and in what ways mature women can be helped to meet the requirements for employment in professional or semiprofessional occupations where manpower shortages exist.

National Manpower Council, *Womanpower* (New York: Columbia University Press, 1957), pp. 31, 35. Copyright held by Henry David. Reprinted by permission.

EDUCATING AMERICAN WOMEN — A CONTRASTING VIEW

In the 1950's there were many different views about the type of education women should have. In the selection that follows, Lynn White, who had been president of Mills College, suggests a special curriculum for college women.

On my desk lies a letter from a young mother, a few years out of college: "I have come to realize that I was educated to be a successful man and now must learn by myself how to be a successful woman." The basic irrelevance of much of what passes as women's education in America could not be more compactly phrased . . .

. . . One may [predict] with confidence that as women begin to make their distinctive wishes felt in curricula terms, not merely will every women's college and coeducational institution offer a firm nuclear course in the Family but from it will radiate curricular series [courses] dealing with food and nutrition, textiles and clothing, health and nursing, house planning and interior decoration, garden design and applied botany, and child development. Each of these series will begin at the non-professional level and continue into professional training for specialized advanced students . . .

. . . Why not study the theory and preparation of Basque paella [rice and seafood dish], of a well-marinated shish-kebab, lamb kidneys sautéed in sherry, and authoritative curry, the uses of herbs, even such simple sophistications as serving cold artichokes with fresh milk. A girl majoring in history or chemistry could well find time for one such course which, we may be sure, would do much to enliven her own life and that of her family and friends in later years. It is rumored that the divorce rate of home economics majors is greatly below that of college women as a whole . . .

Lynn White, *Educating Our Daughters: A Challenge to the Colleges* (New York: Harper and Bros., 1950), pp. 18, 77-78. Abridged and adapted. Reprinted by permission.

ANNE MORROW LINDBERGH REFLECTS ON HER LIFE

Anne Lindbergh, a well-known American writer and the wife of aviator Charles Lindbergh, wrote *Gift From the Sea* in 1955. In this book she reflected on the difficulties of being a modern American woman.

The shape of my life today starts with a family. I have a husband, five children and a home just beyond the suburbs of New York. I have also a craft, writing, and therefore work I want to pursue. The shape of my life is, of course, determined by many other things; my background and childhood, my mind and its education, my conscience and its pressures, my heart and its desires. I want to give and take from my children and husband, to share with friends and community, to carry out my obligations to man and to the world, as a woman, as an artist, as a citizen.

But I want first of all—in fact, as an end to these other desires—to be at peace with myself . . .

I mean to lead a simple life, to choose a simple shell I can carry easily—like a hermit crab. But I do not. I find that my frame of life does not foster simplicity. My husband and five children must make their way in the world. The life I have chosen as wife and mother entrains a whole caravan of complications. It involves a house in the suburbs and either household drudgery or household help which wavers between scarcity and non-existence for most of us. It involves food and shelter; meals, planning, marketing, bills, and making the ends meet in a thousand ways. It involves not only the butcher, the baker, the candlestickmaker, but countless other experts to keep my modern house with its modern "simplifications" . . . functioning properly. It involves health; doctors, dentists, appointments, medicine, cod-liver oil, vitamins, trips to the drugstore. It involves education, spiritual, intellectual, physical; schools, school conferences, car-pools, extra trips for basket-ball or orchestra practice; tutoring; camps, camp equipment and transportation . . .

For life today in America is based on the premise of ever-widening circles of contact and communication . . . My mind reels with it. What a circus act we women perform every day of our lives. It puts the trapeze artist to shame. Look at us. We run a tight rope daily, balancing a pile of books on the head. Baby-carriage, parasol, kitchen chair still under control. Steady now!

This is not the life of simplicity but the life of multiplicity that the wise men warn us of. It leads not to unification but to fragmentation. It does not bring grace; it destroys the soul. And this is not only true of my life, I am forced to conclude; it is the life of millions of women in America. I stress America, because today, the American woman more than any other has the privilege of choosing such a life. Woman in large parts of the civilized world has been forced back by war, by poverty, by collapse, by the sheer struggle to survive, into a smaller circle of immediate time and space, immediate family life, immediate problems of existence. The American woman is still relatively free to choose the wider life . . .

With a new awareness, both painful and humorous, I begin to understand why the saints were rarely married women. I am convinced it has nothing inherently to do as I once supposed with chastity or children. It has to do primarily with distractions. The bearing, rearing, feeding and educating of children; the running of a house with its thousand details; human relationships with their [many] pulls—woman's normal occupations in general run counter to creative life, or contemplative life, or saintly life. The problem is not merely one of *Woman and Career, Woman and the Home, Woman and Independence.* It is more basically: how to remain whole in the midst of the distractions of life; how to remain balanced . . .

Anne Morrow Lindbergh, *Gift From the Sea* (New York: Pantheon, 1955), pp. 22-23, 25-27, 29. Reprinted by permission.

12

The Modern Women's Movement

"Do you believe in Women's Lib?" This question is one that women, old and young, are being asked more and more frequently today. But women find it a difficult question to answer because the term "women's liberation" includes a wide variety of beliefs and actions. All will agree, though, that since the early 1960's women and men in America have been pressing for many changes in society's views and treatment of its female members. There is much disagreement about the directions any changes should take.

Law and Government

In 1963 Betty Friedan's book *The Feminine Mystique* was published. Its main idea was that women were being trapped into the home by a variety of pressures in society. This idea was hotly debated and caused many women to begin rethinking their lives. That same year the Commission on the Status of Women presented its report "American Woman" to the nation. This also helped to make women and men aware of the special role of women in America.

The commission, which had been created by President John F. Kennedy, was chaired by Eleanor Roosevelt until her death shortly before the report was published. The purpose of the commission was to examine women's role and to recommend solutions to combat "the prejudices and outmoded customs [that] act as barriers to the full realization of women's basic rights . . . " The outcome of its study was a report that analyzed women's role and status in such fields as labor and income, marriage and the law and the position of black women in society. In general, the report's recommendations were moderate and did not question such basic assumptions about family life that child care and homemaking were women's jobs. It supported an equal pay act, paid maternity leave, and encouragement of part-time employment, but it did not support an Equal Rights Amendment.

The impact of the commission on American life, however, lay more in its existence than in its recommendations. It was the first official body established by the government to examine the position of American women. It drew national attention to discrimination against women. By 1967 every state had a similar commission.

Since 1963 the federal government has enacted a number of measures designed to eliminate discrimination against women. The first of these was the Equal Pay Act which required that men and women receive equal pay for equal work performed under equal circumstances. In order to get around the law, employers often use different titles for women, such as "executive assistant." Working women find that beliefs supporting unequal pay for women are hard to eliminate. How many working women have been told that "Men have families to support and therefore need more money" or "Women aren't as reliable as men; they are absent more and leave jobs more than men"? Although statistics disprove both assumptions, discrimination continues, and a wide earnings gap is still the reality for many American women. The 1970 census showed that the female who had finished high school earned only 56 percent of the amount earned by men of equivalent age and education. Working women with four years of college earned only 55 percent of the median amount earned by college-educated men—$7,930 as opposed to $13,320.

Women's groups hope that enforcement of the Equal Pay Act will help to eliminate these differences.

The next major piece of legislation affecting women was Title VII of the Civil Rights Act of 1964. It prohibited discrimination by private employers, employment agencies, and unions because of race, color, religion, national origin, or sex. Federal, state, and local governments, as well as educational institutions, were exempted at that time, but in 1972 the Equal Employment Opportunity Acts extended coverage of Title VII to these groups as well.

Women have been moving into jobs traditionally held by men. These jobs often increase the economic potential of women.

The 1964 civil rights bill was originally designed to eliminate discrimination against blacks. But 81-year-old Representative Howard Smith of Virginia, who opposed the bill, tried to kill it. He added a provision outlawing "sex" discrimination in the hope that the bill would be "laughed to death." Liberals and most women's organizations did not want to add "sex" to the bill because they did not want it to be defeated. They also feared that laws protecting working women would be endangered. To the surprise of many, the bill did pass and numerous forms of sex discrimination became illegal.

The sex provision of the Civil Rights Act was often treated as a joke. At a 1965 White House conference someone wondered if the Playboy clubs would have to hire male "bunnies"; some people began referring to the law as the "bunny law." A *New York Times* editorial complained that the Rockettes might have to hire men! The agency responsible for implementing the law, the Equal Employment Opportunity Commission [EEOC] itself wavered in its interpretations of the law.

Laws that provided special protection for working women began to be questioned. Some people felt that a law prohibiting a woman from lifting anything heavier than 30 pounds on the job discriminated against her. Many others, including most women's groups, felt these laws protected women. In 1963, for example, 40 states and the District of Columbia had maximum-hours laws for women. But the passage of Title VII brought many court cases against these laws, and by 1971 only ten states retained such laws without changes.

A landmark case testing protection laws occurred when Lorena Weeks of Georgia took Southern Bell Telephone to court, claiming that she had not been promoted because of a Georgia law that limited the weight of objects a woman could lift on the job. The United States Court of Appeals interpreted Title VII to mean these "protections" discriminated against women.

> Men have always had the right to determine whether the increase in [payment] for strenuous, dangerous, obnoxious, boring or unromantic tasks is worth the [effort]. The promise of Title VII is that women are now to be on equal footing.

The decision was an important one for opponents of protective legislation. Three years later, in April 1971, Southern Bell finally promoted Lorena Weeks and gave her back pay of nearly $31,000. Through such court cases under Title VII, the work and domestic life of American women began to change.

In 1972 the Equal Employment Opportunity Act extended coverage of Title VII to federal, state, and local governments as well as to educational institutions. Some legislators feel that more women will be found in high-level civil service jobs, where they are now only about 1 percent of the workers.

As recently as 1975 there were no women in the United States Senate and only a few female Representatives. But increasing numbers of women gained office on the state and local levels. Ella Grasso of Connecticut became the first female governor elected in her own right and New York State voters elected Mary Ann Krupsak as the state's first female lieutenant governor.

Although attempts are being made to bring women into government, many American leaders often seem to be amused by serious efforts on the part of women. In the summer of 1971 over 200 women organized the National Women's Political Caucus to help put women in high government positions. Such people as *Ms.* editor Gloria Steinem, writer Betty Friedan, and Congresswomen Bella Abzug and Shirley Chisholm participated in the organization of the group. President Nixon and his Secretary of State William Rogers were discussing the Caucus at a picture-taking session. Rogers suggested that the Caucus leaders "looked like a burlesque show," and Nixon asked, "What's wrong with that?" Henry Kissinger, who became Secretary of State after Rogers, was quoted in 1973 as saying:

> For me, women are only amusing, a hobby. No one spends too much time on a hobby.

These attitudes exist on all levels of government and make power for women difficult to achieve.

By the early 1970's women's groups were powerful enough to lobby successfully for enactment of two highly significant pieces of legislation. In 1972 the passage of Title IX of the Education amendments was a major step in prohibiting discrimination in education at all levels. It read:

> No person in the United States shall, on the basis of sex, be excluded from participation in, be denied the benefits of, or be subjected to discrimination under any education program or activity receiving Federal financial assistance.

Shop classes, for example, can no longer be opened only to girls or to boys. Some school districts have ruled that noncontact sports must also be opened to both sexes. Elementary, high school, and college educators are thus forced to take a critical look at their schools, much to the satisfaction of feminists who have criticized sexist practices in schools.

The second major legislative event of the 1970's in the area of women's rights was the passage of the Equal Rights Amendment to the Constitution. The amendment states:

> Equality of rights under the law shall not be denied or abridged by the United States or by any State on account of sex.

The amendment was passed by Congress on March 22, 1972. Thirty-eight states must ratify it by 1979. It had been introduced every year since 1923 when it was first presented by the suffragists of the National Woman's Party. By 1972 many prestigious organizations supported it, including the American Association of University Women, the American Civil Liberties Union, the New York Bar, the Teamsters, the American Federation of Teachers, and the NAACP. But others labeled it a Communist plot and explained that American life would be drastically changed for the worse. Such well-respected Constitutional experts as Senator Sam Ervin of North Carolina opposed it as unnecessary and expressed the fear that its passage would create legal chaos in the country. Some objections to the amendment [ERA] and answers of supporters to those objections are as follows:

1. **Opposed:** The way it is written, ERA would require women to be drafted.

For: No citizen today is drafted because we have a volunteer army. If the draft were resumed, men and women would have to be drafted on the same basis. For example, exemptions for family responsibility would be extended equally to both sexes. With rights come responsibilities.

2. **Opposed:** The ERA will force women to work outside the home because men will no longer be required to support their families.

For: No woman will have to work outside the home under ERA. The single-income family can still exist. If there is a divorce, the one most able to provide will be obligated to provide support.

3. **Opposed:** The ERA will end sex-segregated facilities such as public restrooms and school locker rooms.

For: The ERA does not invalidate an American's right to privacy and does not have this intent.

The most controversial action by the federal government in the early 1970's was the 1973 Supreme Court decision on abortion. A pregnant single woman brought action challenging Texas abortion laws. She wanted an abortion by a competent physician and could not get one legally. She appealed her case to the Court "on behalf of herself and all other women" in a similar position. The Court ruled that for the stage before approximately the first three months of pregnancy, abortion must be permitted, calling on the constitutional protection of an American's right to privacy. Much serious controversy preceded this decision and continued after the Court ruling. Women's groups argued that a woman should be able to control her own body without any interference by the government. Opposing groups, loosely labeled "right-to-life" groups, protested that the government has the obligation to protect life, and that an unborn fetus is alive. Thus, the latter groups argued, abortion should be considered murder. Other organizations disagreed, saying life does not begin until after birth, and the government has never been able to legislate morality. The Court's decision can be overruled only by a Constitutional amendment, and campaigns began in 1973 to pass an amendment to outlaw abortion.

The 1960's and 1970's produced great changes in the legal position of American women. Gradually, as new laws were enforced, women's social position began to change as well.

Feminists Organize

After publication of *The Feminine Mystique* Betty Friedan began to do research in Washington for a second book. There she met others, like herself, who saw the need for an organization to pressure the government to enforce legislation such as the Equal Pay Act. Friedan and others formed the National Organization For Women (NOW) with 300 charter members. Friedan was its first president. Its Bill of Rights, which was written in November 1967, called for a wide variety of changes including passage of the ERA, laws banning sex discrimination, maternity leave benefits, child care centers, and the right of women to be able to control their reproductive lives. Today thousands of women, and some men, belong to NOW and continue to work for reform through legislation.

NOW included among its members women who believed that change could come about through traditional methods of action such as lobbying, political action, and court decisions. But some women began to lose faith in traditional methods and split off to form new, more radical groups. Most of these women saw NOW as too conservative. These were generally younger women who had been involved either in the New Left movement of the 1960's or in the civil rights movement. In both they had felt like "second-class citizens."

At the meetings of the radical New Left Students for a Democratic Society (SDS), women had often felt ignored. They complained about being assigned menial jobs such as making sandwiches or cleaning up. Two of these women, Beverly Jones and Judith Brown, described their feelings about an SDS meeting:

> You are allowed to participate and to speak, only the men stop listening when you do. How many times have you seen a woman enter the discussion only to have it resume at the exact point from which she made her departure, as though she had never said anything at all? How many times have you seen men actually walk out of a room while a woman speaks . . . ?

In 1967 a group of New Left women known as the "radical woman's group" presented a list of demands at the New Politics Convention and were virtually ignored. This treatment was similar to that of the Anti-Slavery Convention held in London more than a century earlier, when Lucretia Mott and Elizabeth Cady Stanton and other women were not allowed to sit on the main floor but were assigned to the balcony.

Women in the civil rights movement often found their position similar to the activist political women. Again, as during the abolitionist period, women were confronted with the problem of working for the equality of another group, the black citizen, while not being taken seriously themselves. In 1964 a few women from a civil rights group, the Southern Non-Violent Coordinating Committee, met to discuss their situation. They agreed that they were being treated as inferior and unequal. These women left the conference and began to meet regularly to discuss women's issues.

Soon they began to disagree about whether or not a woman's group should be formed that would work separately and without men or whether the group should work together with the New Left movement. This disagreement became the basis of the philosophical split that came to dominate the women's movement. One group felt that women were oppressed because of the political-economic structure of America. They believed that the root of the oppression could be found in capitalism, which requires the mother to stay home and bring up the children while the father leaves home each day to work. If this basic economic system did not exist, they argued, we would not have the industrial power we have achieved. Those who supported these ideas generally had worked in the Vietnam War peace movement or the New Left politics. They supported socialism, which they felt would encourage the liberation of women from the home.

Other women felt the economic system was not the cause of the oppression of women. Rather, the problem was male-determined institutions, values, and attitudes, all of which stereotyped people on the basis of sex roles. These attitudes rather than the economic system had to be changed.

Many groups began to form throughout the country, some reflecting the "political-economic" point of view and others the "socially conditioned" one. In September 1968 the Miss America Pageant demonstration brought national attention to the movement that had been labeled "Women's Liberation." The demonstration was held in Atlantic City, New Jersey, in order to protest beauty contests, which the demonstrators felt demeaned women. Radical women from the entire East Coast came to participate. Nothing was burned at the demonstration, but some women had threatened to burn "oppressive" garments such as bras and high-heeled shoes. As a result the term "bra-burners" was used by the press to describe the women. Al-

Militant action, including confrontation, has been used to bring feminist concerns to public attention. Demonstrations have emphasized such issues as the Equal Rights Amendment, abortion, rape, and the need for day care centers.

though most of the publicity was unfavorable, the cause of Women's Liberation gained national attention and attracted many recruits.

As women began to meet and work out their differences, political and personal, they began to realize that many problems which had seemed to be personal were common ones due to social conditioning. They agreed "that what was thought to be a personal problem [had] a social cause and probably a political solution." These casual discussions developed into the technique of "consciousness raising" which began to be widely used as a method of introducing women to the women's movement. Because these discussions worked effectively in small groups, the small group became the organizational unit in the movement. Thousands of American women met to discuss shared feelings and problems that came from being female in America and found that in spite of race or class they had much in common.

> We always stay in touch with our feelings . . . [wrote one participant] We assume that our feelings . . . mean something worth analyzing . . . that our feelings are saying something political . . . In our

groups let's share our feelings and pool them. Let's let ourselves go and see where our feelings lead us. Our feelings will lead us to ideas and then to actions. Our feelings will lead us to our theory, our theory to action, our feelings about that action to new theory and then to new action.

Consciousness raising, although not totally accepted, has provided the basic technique for getting women emotionally and politically involved in the movement for women's liberation from stereotyped roles. However, as was pointed out above, personal insights had to be combined with some kind of action in order for the process to be effective and successful. Many different types of action were proposed and tried, in addition to traditional methods such as those used by NOW.

During the early 1970's a wide variety of groups formed and disbanded. One group, the Redstockings, was founded by two radical members of the movement, Ellen Willis and Shulamith Firestone. The Redstockings believed in militant action and gained national prominence when members disrupted public abortion hearings in New York City and held their own hearings. They used consciousness raising as a tool to teach their members that women must become politically involved in order to exercise power.

The New York Radical Feminists was formed by dissatisfied members of other groups. Radical Feminists wrote and spoke extensively about "male chauvinism"—the belief in male superiority. They discussed the necessity of ridding society of socially-conditioned roles that oppress women and make them second-class citizens.

The combination of the reformist organizations of the women's movement, with their emphasis on working within the system for change, and the radical organizations that provide theory and more dramatic action to call attention to the role of women in America, has been effective in making Americans think about their lives. Most women have at least thought about who they are and how they live. This is often the first step toward change. Even women and men who disagree with feminism have been affected by these ideas and programs.

Minority Women and the Movement

The concern about women's place in society has found comparatively few supporters among minority group women. Black women, American Indian women, and women of Hispanic background have generally not been active in support of women's issues. Their spokeswomen often agree that concerns about male chauvinism, sharing of house-

Mexican-American, Puerto Rican, and other Hispanic women face a double burden of discrimination in the United States. They are often stereotyped as passive, male dominated, and unskilled. But many have become active community leaders. They have also organized self-help groups to improve the role of women in Hispanic society.

work, consciousness raising, and the like are not of primary importance to minority women who struggle daily against racial oppression. They point out that white, middle-class women lead very different lives from black, Hispanic, or American Indian women. Yet many minority women believe that a number of the concerns of the women's movement, such as provision for child care, equal pay and job opportunity, and adequate health care, are relevant to all women regardless of race. Some Mexican-American and Puerto Rican women have formed their own groups to try to improve the lives of women in their communities.

The experiences of black women have led many of them to express concern and even anger about the goals of the women's movement. Slavery, they point out, made it necessary for black women to assume a large portion of responsibility for the family. History made them more independent than most American women. After slavery ended, and until the 1960's, the black man found it difficult to find employment. One sociologist explains:

> The Negro woman, like the white woman, does not represent to the white world as much of an aggressor against the present power structure as does the Negro man.

The black woman often became the sole breadwinner in the family. She rarely had the luxury of simply having to care for her home and

Shirley Chisholm.

family and thus becoming the "dissatisfied housewife" Betty Friedan wrote about in the *The Feminine Mystique*. Stereotypes developed that portrayed the black woman as domineering and always putting down her man. As a result, many black women believe they should "walk behind their man", supporting him in a struggle for racial equality. One woman says:

> I don't think that black women can afford to be competitive with their men and especially now. . . . Some of those women's lib girls are asking for jobs that black men haven't been able to get.

Many black women would agree with the SNCC Black Women's Liberation Committee statement: "Black people are engaged in a life-and-death struggle and the main emphasis of black women must be to combat the capitalist, racist exploitation of black people."

But not all black women would support this idea. In 1972 the Bureau of Labor Statistics, showing the median income of full-time wage earners, illustrated the "double jeopardy" faced by those black and female:

white males earned $10,786
nonwhite* males earned $7,548
white females earned $6,131
nonwhite* females earned $5,320
the majority of nonwhites are black

Black and other nonwhite women thus were the most economically oppressed in American society, and some black leaders feel this will continue until black women join the feminist movement.

Black women in the civil rights movement of the 1960's also encountered the same type of prejudice because of their sex as white women had. Some black women began to feel that a feminist movement as well as a black civil rights movement would be necessary.

Shirley Chisholm was the first black woman elected to the House of Representatives. "I have pointed out time and time again," she has said,

> that the harshest discrimination that I have encountered in the political arena is anti-feminism both from males and brainwashed, Uncle Tom females. When I first announced that I was running for the United States Congress, both males and females advised me, as they had when I ran for the New York State legislature, to go back to teaching—a woman's vocation—and leave the politics to the men.

Other black women who agree that it is necessary to abolish both sexism and racism formed the National Black Feminist Organization in the summer of 1973. Among the founders was Margaret Sloan, an editor of the feminist magazine *Ms.*, who believes that black women must fight racism outside their community and sexism within it. The priorities in the group's platform include community control, black capitalism, improved medical care, improved treatment of black women prisoners, child care, and protection for household workers.

Other black leaders such as activist lawyer Florynce Kennedy and New York City Human Rights Commissioner Eleanor Holmes Norton are working to abolish both sexism and racism. Those combined goals, however, have still not received the support of many members of their community.

Three Feminist Issues—Child Care, The Media, and Education

All feminist groups have given certain issues priority in their work. Three issues—child care, sexism in the media, and sexism in education—provoke much controversy.

Child Care. The need to preserve the nuclear family—mother, father, and children—has been an unquestioned assumption in the United States. It has been generally accepted that one parent—almost always the mother—would stay home until the children were grown. But a study of women and work proves that women are working outside the home in increasing numbers. In 1973 over 35 million women were in the labor force. Nearly one-third of all mothers with preschool children and half the mothers with older children were working, often to keep their families above the poverty level. In the early 1970's, 41 percent of the poor children in the United States were completely dependent upon the earnings of women.

Many women today urge the creation of free child care centers to provide care and education for the children of working parents. More radical women believe that every parent should have the right to free, 24-hour child care. They point out that there are at least 8 million children who are poorly cared for by babysitters or brothers and sisters or no one at all while their parents are at work. Dr. Edward Zigler, a child development expert, said in an interview in *Ms.* magazine, "I've spoken to hundreds of women across the country, rich and poor, women who make $20,000 a year—women whose lives have been blighted because they have been unable to find satisfactory day care. . . . The government helps[industry], but doesn't help mothers."

Supporters of child care centers point out that thousands of parents on welfare could work if child care were provided. They also argue that problems such as juvenile delinquency and drug abuse could be prevented by providing professional care for young children whose parents must work.

In 1971 Congress passed the Comprehensive Child Development Act. The bill provided for the development of child care facilities in the United States, free to some and on an increasing fee scale to others. President Nixon vetoed the bill, expressing the fears of some Americans when he said:

> For the federal government to plunge headlong financially into supporting child development would commit the vast moral authority of the national government to the side of communal approaches to child-rearing over against the family-centered approach.

Those who object to government-supported child care often express fears that forced child care will result; that is, parents will lose their children to the government. They feel child care is communistic and dangerous to freedom. The debate about child care continues and becomes more crucial as more women work outside the home.

Media. Feminists have mounted a wide campaign against sexism in all forms of media. Pointing out that magazines, books, television, radio, and movies have a tremendous influence on Americans, they accuse the media of portraying women and men in stereotyped ways. Some examples:

1. A group called Feminists on Children's Media has published a study of sexism in children's books. This group, and others who have

studied children's school books, found that boys are portrayed as capable, active, and aggressive and performing a variety of roles. They found that girls appear much less frequently and are portrayed as passive and domestic. In one book Johnny says, "I think I will be a dentist when I grow up." Later he says to Betsy, "You can be a dentist's nurse." Betsy's future is portrayed as more limited than Johnny's.

Feminists urge children's book writers to present girls in more human ways, with more alternatives.

2. Feminists have angrily protested television programing for the way it shows women. Soap operas, they say, present women as stereotypes—emotional and always searching after men. The men are the providers. Evening shows rarely have women as the leading character, and if women work they are generally single or widowed. The options for female characters on television seem much more limited than those of the male characters.

There have been some changes in programing and these changes are especially visible in news shows where more women now appear. Often these women are minority group members as well. But news, feminists say, is still *about* men.

One station, ABC-TV in New York City, was actually challenged by feminists when its license came up for renewal. According to the complaint, news about women was usually presented as silly and the newscasters made fun of it or the station neglected major news items

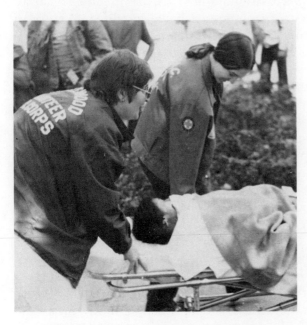

In spite of resistance, women are being admitted to membership in many male-dominated volunteer groups such as ambulance corps. Their performance puts to rest the arguments that they are not "strong enough" or are "too squeamish."

altogether. It is hoped that by taking legal action and by creating publicity, television will change its limited portrayal of women.

3. Women's groups have been particularly active in protesting the image of women presented by most advertisers. Studies show that advertisements very rarely show women in roles other than of housewife and mother. Women become unrealistically ecstatic over white laundry, clean floors, and mirror-finish dishes. Women are often decorative and used as "sex objects" to sell a product. Women's groups call this kind of advertising "sexploitation."

Common stereotypes that advertisements reinforce are those that say, "Women's place is in the home," "Women rarely make important decisions" (they are rarely seen or heard selling major products), "Women are dependent," "Women are primarily sexual objects." For example an ad for a sports car showed a sexy woman perched on top of the car, implying that the buyer—a man—would get her if he bought that car.

Men are also portrayed in stereotyped ways—aggressive, unemotional, strong. Women's groups such as NOW are working to eliminate stereotypes and to pressure advertisers by boycotting products that portray women in demeaning or fixed roles.

Education. Title IX of the Education Amendments of 1972 prohibits sex discrimination in educational programs receiving federal assistance. Feminists such as Anne Grant, the Education Task Force director of NOW, believe that the elimination of sex bias in schools is absolutely necessary in order for women to achieve equality in American life. Such sex bias, Grant feels, has been considerable in American education. Women's groups are working to make certain that Title IX is enforced to end discrimination.

The implications of this act are great. If a course cannot be taught to both girls and boys equally, it must be changed or eliminated. This includes such classes as home economics, industrial arts, sciences, career education, and in some cases, physical education.

Female teachers are pressing for revised maternity leave laws that do not force them to leave after five or seven months of pregnancy if they are able to work longer. And one man in New York City has challenged the maternity leave policy of its school board. He wished to take paternity leave to care for his child while his wife worked. When the Board of Education denied this, he went to court and won his case.

Students themselves have brought court cases to end sex discrimination. Alice de Rivera won the right to attend all-male Stuyvesant High School in New York City in 1969. Bonnie Cruz Sanchez went to court to force her school to allow her to take a metal-working shop course. She won both her case and the school's top metal work prize for 1970. Her mother supported her because she too had been denied the same right when she went to high school.

In addition, hundreds of schools and colleges have introduced women's studies programs. These courses are designed to study women's historical and contemporary roles in society.

At all levels of education, in courses, administration, allocation of professorships, textbooks, and in extracurricular activities, women are pressing to be treated without bias. Not all parents or students agree with this trend in education and many worry that the traditional structure of American society will change tremendously if these trends continue. Surely the issue will continue to be debated.

Summary

The 1960's and early 1970's have been years of great change in the lives of many American women. Wide-ranging legislation has attempted to end the economic, political, and social discrimination against women that has existed in American life for three centuries. Other activities have caused women and men to look carefully at their lives and to examine and question both their behavior and their assumptions about that behavior. Although some Americans continue to believe that women belong in the home, many others have come to believe that each person, female or male, should be allowed to choose the role that suits her or him best.

THE EQUAL RIGHTS AMENDMENT—PRO AND CON

The Equal Rights Amendment to the Constitution was passed by Congress in 1972 and went to the states for ratification. It continues to have strong supporters and strong opposition. Representative Emanuel Celler opposed the amendment in Congressional debate and Representative Edith Green supported it.

Representative Celler: . . . Feminists clamor for equal rights. Nobody can deny that women should have equality under the law. But ever since Adam gave up his rib to make a woman, throughout the ages we have learned that physical, emotional, psychological and social differences exist and dare not be disregarded . . . Beyond that, let me say that there is as much difference between a male and a female as between a horse chestnut and a chestnut horse—and as the French say, Vivé le difference.

Any attempt to pass an amendment that promises to wipe out the effects of these differences is about as abortive as trying to fish in a desert—and you cannot do that.

There is no really genuine equality and I defy anyone to tell me what "equality" in this amendment means. Even your five fingers—one is not equal to the other—they are different.

You know, as a matter of fact, there is only one place where there is equality—and that is in the cemetery.

Women have thrown off many shackles with the help of men. I admit some shackles remain. Our duty is to abolish distinctions based on sex except such as are reasonably justified by differences in physical structure or biological or social function. The equal rights amendment would eliminate all distinctions in legal treatment of men and women even when the fundamental reasonableness and common sense of such differences is apparent . . . It would require [unusual ability] to predict the effects of this amendment. Scores and scores of laws—State, municipal, and Federal Government—make distinctions in their applications, and, therefore, it would be impossible to determine exactly what the consequences would be . . .

Representative Green: . . . Mr. Speaker, after listening to some of the debate, may I say it actually seems incredible to me that in the last quarter of the 20th century we are still debating whether or not the majority of the American people have equal rights under the Constitution.

It has been said that if this amendment is passed it will create profound social changes. May I say to you, it is high time some profound social changes were made in our society . . . I hope that the debate today will not be based on "vive le difference" arguments, but rather with the words of Walt Whitman in mind: "That whatever degrades another degrades me, and whatever is said or done returns at last to me."

If we have the power and we do not act to remove the barriers that result in waste and injustice and frustration, then society is the loser, and any kind of discrimination is degrading to the individual and harmful to society as a whole.

Women know that there is no such thing as equality *per se* but only equal opportunity to—and this is what women want: equal rights and equal opportunity to make the best one can of one's life within one's capability and without fear of injustice or oppression or denial of those opportunities . . .

Congressional Record, Vol. 116, Part 21, 91st Congress, 2nd Session, pp. 28000-28001, 28014.

WOMEN AND THE WORLD OF WORK

The following charts and graphs tell the story of working women: 1. the gap between what they earn and what men doing comparable work make, 2. the high percentage of working women who are married, and 3. the number of nonwhite women who work as compared to white women.

Median Earnings of Full-Time Year-Round Workers,[1] by Sex, 1955-70[2]

Year	Median earnings		Women's median earnings as percent of men's
	Women	Men	
1970	$5,323	$8,966	59.4
1969	4,977	8,227	60.5
1968	4,457	7,664	58.2
1967	4,150	7,182	57.8
1966	3,973	6,848	58.0
1965	3,823	6,375	60.0
1964	3,690	6,195	59.6
1963	3,561	5,978	59.6
1962	3,446	5,794	59.5
1961	3,351	5,644	59.4
1960	3,293	5,417	60.8
1959	3,193	5,209	61.3
1958	3,102	4,927	63.0
1957	3,008	4,713	63.8
1956	2,827	4,466	63.3
1955	2,719	4,252	63.9

[1] Worked 35 hours or more a week for 50 to 52 weeks.

[2] Data for 1967-70 are not strictly comparable with those for prior years, which are for wage and salary income only and do not include earnings of self-employed persons.

Source: U.S. Department of Commerce, Bureau of the Census: Current Population Reports, P-60.

Median Wage or Salary Income of Full-Time Year-Round Workers,
by Sex and Selected Major Occupation Group, 1970

Major occupation group	Median wage or salary income		Women's median wage or salary income as percent of men's
	Women	Men	
Professional and technical workers	$7,878	$11,806	66.7
Nonfarm managers, officials, and proprietors	6,834	12,117	56.4
Clerical workers	5,551	8,617	64.4
Sales workers	4,188	9,790	42.8
Operatives	4,510	7,623	59.2
Service workers (except private household)	3,953	6,955	56.8

Source: U.S. Department of Commerce, Bureau of the Census: Current Population Reports, P-60, No. 80.

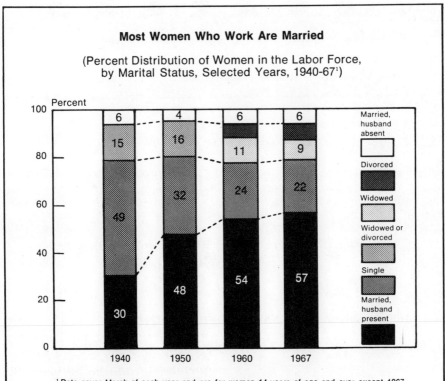

Most Women Who Work Are Married

(Percent Distribution of Women in the Labor Force,
by Marital Status, Selected Years, 1940-67[1])

[1] Data cover March of each year and are for women 14 years of age and over except 1967 which are for 16 and over.

Source: U.S. Department of Labor, Bureau of Labor Statistics;
        U.S. Department of Commerce, Bureau of the Census.

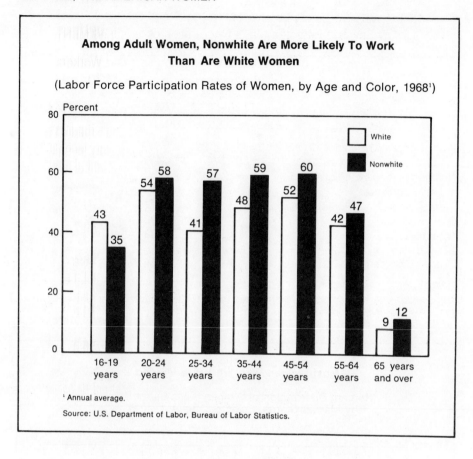

**Among Adult Women, Nonwhite Are More Likely To Work
Than Are White Women**

(Labor Force Participation Rates of Women, by Age and Color, 1968[1])

[1] Annual average.

Source: U.S. Department of Labor, Bureau of Labor Statistics.

WORKING WOMEN—THE MYTH AND THE REALITY

Many stereotypes shape our thinking about women. For example, it is often said that "a woman's place is in the home" and it is generally believed that is where they are. But the statistics tell us that over 35 million women were working in 1973, over half because they had to.

Male Workers More Equal Than Female Workers?
No! All Workers are Equal.

THE MYTH	THE REALITY
A woman's place is in the home.	Homemaking in itself is no longer a full-time job for most people. Goods and services formerly produced in the home are now commercially available; laborsaving devices have lightened or eliminated much work around the home.

THE MYTH

Women aren't seriously attached to the labor force; they work only for extra pocket money.

Women are out ill more than male workers; they cost the company more.

Women don't work as long or as regularly as their male coworkers; their training is costly—and largely wasted.

THE REALITY

Today more than half of all women between 18 and 64 years of age are in the labor force, where they are making a substantial contribution to the nation's economy. Studies show that nine out of ten girls will work outside the home at some time in their lives.

Of the nearly 34 million women in the labor force in March, 1973, nearly half were working because of pressing economic need. They were either single, widowed, divorced, or separated or had husbands whose incomes were less than $3,000 a year.

A recent Public Health Service study shows little difference in the absentee rate due to illness or injury: 5.9 days a year for women compared with 5.2 for men.

A declining number of women leave work for marriage and children. But even among those who do leave, a majority return when their children are in school. Even with a break in employment, the average woman worker has a worklife expectancy of 25 years as compared with 43 years for the average male worker. The single woman averages 45 years in the labor force.

Studies on labor turnover indicate that net differences for men and women are generally small. In manufacturing industries the 1968 rates of accessions per 100

THE MYTH

THE REALITY

employees were 4.4 for men and 5.3 for women; the respective separation rates were 4.4 and 5.2.

Married women take jobs away from men; in fact, they ought to quit those jobs they now hold.

There were 19.8 million married women (husbands present) in the labor force in March 1973; the number of unemployed men was 2.5 million. If all the married women stayed home and unemployed men were placed in their jobs, there would be 17.3 million unfilled jobs.

Moreover, most unemployed men do not have the education or the skill to qualify for many of the jobs held by women, such as secretaries, teachers, and nurses.

Women should stick to "Women's jobs" and shouldn't compete for "men's jobs."

Job requirements, with extremely rare exceptions, are unrelated to sex. Tradition rather than job content has led to labeling certain jobs as women's and others as men's. In measuring 22 inherent aptitudes and knowledge areas, a research laboratory found that there is no sex difference in 14, women excel in 6, and men excel in 2.

Women don't want responsibility on the job; they don't want promotions or job changes which add to their load.

Relatively few women have been offered positions of responsibility. But when given these opportunities, women, like men, do cope with job responsibilities in addition to personal or family responsibilities. In 1973, 4.7 million women held professional and technical jobs; another 1.6 million worked as nonfarm managers and ad-

THE MYTH   THE REALITY

ministrators. Many others held supervisory jobs at all levels in offices and factories.

The employment of mothers leads to juvenile delinquency.

Studies show that many factors must be considered when seeking the causes of juvenile delinquency. Whether or not a mother is employed does not appear to be a determining factor.

These studies indicate that it is the quality of the mother's care rather than the time consumed in such care which is of major significance.

Men don't like to work for women supervisors.

Most men who complain about women supervisors have never worked for a woman.

In one study where at least three-fourths of both the male and female respondents (all executives) had worked with women managers, their evaluation of women in management was favorable. On the other hand, the study showed a traditional/cultural bias among those who reacted unfavorably to women as managers.

In another survey in which 41 percent of the reporting firms indicated that they hired women executives, none rated their performance as unsatisfactory; 50 percent rated them adequate; 42 percent rated them the same as their predecessors; and 8 percent rated them better than their predecessors.

U. S. Department of Labor, Women's Bureau, "The Myth and the Reality," (Washington, 1974), revised.

THE SUPREME COURT RULES ABORTION IS LEGAL

On January 22, 1973 the Supreme Court ruled on the abortion question. The issue had been emotional and controversial, and remains one of the most controversial issues in spite of the Court's decision. The following presents the majority view of the Court and a dissenting view of one of the Justices.

Mr. Justice Blackmun delivered the opinion of the Court.

. . . We forthwith acknowledge our awareness of the sensitive and emotional nature of the abortion controversy, of the vigorous opposing views, even among physicians, and of the deep and seemingly absolute convictions that the subject inspires. One's philosophy, one's experiences, one's exposure to the raw edges of human existence, one's religious training, one's attitude toward life and family and their values, and the moral standards one establishes and seeks to observe, are all likely to influence and to color one's thinking and conclusions about abortion.

In addition, population growth, pollution, poverty, and racial overtones tend to complicate and not to simplify the problem.

Our task, of course, is to resolve the issue by constitutional measurement free of emotion . . .

I

The Texas statutes that concern us here [against abortion] . . . make it a crime to "procure an abortion" as therein defined, or to attempt one, except with respect to "an abortion procured or attempted by medical advice for the purpose of saving the life of the mother." Similar statutes are in existence in a majority of the States . . .

V

The principal thrust of appellant's [the person appealing the case] attack on the Texas statutes is that they improperly invade a right, said to be possessed by the pregnant woman, to choose to terminate her pregnancy. Appellant would discover this right in the concept of personal "liberty" embodied in the Fourteenth Amendment's Due Process Clause; or in personal, marital, familial, and sexual privacy said to be protected by the Bill of Rights . . .

VIII

The Constitution does not explicitly mention any right of privacy. In a line of decisions, however . . . the Court has recognized that a right of personal privacy, or a guarantee of certain areas or zones of privacy, does exist under the Constitution . . .

This right of privacy, whether it be founded in the Fourteenth Amendment's concept of personal liberty and restrictions upon state action, as we feel it is, or, as the District Court determined, in the Ninth Amendment's reservation of rights to the people, is broad enough to encompass a woman's decision whether or not to terminate her pregnancy. The detriment that the State would impose upon the pregnant woman by denying this choice altogether is apparent. Specific and direct harm medically diagnosable even in early pregnancy may be involved. Maternity, or additional offspring, may force upon the woman a distressful life and future. Psychological harm may be imminent. Mental and physical health may be taxed by child care. There is also the distress, for all concerned, associated with the unwanted child, and there is the problem of bringing a child into a family already unable, psychologically and otherwise, to care for it. In other cases, as in this one, the additional difficulties and continuing stigma of unwed motherhood may be involved. All these are factors the woman and her responsible physician necessarily will consider in consultation.

On the basis of elements such as these, appellants and some [who support them] argue that the woman's right is absolute and that she is entitled to terminate her pregnancy at whatever time, in whatever way, and for whatever reason she alone chooses. With this we do not agree . . . [A] state may properly assert important interests in safeguarding health, in maintaining medical standards, and in protecting potential life . . .

We therefore conclude that the right of personal privacy includes the abortion decision, but that this right is not unqualified and must be considered against important state interests in regulation. [Thus, the Court ruled that *after the first three months* the State could regulate abortion in various degrees and after approximately six months could ban it altogether. During the first three months the decision was left up to the woman and the attending physician.]

Dissenting, Justice White:

At the heart of the controversy in these cases are those recurring pregnancies that pose no danger whatsoever to the life or health of the mother but are nevertheless unwanted for any one or more of a variety of reasons—convenience, family planning, economics, dislike of children, the embarrassment of illegitimacy, etc. The common claim before us is that for any one of such reasons, or for no reason at all, and without asserting or claiming any threat to life or health, any woman is entitled to an abortion at her request if she is able to find a medical advisor willing to undertake the procedure . . .

The Court apparently values the convenience of the pregnant mother more than the continued existence and development of the life or potential life which she carries. Whether or not I might agree with that marshalling of values, I can in no event join the Court's judgment because I find no constitutional warrant for imposing such an order of priorities on the people and legislatures of the States . . . This issue, for the most part, should be left with the people and to the political processes the people have devised to govern their affairs. . . .

Supreme Court of the United States, *Jane Roe et. al. appellants v. Henry Wade*, January 22, 1973, pp. 1-3, 14, 36-39; pp. 1-2 dissenting.

THE NOW BILL OF RIGHTS

The National Organization for Women was founded in 1966 with Betty Friedan as its first president. Its goal was to "take action to bring women into full participation in the mainstream of American society now, assuming all the privileges and responsibilities thereof in truly equal partnership with men." Members of the organization wrote a bill of rights for women at the first national conference in 1967.

I   Equal Rights Constitutional Amendment

II   Enforce Law Banning Sex Discrimination in Employment

III   Maternity Leave Rights in Employment and in Social Security Benefits

IV   Tax Deduction for Home and Child Care Expenses for Working Parents

V   Child Care Centers

VI   Equal and Unsegregated Education

VII   Equal Job Training Opportunities and Allowances for Women in Poverty

VIII   The Right of Women to Control Their Reproductive Lives

WE DEMAND:

I. That the United States Congress immediately pass the Equal Rights Amendment to the Constitution to provide that "Equality of rights under the law shall not be denied or abridged by the United States or by any State on account of sex," and that such then be immediately ratified by the several States.

II. That equal employment opportunity be guaranteed to all women, as well as men, by insisting that the Equal Employment Opportunity Commission enforce the prohibitions against sex discrimination in employment under Title VII of the Civil Rights Act of 1964 with the same vigor as it enforces the prohibitions against racial discrimination.

III. That women be protected by law to ensure their rights to return to their jobs within a reasonable time after childbirth without loss of seniority or other accrued benefits, and be paid maternity leave as a form of social security and/or employee benefit.

IV. Immediate revision of tax laws to permit the deduction of home and child care expenses for working parents.

V. That child care facilities be established by law on the same basis as parks, libraries, and public schools, adequate to the needs of children from the pre-school years through adolescence, as a community re-source to be used by all citizens from all income levels.

VI. That the right of women to be educated to their full potential equally with men be secured by Federal and State Legislation, eliminating all discrimination and segregation by sex, written and unwritten, at all levels of education, including colleges, graduate and professional schools, loans and fellowships, and Federal and State training programs such as the Job Corps.

VII. The right of women in poverty to secure job training, housing, and family allowances on equal terms with men, but without prejudice to a parent's right to remain at home to care for his or her children; revision of welfare legislation and poverty programs which deny women dignity, privacy, and self-respect.

VIII. The right of women to control their own reproductive lives by removing from penal codes laws limiting access to contraceptive information and devices and laws governing abortion.

NOW *Bill of Rights,* National Organization for Women, Inc. Reprinted by permission.

THE POLITICS OF HOUSEWORK

In 1968 Pat Mainardi published a short paper, "The Politics of Housework," in which she showed how housework defines the basic roles women play in our society. Even when the husband offers to "help" in the house, she wrote, he often finds "excuses" to stop. Mainardi suggests that society's values must change if women and men are going to be able to modify their roles significantly.

> Though women do not complain of the power of husbands, each complains of her own husband, or of the husbands of her friends. It is the same in all other cases of servitude; at least in the commencement of the emancipatory movement. The serfs did not at first complain of the power of the lords, but only of their tyranny.

John Stuart Mill,
On the Subjection of Women

Liberated women—very different from Women's Liberation! The first signals all kinds of goodies. . . . The other signals— HOUSEWORK. The first brings sex without marriage, sex before marriage, cozy housekeeping arrangements ("I'm living with this chick") and the self-content of knowing that you're not the kind of man who wants a doormat instead of a woman. That will come later. After all, who wants that old commodity anymore, the Standard American Housewife, all husband, home and kids. The New Commodity, The Liberated Woman, has sex a lot and has a Career, preferably something that can be fitted in with the household chores—like dancing, pottery, or painting.

On the other hand is Women's Liberation—and housework. What? You say this is all trivial? Wonderful! That's what I thought. It seemed perfectly reasonable. We both had careers, both had to work a couple of days a week to earn enough to live on, so why shouldn't we share the housework? So I suggested it to my mate and he agreed—most men are too hip to turn you down flat. You're right, he said. It's only fair.

Then an interesting thing happened. I can only explain it by stating that we women have been brainwashed more than even we can imagine. Probably too many years of seeing television women in ecstasy over their shiny wax floors or breaking down over their dirty shirt collars. Men have no such conditioning. They recognize the essential fact of housework right from the very beginning. Which is that it stinks.

Here's my list of dirty chores: buying groceries, carting them home and putting them away; cooking meals and washing dishes and pots; doing the laundry, digging out the place when things get out of control; washing floors. The list could go on but the sheer necessities are bad enough. All of us have to do these things, or get someone else to do them for us. The longer my husband contemplated these chores, the more repulsed he became, and so proceeded the change from the normally sweet considerate Dr. Jekyll into the crafty Mr. Hyde who would stop at nothing to avoid the horrors of—housework. As he felt himself backed into a corner laden with dirty dishes, brooms, mops and reeking garbage, his front teeth grew longer and pointier, his fingernails haggled and his eyes grew wild. Housework trivial? Not on your life! Just try to share the burden.

So ensued a dialogue that's been going on for several years. Here are some of the high points:

* "I don't mind sharing the housework, but I don't do it very well. We should each do the things we're best at." MEANING: Unfortunately I'm no good at things like washing dishes or cooking. What I do best is a little light carpentry, changing light bulbs, moving furniture (how often do *you* move furniture?) ALSO MEANING: Historically the

lower classes (black men and us) have had hundreds of years experience doing menial jobs. It would be a waste of manpower to train someone else to do them now. ALSO MEANING: I don't like the dull stupid boring jobs, so you should do them.

* "I don't mind sharing the work, but you'll have to show me how to do it." MEANING: I ask a lot of questions and you'll have to show me everything every time I do it because I don't remember so good. Also don't try to sit down and read while I'm doing my jobs because I'm going to annoy hell out of you until it's easier to do them yourself.

* "We used to be so happy!" (Said whenever it was his turn to do something.) MEANING: I used to be so happy. MEANING: Life without housework is bliss. No quarrel here. Perfect Agreement.

* "We have different standards, and why should I have to work to your standards? That's unfair." MEANING: If I begin to get bugged by the dirt and crap I will say, "This place sure is a sty" or "How can anyone live like this?" and wait for your reaction. I know that all women have a sore called "Guilt over a messy house" or "Household work is ultimately my responsibility." I know that men have caused that sore— if anyone visits and the place is a sty, they're not going to leave and say, "He sure is a lousy housekeeper," you'll take the rap in any case. I can outwait you. ALSO MEANING: I can provoke innumerable scenes over the housework issue. Eventually doing all the housework yourself will be less painful to you than trying to get me to do half. Or I'll suggest we get a maid. She will do my share of the work. You will do yours. It's women's work . . .

* "In animal societies, wolves, for example, the top animal is usually a male even where he is not chosen for brute strength but on the basis of cunning and intelligence. Isn't that interesting?" MEANING: I have historical, psychological, anthropological and biological justification for keeping you down. How can you ask the top wolf to be equal? . . .

* "Man's accomplishments have always depended on getting help from other people, mostly women. What great man would have accomplished what he did if he had to do his own housework?" MEANING: Oppression is built into the system and I, as the white American male, receive the benefits of this system. I don't want to give them up. . . .

Pat Mainardi, "The Politics of Housework," 1968. Reprinted by permission of KNOW, INC, Pittsburgh, Pa.

RETHINKING ROLES

Women who wish to go back to work often find that they still carry the whole burden of doing housework along with their outside employment. Gabrielle Burton, a Maryland writer and mother describes how she attempted to deal with this problem.

After whistling for eight years, I finally admitted that I had had bad career guidance; I was unhappy in my profession; and I wanted to change my job. I kept [gathering] my little logics until they presented a decent case. Then I gathered my courage and presented it.

"Roger?" [her husband] I said.

"Yes, dear?"

"I'd like to talk about something."

"Yes, dear?"

Then I fumbled and mumbled something like this:

"The house is there for the benefit of everyone in the family. The responsibility for it should be divided. At one time in my life, I volunteered to assume everyone's responsibility. It's time for me to be moving on. This will necessitate everyone reassuming his personal responsibility for the functioning of the house."

At this point, you explain that you're going back to school to become a brain surgeon, or write full-time (that's me, saying that), or you're going to raise the kids REALLY without cluttering it up with diverse other full-time gardening, cleaning, or maintenance jobs. If your husband says, "Yeah! And who's gonna pay for all this, sister?" you might point out that a large Eastern bank estimates your annual services are worth $10,000 [as a housewife] and you'll deduct your tuition from back wages. But this kind of tit for tat is a dead end route. Either he thinks you're making a contribution and have some personal rights or he doesn't. You might as well find out how the wind blows.

There are some women who truly love being housewives and that's [praiseworthy]. The whole point of liberation is that everyone makes her own choice . . .

There are other women who have eagerly claimed the house as "theirs." Women have so pitifully little that we can call our own, that we brought out of our own efforts or contacts. Most of us get our money, our friends, our status from our husbands. We are pleased to have something be "ours." This is the "Queen of the Castle" syndrome. This is "my" house, "my" kitchen, "my" oregano. If one wants that, fine, but I have gladly relinquished the ownership of the oregano, along with the responsibility for it. Whoever uses it, takes charge of it.

Roger agreed:

—that the house does benefit all of us;

—that a benefit implies a responsibility;

—that if I didn't want to be Queen of the Castle anymore, I should have a right to relinquish it;

—that I hadn't shown any great aptitude for housework and eight years was a reasonable trial;

—that I had a right to try something else.

That left us with a big house, four little kids, and one established career. I don't believe in servants so the solution had to be worked out among ourselves. The children are 7, 6, 3, and 7 months [Burton has since had an additional child] . . .

We proceeded to make a schedule. Five jobs are written on slips of paper. On Sunday nights these are shaken in a fish bowl and each person chooses a task for the week. (This silly ceremony is preferred by our kids, who like to feel an element of chance in life. Roger and I would rather throw dice.)

The jobs are recurrent maintenance jobs, the bare necessity to keep the house from collapse. They are:

1. Trash. Empty every wastebasket in the house. Deposit all in outdoor cans daily.

2. Upstairs pick-up. Carry a basket from room to room. Put everything in it that's out of place. Take care of your own things from it. Announce to family that things may now be claimed. There is a one-half hour limit on claiming things, after which they are given away or thrown away.

3. Downstairs pick-up. Same as No. 2 but done on the main floor.

4. Baby. Feed and/or entertain her when parents are busy or tired. Take care of all her things that show up in the pick-up basket. Run and fetch.

5. Bathrooms. Keep from looking like disaster areas. Pick up fallen towels, chip away mounds of toothpaste, a little polishing here and there.

A job is taken for one week, unless one gripes continuously. Then it's taken for two weeks . . .

In the beginning, the children required great supervision to complete their tasks. Weary, time-consuming training is necessary. Naturally you can do everything quicker yourself. That's the question: Do you want to go on the rest of your life doing everything? . . .

Gabrielle Burton, *I'm Running Away From Home, But I'm Not Allowed To Cross the Street: A Primer on Women's Liberation* (Pittsburgh: KNOW, Inc., 1972), pp. 58-62. Reprinted by permission.

ON BEING BLACK AND FEMALE

In the following article, writer Renee Ferguson discusses the varying ideas about women's liberation held by American black women. Many are involved with getting civil rights for blacks, while others see the struggle for equality for women as part of the larger struggle for black freedom. Ferguson explains why relatively few black women are in the women's movement.

The women's liberation movement touches some sensitive nerves among black women—but they are not always the nerves the movement seems to touch among so many whites.

At a time when some radical white feminists are striving for a different family structure, many black women are trying to stabilize their families. They are making a special effort, in a great number of cases, to assume the wife and mother role more effectively. Whether a black woman feels that she can relate to the women's liberation movement and the extent to which she is or is not involved in it may well depend on her age and her experiences.

Dr. Anna Hedgeman, for instance, who takes pride in the fact that she lived in Harlem for most of the thirty years she has lived in New York, is a strong advocate of the woman's liberation movement. She believes that there is no way in which black women in America are uninvolved in the movement. "We as Afro-American women have to face the problems of total discrimination in our society," Dr. Hedgeman says. "We have had the extra burden of being women. But if you just review the problems that women face you need only substitute the word Afro-American people for the word women and you have the same problems—job discrimination, want ads that discriminate and false stereotypes."

On the other hand, Howard University senior and Student Association Secretary Pamely Preston doesn't think that the women's liberation movement has any meaning for black women. "As far as I'm concerned the women's liberation movement is trite, trivial and simple. It's just another white political fad," Miss Preston says. "Black people have some of the same problems that they had when they were first brought to this country. That's what we've got to deal with." If the relatively modest turnout of black women for the recent Women's Liberation Day demonstrations is any indication of the black women's interest in the movement, then perhaps Miss Preston's attitude is indicative of the way most black women feel.

These vastly differing attitudes raise a real question about the extent to which the women's liberation movement means very much to black women. Do black women and white women have the same social, economic and political priorities and problems and how do they affect the status of the women's liberation movement in the minds of black women?

In a 1963 article which appeared in the *Washington Post,* the President of the National Council of Negro Women, Dorothy Height, said, "A Negro woman has the same kind of problems as other women, but she can't take the same things for granted. For instance, she has to raise children who seldom have the same sense of security that white children have when they see their father accepted as a successful member of the community. A Negro child's father is ignored as though he didn't exist."

The instability of the black inner-city family has been the subject of concern and study by sociologists for years . . .

Local singer Marjorie Barnes in citing the problems of the instability of black families as one of her main reasons for noninvolvement in the women's liberation movement, says, "I don't think that black women can afford to be competitive with their men—especially now. Competing with them for jobs would just add to the problem that already exists. Black women have been able to find work when their husbands couldn't and have often been the head of the family not because they wanted to be but out of economic necessity. Some of those women's lib girls are asking for jobs that black men haven't been able to get."

Miss Barnes adds, "Black women have the additional problem of raising their children in crime ridden neighborhoods and they've got to see to it that their children receive a decent basic education. Most black women don't have time to take up a white middle class cause like women's lib unless they're trying to hide from the realities of the struggle for black liberation." . . .

Perhaps the lack of involvement of black women in the women's liberation movement can best be explained in terms of priorities. The priorities of black women versus the priorities of white women.

Obviously the first priority of virtually all black people is the elimination of racial prejudice in America—in effect the liberation of black people. Second in importance is the black family problem of establishing a decent way of life in America as it exists today. When racism in America is eliminated, then perhaps the black family's stability problem will disappear and more black women will be able to give first priority to the elimination of oppression because of sex.

Renee Ferguson, "Women's Liberation Has A Different Meaning for Blacks," *The Washington Post,* October 3, 1970. Reprinted by permission.

SEX DISCRIMINATION IN EDUCATION

In 1971, Bonnie Edelhart, a junior high school student, brought suit against Harold Baron, Principal of JHS 217 and Hugh McDougall, District Superintendent of District 28 in New York City because she was not allowed to take shop classes. Title IX of the Education Act prohibits such sex-segregated classes.

I asked Miss Jonas if my daughter [Bonnie] could take metal working or mechanics, and she said there is no freedom of choice. That is what she said.

THE COURT: That is it?

THE WITNESS: I also asked her whose decision this was, that there was no freedom of choice. And she told me it was the decision of the Board of Education.

I didn't ask her anything else because she clearly showed me that it was against the school policy for girls to be in the class. She said it was a Board of Education decision.

Question: Did she use that phrase, "no freedom of choice"?

Answer: Exactly that phrase; no freedom of choice. That is what made me so angry that I wanted to start this whole thing.

Question: Now, after this lawsuit was filed, they then permitted you to take the course; is that correct?

Answer: No, we had to fight about it for quite a while.

Question: But eventually, they did let you in the second semester?

Answer: They only let me in there.

Question: You are the only girl?

Answer: Yes.

Question: How did you do in the course?

Answer: I got the medal for it from all the boys there.

Question: Will you show the court?

Answer: Yes (indicating).

Question: And what does the medal say?

Answer: Metal 1970 Van Wyck [High School].

Question: And why did they give you that medal?

Answer: Because I was the best out of all the boys.

THE COURT: I do not want any giggling or noises in the courtroom. Just do the best you can to control yourself or else I will have to ask you to leave the courtroom.

Question: Did anyone at the Board of Education ever tell you anything to do about this matter?

Answer: Well, eventually I was told that because the school was decentralizing that I should go back to the school for this problem; that it wouldn't be a matter of the Central Board any more.

Question: And did you do that?

Answer: Yes, I did. I called the school. I spoke to Mr. Baron. . . , and he said that we have too many boys in the school to be able to allow the girls to take metal work and mechanics.

Question: Mrs. Edelhart, when you were in high school, did you attempt to take a metal working course?

MR. MAURER: Objection.

THE COURT: How long ago was it?

THE WITNESS: About twenty years ago.

THE COURT: Objection sustained. Unrelated.

MR. ENNIS: Your Honor, I wish to show that it is related, in this sense. I wish to show that the only named plaintiff in this case was the named plaintiff because she had the support of her mother. She had the support of her mother because her mother was also denied permission to take a metalwork class when she was in high school, and it is because of that continuing problem.

THE COURT: I am not persuaded. The objection is sustained.

Question: Mrs. Edelhart, do you think that having taken the course it was valuable for your daughter?

MR. MAURER: Objection.

Answer: Yes, I do.

THE COURT: What is the relevancy of that?

MR. ENNIS: Well, Your Honor, I wish to establish that, having taken that course, [Bonnie] was a more self-reliant and capable individual than she was before.

THE COURT: Let us assume that is so. What has that got to do with policy?

MR. ENNIS: It has to do with whether or not that policy is damaging the lives of female students in high school. We intend to show that it is; that the Board of Education policy is depriving female students of the opportunity to become self-reliant people.

THE COURT: Do you expect to offer any statistics on it, or do you expect to rely on the testimony?

MR. ENNIS: We will offer statistics, Your Honor.

Case of Bonnie Edelhart, cited in the "Report on Sex Bias in the Public Schools," Education Committee, NOW (New York, 1973), Cover and pp. 6-7. Reprinted by permission.

A YOUNG MOTHER'S FEELINGS ABOUT HER CHILD

Eileen Jacobson is a young mother with a four year old girl named Rachel. Eileen feels that child care offers both her and Rachel freedom. Eileen believes that a woman must not only be free (if that is what she chooses) to work but also to create, to study, and to be. This attitude toward life might change some of the basic ideas and values of our society.

I am a person. I am an adult. I am a woman. I am a mother. I love my daughter. I think she is bright, fun, exciting. Everything a four year old can be, she is. She is a child.

For the first year and a half of her life, I was her constant companion. Although I enjoyed much of our time together, I found myself getting smaller mentally and larger physically. I often felt a great need to be alone or with other adults. To read mature books that I could think about as an adult. To be in the company of other adults and discuss something besides the advantages of breast feeding and the progress of toilet training.

I am one of those women who detest housework, yet I love a clean house, so I hire someone to do it for me. And I pay him a fair wage. I also dislike spending my entire day entertaining my child, despite the fact that I love her, so she goes to a child care center. I know other women who have made play schools of part of their homes, spend most of their time with their children, and really enjoy it. I think that's fine, but it's not for me.

I believe that both men and women should have a choice as to how they will spend their time and that neither should be judged by their choices. My husband does not love our daughter any less because he chooses to have a full time job and is, therefore, away from her for most of the day. It is interesting that no one would think of making this assumption about his feelings.

Similarly, I choose to spend my days in my own way, sometimes resulting in monetary gain, and often with just personal creativity and enjoyment. I feel I need and deserve this ability to be in a world of my choosing. And for the same reason that my husband and my daughter need and deserve it. Each of us is a person.

I believe I and my husband are the most important people in my daughter's life. But I don't think her happiness or her security are dependent upon his or my constant presence. The fact that she knows we love her gives her security. The fact that the time spent with her is important to us all makes us all happy.

But, because I care about my child, the only way that I can truly be free to make a choice for myself, is to have a place for her to spend her time which will provide the acceptance, warmth and stimulation that I would and could give her, if that were my choice. And certainly, the cost of this care must be within the possibilities of our limited budget.

I think my daughter benefits from having a mother who has had a choice. I know I do.

From personal correspondence between Eileen Jacobson and the authors.

Suggestions for Further Reading

GENERAL WORKS

Auchincloss, Louis, *Pioneers and Caretakers: A Study of Nine American Women Novelists,* Minneapolis, Minnesota: University of Minnesota Press, 1965.

Baynick, David King, *Pioneers in Petticoats,* New York: Crowell, 1959. (collective biography)

Beard, Mary, ed., *America Through Women's Eyes,* New York: Macmillan, 1934. Reprinted 1968.

Calhoun, Arthur Wallace, *A Social History of the American Family,* New York: Barnes and Noble, 1960.

Cott, Nancy F., ed., *The Root of Bitterness: Documents of the Social History of American Women,* New York: Dutton, 1972. (paper)

Douglas, Emily Taft, *Remember the Ladies: The Story of Great Women Who Helped Shape America,* New York: Putnam, 1966.

Flexner, Eleanor, *Century of Struggle: The Woman's Rights Movement in the United States,* Cambridge, Massachusetts: Harvard University Press, 1959. (paper)

Handlin, Oscar and Mary, *Facing Life: Youth and the Family in American History,* Boston: Little, Brown, 1971. (paper)

Harris, Janet, *A Single Standard,* New York: McGraw Hill, 1971. (historical and contemporary issues)

Hollander, Phyllis, *American Women in Sports*, New York: Grosset and Dunlap, 1972.

Hume, Ruth Fox, *Great Women of Medicine*, New York: Random House, 1964.

Ingraham, Claire and Leonard, *An Album of Women in American History*, New York: Franklin Watts, 1972.

James, Edward T. and Janet W., *Notable American Women 1607-1950: A Biographical Dictionary*, 3 volumes, Cambridge, Massachusetts: Belknap Press, Harvard University, 1971. (paper)

Jensen, Oliver, *The Revolt of American Women: A Pictorial History of the Century of Change . . .* , New York: Harcourt, Brace, 1952. (paper)

Kraditor, Aileen, ed., *Up From the Pedestal*, Chicago: Quadrangle, 1968. (paper) (selected writings in the history of feminism)

Lerner, Gerda, ed., *Black Women in White America: A Documentary History*, New York: Pantheon, 1972. (paper)

————, *The Woman in American History*, Reading: Massachusetts, Addison Wesley, 1971. (paper)

Merriam, Eve, ed., *Growing Up Female in America—Ten Lives*, Garden City, New York: Doubleday, 1971. (paper)

Newcomer, Mabel, *A Century of Higher Education for American Women*, New York: Harper, 1959.

Riegel, Robert, *American Women: A Story of Social Change*, Rutherford, New Jersey: Farleigh Dickinson University Press, 1970.

Ross, Ishbel, *Charmers and Cranks: Twelve Famous American Women Who Defied Conventions*, New York: Harper, 1965.

Ross, Pat, ed., *Young and Female: Personal Accounts of Turning Points in the Lives of Eight American Women*, New York: Random House, 1972. (paper)

Schneir, Miriam, *Feminism: The Essential Historical Writings*, New York: Random House, 1972. (paper)

Scott, Anne Firor, ed., *Women in American Life*, Boston: Houghton Mifflin, 1970. (paper)

Smith, Page, *Daughters of the Promised Land: Women in American History*, Boston: Little, Brown, 1970. (paper)

Sochen, June, *Movers and Shakers: American Women Thinkers and Activists 1900-1970*, New York: Quadrangle, 1973. (paper)

Whitton, Mary Ormsbee, *These Were the Women U.S.A. 1776-1860*, New York: Hastings House, 1954.

Wilcox, R. Turner, *Five Centuries of American Costume*, New York: Scribner's, 1963.

Yost, Edna, *Women of Modern Science*, New York: Dodd Mead, 1959.

CHAPTER 1. THOSE WHO CAME FIRST

Bacon, Martha, *Puritan Promenade,* Boston: Houghton Mifflin, 1964.

Benson, Mary, *Women in 18th Century America,* New York: Columbia University Press, 1935.

Dexter, Elizabeth, *Colonial Women of Affairs,* Boston: Houghton Mifflin, 1931.

Graham, Shirley, *The Story of Phillis Wheatley,* New York: Messner, 1949.

Holliday, Carl, *Woman's Life in Colonial Days,* New York: Ungar, 1960. (reprint)

Ravenal, Harriet, *Eliza Pinckney,* New York: Scribner's, 1896. Reprinted 1967.

Spruill, Julia C., *Women's Life and Work in the Southern Colonies,* Chapel Hill, North Carolina: University of North Carolina Press, 1938. (paper)

CHAPTER 2. FORMATION OF A NEW NATION

Blumenthal, Walter Hart, *Women Camp Followers of the Revolution,* Philadelphia: George S. MacManus, 1952. Reprinted 1974.

Brown, Alice, *Mercy Warren,* New York: Scribner's, 1896. Reprinted 1968.

Ellet, Elizabeth F., *The Women of the American Revolution,* Philadelphia: George W. Jacobs, 1900. Reprinted 1969.

Evans, Elizabeth, *Weathering the Storm: Women of the American Revolution,* New York: Scribner's, 1975.

Fritz, Jean, *Cast for a Revolution: Some American Friends and Enemies 1728-1814,* Boston: Houghton Mifflin, 1972. (Mercy Warren)

Morris, Margaret, *Margaret Morris, Her Journal,* Philadelphia: George S. MacManus, 1949. Reprinted 1969.

CHAPTER 3. WESTWARD THE NATION

Brown, Dee, *The Gentle Tamers: Women of the Old Wild West,* New York: Putnam, 1958. (paper)

Easton, Jeannette, *Narcissa Whitman, Pioneer of Oregon,* New York: Harcourt, Brace, 1941.

Harman, S. W., *Belle Starr: The Female Desperado,* Houston: Frontier Press of Texas, 1954.

Johnson, Dorothy Mane, *Some Went West,* New York: Dodd Mead, 1965.

Miller, Helen Markley, *Woman Doctor of the West,* New York: Messner, 1960. (Bethenia Owens-Adair)

Ross, Nancy, *Westward the Women,* New York: Knopf, 1944. (paper)

CHAPTER 4. AN ERA OF REFORM

Baker, Rachel and Merlen, Johanna Baker, *America's First Woman Astronomer: Maria Mitchell,* New York: Messner, 1960.

Dexter, Elizabeth, *Career Women of America, 1776–1840,* New Hampshire: Marshall Jones, 1950.

Flexner, Eleanor,*Mary Wollstonecraft,* New York: Coward McCann and Geoghegan, 1972. (paper)

Harveson, Mae Elizabeth, *Catherine Esther Beecher: Pioneer Educator,* Philadelphia: Science Press Printing Co., 1932. Reprinted 1969.

Hays, Elinor Rice, *Those Extraordinary Blackwells,* New York: Harcourt, Brace, 1967.

Longsworth, Polly, *Emily Dickinson: Her Letter to the World,* New York: Crowell, 1965.

Lutz, Alma,*Emma Willard: Pioneer Educator of American Women,* Boston: Beacon Press, 1964.

McFerran, Ann, *Elizabeth Blackwell: First Woman Doctor,* New York: Grosset and Dunlap, 1966.

Marshall, Helen E., *Dorothea Dix: Forgotten Samaritan,* Chapel Hill, North Carolina: University of North Carolina Press, 1937. Reprinted 1967.

Miller, Perry, ed., *Margaret Fuller: American Romantic, A Selection from Her Writings and Correspondence,* New York: Doubleday, 1963. (paper)

Pinchbeck, Ivy,*Women Workers and the Industrial Revolution, 1750–1850,* New York: F.S. Crofts, 1930.

Worthington, Marjorie,*Miss Alcott of Concord,* Garden City, New York: Doubleday, 1958.

CHAPTER 5. ABOLITION AND WOMEN'S RIGHTS

Bayliss, John F., ed., *Black Slave Narratives,* New York: Macmillan, 1970. (paper)

Bernard, Jacqueline, *Journey Toward Freedom: The Story of Sojourner Truth,* New York: Norton, 1967. (paper)

Bradford, Sarah,*Harriet Tubman: the Moses of Her People,* New York: G. Lockwood and Son, 1886. Reprinted 1961.

Buckmaster, Henrietta, *Flight to Freedom: The Story of the Underground Railroad,* New York: Crowell, 1958. (paper)

Cromwell, Otelia, *Lucretia Mott,* Cambridge, Massachusetts: Harvard University Press, 1958.

Fauset, Arthur, *Sojourner Truth: God's Faithful Pilgrim,* Chapel Hill, North Carolina: University of North Carolina Press, 1938. Reprinted 1971.

Fields, Annie, ed., *Harriet Beecher Stowe: Life and Letters,* Boston: Houghton Mifflin, 1898. Reprinted 1970.

Gurko, Miriam, *The Ladies of Seneca Falls: The Birth of the Woman's Rights Movement,* New York: Macmillan, 1974.

Hays, Elinor Rice, *Morning Star: A Biography of Lucy Stone,* New York: Harcourt, Brace, 1961.

Lerner, Gerda, *The Grimké Sisters From North Carolina: Rebels Against Slavery,* Boston: Houghton Mifflin, 1967. (paper)

Lutz, Alma, *Crusade For Freedom: Women in the Anti-Slavery Movement,* Boston: Beacon Press, 1968.

Meltzer, Milton, *Tongue of Flame: The Life of Lydia Maria Child,* New York: Crowell, 1965.

Ortiz, Victoria, *Sojourner Truth: A Self-Made Woman.* Philadelphia: Lippincott, 1974.

Perkins, A. J. and Woolfson, Theresa, *Frances Wright, Free Enquirer,* New York: Harper, 1939. Reprinted 1972.

Petry, Ann, *Harriet Tubman, Conductor on the Underground Railroad,* New York: Crowell, 1955.

Sterling, Dorothy, *Freedom Train: Story of Harriet Tubman,* New York: Doubleday, 1954.

———, *Lucretia Mott: Gentle Warrior,* New York: Doubleday, 1964.

Suhl, Yuri, *Ernestine Rose and the Battle for Human Rights,* New York: Reynal, 1959.

Wagenknecht, Edward, *Harriet Beecher Stowe: The Known and the Unknown,* New York: Oxford University Press, 1965.

Wilson, Forrest, *Crusader in Crinoline: The Life of Harriet Beecher Stowe,* Philadelphia: Lippincott, 1941.

Wise, Winifred E., *Harriet Beecher Stowe: Woman with a Cause,* New York: Putnam, 1965

Wright, Constance, *Fanny Kemble and the Lovely Land,* New York: Dodd Mead, 1972.

Yates, Elizabeth, *Prudence Crandall: Woman of Courage,* New York: Dutton, 1968.

CHAPTER 6. THE CIVIL WAR AND RECONSTRUCTION

Booker, Simeon, *Susie King Taylor: Civil War Nurse,* New York: McGraw Hill, 1969.

Dannett, Sylvia G., ed., *Noble Women of the North,* New York: Yoseloff, 1959.

Forten, Charlotte, *The Journal of Charlotte L. Forten: A Free Negro in the Slave Era,* New York: Collier Books, 1961. (paper)

Greenbie, Marjorie, *Lincoln's Daughters of Mercy,* New York: Putnam, 1944. (about the Sanitary Commission)

Massey, Mary Elizabeth, *Bonnet Brigades,* New York: Knopf, 1966.

Moore, Frank, *Women of the War: Their Heroism and Self-Sacrifice,* Hartford: S.S. Scranton, 1866.

Ross, Ishbel, *Angel of the Battlefield: The Life of Clara Barton,* New York: Harper, 1956.

Talmadge, Marian and Gilmore, Iris, *Emma Edmonds: Nurse and Spy,* New York: Putnam, 1970.

Turner, Justin G. and Turner, Linda Levitt, *Mary Todd Lincoln: Her Life and Letters,* New York: Knopf, 1972.

Young, Agnes Brooks, *The Women and the Crisis: Women of the North in the Civil War,* New York: McDowell, Obolensky, 1959.

CHAPTER 7. REFORM AND THE PROGRESSIVE ERA

Baker, Nina Brown, *Nelly Bly, Reporter,* New York: Holt, 1956. (paper)

Beals, Carleton, *Cyclone Carry: The Story of Carry Nation,* Philadelphia: Chilton, 1962.

Duster, Alfreda, ed., *Crusade for Justice: The Autobiography of Ida B. Wells,* Chicago: University of Chicago Press, 1970.

Earhart, Mary, *Frances Willard: From Prayers to Politics,* Chicago: University of Chicago Press, 1944.

Goldmark, Josephine, *Impatient Crusader: Florence Kelley's Life Story,* Urbana, Illinois: University of Illinois Press, 1953.

Lavine, Sigmund A., *Evangeline Booth: Daughter of Salvation,* New York: Dodd Mead, 1970. (Salvation Army)

Linn, James Weber, *Jane Addams: A Biography,* New York: Appleton-Century, 1935. Reprinted 1968.

McKown, Robin, *The World of Mary Cassatt,* New York: Crowell, 1972.

Meigs, Cornelia, *Jane Addams: Pioneer for Social Justice,* Boston: Little, Brown, 1970.

O'Neill, William, *Everyone Was Brave: The Rise and Fall of Feminism in America,* Chicago: Quadrangle, 1969. (paper)

Taylor, Robert Lewis, *Vessel of Wrath: The Life and Times of Carry Nation,* New York: New American Library, 1966.

Wise, Winifred E., *Jane Addams of Hull-House: A Biography,* New York: Harcourt, Brace, 1963.

CHAPTER 8. SUFFRAGE AT LAST

Anthony, Katherine S., *Susan B. Anthony,* Garden City, New York: Doubleday, 1954. Reprinted 1974.

Catt, Carrie Chapman and Shuler, Nettie Rogers, *Woman Suffrage and Politics,* New York: Scribner's, 1923. (paper)

Clarke, Mary Stetson, *Bloomers and Ballots: Elizabeth Cady Stanton and Women's Rights,* New York: Viking, 1972.

Faber, Doris, *Oh Lizzie! The Life and Times of Elizabeth Cady Stanton,* New York: Lothrop, Lee and Shepard, 1972. (paper)

_____, *Petticoat Politics: How American Women Won the Right to Vote,* New York: Lothrop, Lee and Shepard, 1967.

Flexner, Eleanor, *Century of Struggle: The Woman's Rights Movement in the United States,* Cambridge, Massachusets: Harvard University Press, 1959. (paper)

Grimes, Alan Pendleton, *The Puritan Ethic and Woman Suffrage,* New York: Oxford University Press, 1967.

Kraditor, Aileen, *Ideas of the Woman Suffrage Movement, 1890–1920,* New York: Columbia University Press, 1965. (paper)

Lutz, Alma, *Created Equal: A Biography of Elizabeth Cady Stanton,* New York: John Day, 1940. Reprinted 1973.

_____, *Susan B. Anthony: Rebel, Crusader, Humanitarian,* Boston: Beacon Press, 1959.

Peck, Mary Grace, *Carrie Chapman Catt,* New York: H.W. Wilson, 1944.

Severn, Bill, *Free But Not Equal: How Women Won the Right to Vote,* New York: Messner, 1967.

Stanton, Elizabeth Cady, *Eighty Years and More,* London: Fisher and Unwin, 1898. (paper)

Stevens, Doris, *Jailed For Freedom,* New York: Boni and Liveright, 1920.

Stevenson, Janet, *Women's Rights,* New York: Franklin Watts, 1972.

CHAPTER 9. WORLD WAR I AND THE TWENTIES

Allen, Frederick Lewis, *Only Yesterday: An Informal History of the 1920's,* New York: Harper, 1931. (paper)

Anderson, Mary, *Woman at Work: The Autobiography of Mary Anderson as told to Mary N. Winslow,* Minneapolis, Minnesota: University of Minnesota Press, 1951. Reprinted 1973.

Brown, Marion Marsh and Crone, Ruth, *Willa Cather: The Woman and Her Works,* New York: Scribner's, 1970.

Coigney, Virginia, *Margaret Sanger: Rebel With a Cause,* New York: Doubleday, 1969.

Douglas, Emily Taft, *Margaret Sanger: Pioneer of the Future,* New York: Holt, 1970.

Duncan, Isadora, *My Life,* New York: Liveright, 1933. (paper)

Gurko, Miriam, *Restless Spirit: The Life of Edna St. Vincent Millay,* New York: Crowell, 1962.

Lader, Lawrence and Meltzer, Milton,*Margaret Sanger: Pioneer of Birth Control,* New York: Crowell, 1969.

Milford, Nancy, *Zelda,* New York: Harper, 1970. (paper)

Sanger, Margaret, *An Autobiography,* New York: Norton, 1938. (paper)

Stevenson, Elizabeth,*Babbitts and Bohemians: The American 1920's,* New York: Macmillan, 1967. (paper)

Windeler, Robert, *Sweetheart: The Story of Mary Pickford,* New York: Praeger, 1974.

CHAPTER 10. THE DEPRESSION AND WORLD WAR II

Blassingame, Wyatt,*Combat Nurses of World War II,* New York: Random House, 1967.

Burke, John, *Winged Legend: The Story of Amelia Earhart,* New York: Putnam's, 1970.

Eaton, Jeannette, *The Story of Eleanor Roosevelt,* New York: Morrow, 1956.

Hall, Helen,*Unfinished Business in Neighborhood and Nation,* New York: Macmillan, 1971. (Henry Street Settlement)

Holt, Rackham, *Mary McLeod Bethune,* Garden City, New York: Doubleday, 1964.

Lash, Joseph,*Eleanor and Franklin,* New York: Norton, 1971. (paper)

Pruette, L., *Women Workers Through the Depression,* New York: Macmillan, 1934.

Strippel, Dick,*Amelia Earhart: The Myth and the Reality,* New York: Exposition, 1972.

CHAPTER 11. LIFE IN THE FIFTIES

Anderson, Marian,*My Lord, What a Morning,* New York: Viking, 1956. (paper)

Gibson, Althea, *I Always Wanted to Be Somebody,* New York: Harper, 1958. (paper)

Lundberg, Ferdinand and Farnham, Marynia,*Modern Woman: The Lost Sex,* New York: Harper, 1947.

Myrdal, Alva and Klein, Viola, *Women's Two Roles, At Home and Work,* London: Routledge and Kegan Paul, 1956. (paper)

Smuts, Robert,*Women and Work in America,* New York: Columbia University Press, 1959. (paper)

CHAPTER 12. THE MODERN WOMEN'S MOVEMENT

Abzug, Bella, *Bella! Ms. Abzug Goes to Washington,* New York: Saturday Review Press, 1972.

Adams, Elsie, and Briscoe, Mary Louise, eds., *Up Against the Wall, Mother: On Women's Liberation,* Beverly Hills, California: Glencoe Press, 1971. (paper) (anthology of readings on the women's movement)

Amundsen, Kirsten, *The Silenced Majority: Women and American Democracy,* Englewood Cliffs, New Jersey: Prentice Hall, 1971. (paper)

Babcox, Deborah, and Belkin, Madeline, *Liberation Now! Writings From the Women's Liberation Movement,* New York: Dell, 1971. (paper)

Bird, Caroline, *Born Female: The High Cost of Keeping Women Down,* New York: McKay, 1968. (paper)

Boston Women's Health Collective, *Our Bodies, Ourselves,* New York: Simon and Schuster, 1973. (paper) (guide to health and sexuality)

Brenton, Myron, *The American Male,* New York: Coward-McCann, 1966. (paper)

Brownmiller, Susan, *Shirley Chisholm,* New York: Doubleday, 1970. (paper)

Cade, Toni, *The Black Woman: An Anthology,* New York: New American Library, 1970.

Carson, Josephine, *Silent Voices: The Southern Negro Woman Today,* New York: Delacorte, 1969. (paper)

Chamberlin, Hope, *Minority of Members: Women in the U.S. Congress,* New York: Praeger, 1973. (paper)

Chapin, June, and Branson, Margaret, *Women: The Majority Minority,* Boston: Houghton Mifflin, 1973. (paper)

Chisholm, Shirley, *Unbought and Unbossed,* Boston: Houghton Mifflin, 1970. (paper)

DeCrow, Karen, *A Young Woman's Guide to Liberation,* New York: Bobbs-Merrill, 1971. (paper)

Gornick, Vivian, and Moran, Barbara, eds., *Woman in Sexist Society: Studies in Power and Powerlessness,* New York: Basic Books, 1971. (paper)

Greer, Germaine, *The Female Eunuch,* New York: McGraw Hill, 1971. (paper)

Guffy, Ossie, as told to Ledner, Caryl, *Ossie: The Autobiography of a Black Woman,* New York: Norton, 1971. (paper)

Harrison, Barbara, *Unlearning the Lie: Sexism in School,* New York: Liveright, 1973. (paper)

Hole, Judith, and Levine, Ellen, *Rebirth of Feminism,* New York: Quadrangle, 1971. (paper)

Kanowitz, Leo, *Women and the Law: The Unfinished Revolution,* Albuquerque, New Mexico: University of New Mexico Press, 1969. (paper)

Ladner, Joyce A., *Tomorrow's Tomorrow: The Black Woman,* Garden City, New York: Doubleday, 1971. (paper)

Maccoby, Eleanor E., ed., *The Development of Sex Differences,* Stanford, California: Stanford University Press, 1966.

McHugh, Mary, *The Woman Thing,* New York: Praeger, 1973.

Mailer, Norman, *The Prisoner of Sex,* Boston: Little Brown, 1971. (paper)

Medea, Andrea and Thompson, Kathleen, *Against Rape,* New York: Farrar, Straus, and Giroux, 1974. (paper)

Merriam, Eve, *After Nora Slammed the Door, American Women in the 1960's: the Unfinished Revolution,* Cleveland: World, 1964.

Morgan, Robin, ed., *Sisterhood is Powerful: An Anthology of Writings from the Women's Liberation Movement,* New York: Random House, 1970. (paper)

New York City Commission on Human Rights, *Women's Role in Contemporary Society: A Report,* New York: Avon, 1972. (paper)

Ross, Susan, *The Rights of Women: ACLU Handbook,* New York: Avon, 1973. (paper)

Sakol, Jeannie and Goldberg, Lucianne, *Purr, Baby, Purr,* New York: Hawthorn, 1972. (paper) (in praise of traditional femininity)

Vilar, Esther, *The Manipulated Man,* New York: Farrar, Straus, and Giroux, 1973. (paper)

Index